...cts
Made Easy

Volatile Markets Made Easy

Trading Stocks and Options for
Increased Profits

Guy Cohen

Vice President, Publisher: Tim Moore
Associate Publisher and Director of Marketing: Amy Neidlinger
Executive Editor: Jim Boyd
Editorial Assistants: Myesha Graham, Pamela Boland
Operations Manager: Gina Kanouse
Digital Marketing Manager: Julie Phifer
Publicity Manager: Laura Czaja
Assistant Marketing Manager: Megan Colvin
Cover Designer: Alan Clements
Managing Editor: Kristy Hart
Project Editors: Chelsey Marti and Anne Goebel
Copy Editor: Language Logistics, LLC
Proofreader: Kathy Ruiz
Indexer: Lisa Stumpf
Senior Compositor: Gloria Schurick
Manufacturing Buyer: Dan Uhrig

FT Press offers excellent discounts on this book when ordered in quantity for bulk
purchases or special sales. For more information, please contact U.S. Corporate and
Government Sales, 1-800-382-3419, corpsales@pearsontechgroup.com. For sales
outside the U.S., please contact International Sales at international@pearson.com.

ISBN-10: 0-13-335383-4
ISBN-13: 978-0-13-335383-9

Pearson Education LTD.
Pearson Education Australia PTY, Limited.
Pearson Education Singapore, Pte. Ltd.
Pearson Education North Asia, Ltd.
Pearson Education Canada, Ltd.
Pearson Educación de Mexico, S.A. de C.V.
Pearson Education—Japan
Pearson Education Malaysia, Pte. Ltd.

This product is printed digitally on demand. This book is the paperback version of an original
hardcover book.

This book is dedicated to those who want to make money from trading.

Contents

Foreword

All through my career, I have been fascinated with the technical approach to trading. At first, I was convinced that technical patterns predicted the future.

I studied the masters—Gann, Elliott, and techniques like Fibonacci—and began to apply the principles to my trading. When I trade full time, I draw my own charts. What I found was that technical analysis could explain the past but not the future.

However, I found that the technical approach could and did help me find winning trades. And even better, it helped me to exit the trade without giving back my profits. Guy Cohen has articulated in eight chapters what I spent 30 years to learn.

Volatile Markets Made Easy is not just a book; it is a full course of instruction. The student will discover so many gems of knowledge that will help with their trading throughout his or her career that this book will never be far away.

Technicians can make their language confusing and difficult to understand. That is what I call job security. In *Volatile Markets Made Easy*, Guy Cohen simplifies the terms and gives the reader a road map that is easy to follow and less, well, technical.

Follow the principles clearly expressed in these pages and you will trade with greater confidence and, in my opinion, trade more profitably.

There is only one reason to trade and that is to win, make money, and enjoy a lifestyle like no other. Take command; follow the guide in the chapters before you. It will be a rewarding journey.

—Ned W. Bennett
CEO/Cofounder, optionsXpress, Inc.
March 16, 2009

Acknowledgments

First, I want to say a big thank you to my colleagues at Flag-Trader. Their skill and diligence has been instrumental in improving my trading skills. Also to my business advisor and trusted friend, Howard Weisberg, whose wise counsel has proved priceless over the years. Finally, to my students all over the world, who have taught me far more than I've taught them.

About the Author

Guy Cohen is the author of the best-selling trading books: *Options Made Easy*, *The Bible of Options Strategies*, and now, *Volatile Markets Made Easy*. He has extensive experience of the options and stock markets and his clients include NYSE Euronext, the largest stock exchange in the world.

Guy is also the creator of trading products Flag-Trader, OptionEasy, and Illuminati-Trader.

Specializing in trading applications Guy has developed comprehensive trading and training models, all expressly designed for maximum user-friendliness.

An entertaining speaker, Guy has an MBA (Finance) from City University Cass Business School, London.

Preface

In June 2008 the S&P 500 fell by 125 points, and the Dow Jones 30 Index fell by 1350 points. Several of my students more than doubled their money during that same time. They did it by using the techniques and strategies contained in this book.

This book is about making money. That's my job here, to help you make money by trading the financial markets.

This is a down-to-earth book aimed at helping anyone who doesn't have the advantage of trading within the bid-ask spread, who typically places trades via an online or full-service broker or in some countries via a spread betting firm. This book is for all private investors. There are wonderful texts for mathematicians—I've read a good number of them—but this book does not aspire to be one of them. My goal is to provide you with a sense of how to trade profitably from the principles I outline.

There's a big secret that I'm going to share with you. You *can* make money trading the markets, and you can do it by using these methods. But until you wholeheartedly embrace the concept of *wealth psychology*, you won't have cracked it to your fullest potential. What's more, until you have adopted the right mindset, not just for trading but for creating wealth as a whole, there exists the potential for a "retracement" for want of a better expression. How many times have you heard of people making fabulous fortunes only to blow it a few months or years later? Lots! And you may personally know a few like that too. I know I do.

As the title suggests, this book focuses on how to make money from strategies that take advantage of volatility in the markets. I should distill this further by saying that we're talking here about profiting primarily from *increasing* volatility. The strategies contained here will all put you in a "long" position whereby your risk will always be limited and definable. In other words, the strategies in this book will make you a net buyer of options. As such, your upside will typically be unlimited. I'm not going to be addressing short options strategies here.

There are several worthy short strategies that can work over and over again month after month. However, short strategies can put you in an unlimited loss position and typically have limited upsides. I'm aware of many people who made their living by selling short options during the late 1990's tech bubble and who indeed made fortunes from doing so. But when the market turned, so did their fortunes and in many cases their livelihoods, their homes, their children's education...you get the picture.

The point is, there's plenty of profit to be gleaned with long strategies with unlimited upside and limited downside, so we'll focus on those and make sure we do them right.

For now, here's a summary of what you're about to learn in this book.

Chapter 1 is an introduction to options. If you're already familiar with this topic, you should still go through it as a review before reading the other options chapters in the book.

In **Chapter 2** I explain my preferred technical chart patterns and why I like to trade them from a practical viewpoint. This chapter is focused on my favorite patterns and is not intended to be an almanac on all the chart patterns known to man. The aim is to be crystal clear as to what you should be looking for and why that's such a valuable approach to take.

We return back to options in **Chapter 3** where I summarize the Greeks. The Greeks are sensitivities to various factors affecting the pricing of options. These sensitivities have a direct effect on your trading.

Chapters 4 through 6 take you through my six favored options strategies. The aim is to trade safely, profitably, and with manageable risk at all times. Only when you witness the pitfalls of a strategy can you decide whether or not it's right for you. In Chapter 6 I explain how to maximize your income return by trading options—without having to risk too much. The only way to demonstrate this properly is to show you how some traders get it wrong by exposing themselves to inordinate amounts of risk, in many cases without even knowing they're doing it.

In **Chapter 7** we run through the steps of creating a trading plan. The steps are universal for all strategies.

Chapter 8 is the most technically challenging part of the book in which I go through some of the mathematical algorithms that define the whole subject of options trading. This chapter is mathematical in nature but has a practical element to it.

Finally, in **Chapter 9** I show you how to implement a trading plan for each of the six favored strategies so you can see how the processes work in practice and what you'll need to do as you start to implement your new trading program.

What distinguishes this book from others out there is that it is completely practical throughout. This isn't a book about theory. It's real world stuff, real *trading* world stuff, that is. I focus on six strategies that will bear fruit for you if you follow the rules and adhere to the certain principles outlined throughout this book. The most successful traders stick to just a few strategies that they understand intimately. This is what you should aspire to do as well.

I sincerely hope you enjoy reading this book and profit from it. I'm committed to communicating in a practical and down-to-earth way the same qualities I bring to my workshops and software products. Trading is a serious business, but it can be enjoyable too, especially when you're organized, disciplined, and committed to following sound principles. Those principles are laid out in this book with a sense of enthusiasm, fun, and humor that hopefully you can take with you.

Good luck!

chapter 1

Introduction to Options

This book is concerned with making money from the financial markets. If you pick up just one thing from it that you use successfully for the rest of your life, it will be worth it. And I believe you will.

During this chapter I provide a basic overview of options and set the basic foundations that you will need for the chapters ahead.

Definition of an Option

An *option* conveys the right, not the obligation, to buy (or sell) an asset at a fixed price before a predetermined date.

Here are the salient components of that definition:

- the right, not the obligation
- to buy or sell an asset
- at a fixed price
- before a predetermined date

These components play important roles in the valuation of an option. Remember that the option itself has a value (known as the *premium*), which we dissect later after we finish with the definitions.

Calls and Puts

The two types of options are calls and puts.

- A call is an option to BUY.
- A put is an option to SELL.

Therefore:

- A *call option* is the right, not the obligation, to buy an asset at a fixed price before a predetermined date.
- A *put option* is the right, not the obligation, to sell an asset at a fixed price before a predetermined date.

Right Versus Obligation

Let's now look at that definition and consider each part, starting with the "right, not the obligation to buy or sell an asset."

Buying Gives You the Right; Selling Imposes a Potential Obligation

- Buying a call conveys the *right*, not the obligation, to *buy* an underlying security (such as 100 shares of stock).
- Buying a put conveys the *right*, not the obligation, to *sell* an underlying security.
- Remember, when you buy an option you are *not* obligated to buy or sell the underlying instrument—you simply have the *right* to do so at the fixed (exercise or strike) price.
- Your maximum risk, when you buy an option, is simply the price you paid for it. In other words, your risk is limited.

Remember, when you buy something, you can only lose what you paid for it. Your upside potential is unlimited as there is theoretically no limit to what something could be valued at later. In this way, when you buy something, you want the price to rise so you can make a profit.

Similarly, when you sell something, your upside is capped to what you receive for it. However, if you sell stock you don't yet own (that is, you *short* stock), you must eventually buy it back in order to close your position. In this way, when we short stock, we want the price to fall so we can buy it back at a lower price and make a profit.

Selling (Naked) Imposes the Obligation

Now here's where things can get a little upside-down, so if you're new to this, take it slowly! This is also where my "Rule of the Opposites" comes into play.

> **Rule of the Opposites**
>
> *Buying a call = right to buy the stock*
> *Selling a call = obligation to sell the stock*
> *Buying a put = right to sell the stock*

- Selling a call *obliges* you to *deliver* (or sell) the underlying asset to the call buyer if he exercises his right to buy from you.

- Selling a put *obliges* you to *buy* the underlying asset from the put buyer if he exercises his right to sell to you.

- Selling options naked means you haven't bought a position in the underlying stock or hedged your position with an option to protect yourself. Selling naked therefore gives you an *unlimited* risk profile, as the term *naked* infers.
  Combined with the fact that you are obliged to do something, this is not a recommended strategy. There's a time and a place for strategies like this, but only advanced traders should contemplate selling naked options, and even they will typically have a protective strategy in mind in order to cover their exposure.

Figure 1.1   Interaction of option buyer and seller

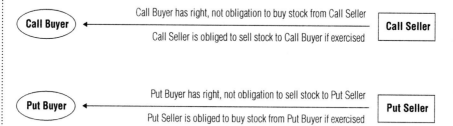

Fixed Price

Now let's look at the words "at a fixed price" from the option definition.

Exercise (or Strike) Price

The *exercise* or *strike price* is the fixed price at which the option can be exercised.

So if you buy a call option that has a strike price of $30, then you have bought yourself the option to buy the underlying stock at a price of $30 per share.

However, in the real world you will only want to exercise your right to buy that asset at $30 if the underlying asset is actually worth more than $30 in the market. Otherwise there would be no point. It would mean buying the asset for $30, when it's only actually worth, say, $25 in the marketplace. No one would do that because they could buy it for $25 in the market, which is clearly better value.

Expiration Date

The definition of an option finishes with the words, "before a predetermined date" or its *expiration date*—the date before which the option can be exercised.

Rule of the Opposites

Option Values at Expiration
Call = stock – strike
Put = strike – stock

- At expiration, the call option's own value is only worth the price of the asset less the strike price.

- At expiration, the put option's own value is only worth the strike price less the price of the asset.

(For U.S. equity options, the expiration dates fall on the Saturday after the third Friday of every month.)

Types of Calls and Puts

Options can be either *American*-style or *European*-style.

- American-style options allow the option buyer to exercise the option (that is, buy or sell the underlying asset) at any time before the expiration date.

- European-style options do *not* allow the option buyer to exercise the option before the expiration date.

All U.S. equity options are American-style, which are technically more valuable than European-style options because of their greater flexibility. Being able to exercise before expiration is more valuable than not being able to. However, this is rarely advisable for reasons that I explain later on.

As a rule, stock options are usually American-style.

The Valuation of Options

Options have a value, known as the *premium*, and are totally separate entities to the underlying assets from which they are derived (hence the term derivative). So for example, a stock is not an option, but you can have options to buy or sell stocks. The option premium can be split into two parts:

- *Intrinsic value*
- *Time value*

Generally speaking:

- Intrinsic value is that part of the option's value that is *In the Money* (ITM).
- Time value is the remainder of the option's value. *Out of the Money* (OTM) options will have no Intrinsic Value, and their price will solely be based on Time Value. Time Value is another way to express hope value. This hope is based on the amount of time left to expiration and the price of the underlying asset.

  - A call is *In the Money* when the underlying asset price is greater than the strike price.
  - A call is *Out of the Money* when the underlying asset price is less than the strike price.
  - A call is *At the Money* when the underlying asset price is the same as the strike price.

With puts, it works the **opposite** way:

- A put is *In the Money* when the underlying asset price is less than the strike price.
- A put is *Out of the Money* when the underlying asset price is greater than the strike price.
- A put is *At the Money* when the underlying asset price is the same as the strike price.

Rule of the Opposites

In the Money
Calls: stock > strike
Puts: stock < strike
Out of the Money
Calls: stock < strike
Puts: stock > strike

Figure 1.2   Option premium components

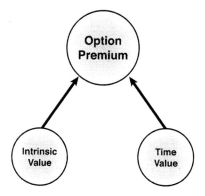

Now that we know the basic components of an option's premium, let's look at some simple calculations for intrinsic and time value for both calls and puts.

Intrinsic and Time Value for Calls

Here's what you need to remember in order to calculate intrinsic and time value for calls.

- call intrinsic value = stock price – strike price
- call time value = premium – intrinsic value
- the minimum intrinsic value is zero; it cannot be negative
- call premium = intrinsic value + time value

Table 1.1

Stock price		34.00
Call premium		5.70
Strike price		30.00
Time to expiration		3 months
Intrinsic Value	Stock–strike 34.00-30.00	4.00
Time Value	Premium–intrinsic 5.70-4.00	1.70
Stock price		34.00
Call premium		1.40
Strike price		35.00
Time to expiration		20 days
Intrinsic Value	Stock-strike 34.00-35.00	0.00
Time Value	Premium-intrinsic 1.40-0.00	1.40

Intrinsic and Time Value for Puts

Now here are the calculations for puts:

- put intrinsic value = strike price – stock price
- put time value = premium – intrinsic value

- the minimum intrinsic value is zero; it cannot be negative
- put premium = intrinsic value + time value

Table 1.2

Stock price		37.00
Put premium		4.80
Strike price		40.00
Time to expiration		1 month
Intrinsic Value	Strike-stock 40.00-37.00	**3.00**
Time Value	Premium-intrinsic 4.80-3.00	**1.80**
Stock price		55.00
Put premium		1.90
Strike price		50.00
Time to expiration		1 month
Intrinsic Value	Strike-stock 50.00-55.00	**0.00**
Time Value	Premium-intrinsic 1.90-0.00	**1.90**

We can see that intrinsic value is easy to calculate, and from there we can easily determine the time value portion of the total premium. However, there are many elements that make up the composition of time value.

In total, there are seven factors that converge together to make up the value of an option premium.

Remember, an option is defined as *the right, not the obligation, to buy or sell an asset at a fixed price before a predetermined date.*

Let's take the seven factors one at a time:

Table 1.3   Seven Factors that Affect Option Premiums

From Definition	Note
"Buy or sell"	The *type of option* (call or put) will affect the option premium.

Table 1.3   continued

From Definition	Note
"Underlying asset"	The *underlying asset price* will affect the option premium.
"At a fixed price"	The strike price will affect the option premium.
"Before a predetermined date"	The *expiration date* will affect the option premium.

There are three other major influences on option pricing:

Volatility	Volatility is a crucial and major influence in the pricing of options. Understanding volatility gives the options trader the ability to select specific trades most profitably. The most advanced traders always use volatility to their advantage.
Risk-free interest rate	This is the short-term rate of government money. It is known as "risk free," owing to the perceived covenant strength of (developed world economy) governments.
Dividends	This applies to any asset that offers an income "reward" for owners of the underlying asset. For stock options this will be the dividend payable.

So in summary, option premiums are affected by

1. the type of option (call or put)
2. the price of the underlying asset
3. the strike price
4. the expiration date
5. volatility – implied and historical
6. risk-free interest rate
7. dividends

Why Trade Options?

With the flexibility afforded to a trader by these remarkable financial instruments, there are myriad reasons to include options as part of your trading arsenal. The effort involved in your own due diligence is well worth it, but it will take some time and dedication. There are many so-called gurus out there, and yet I'm often horrified by what my students tell me they've learned from instructors whose knowledge appears to be wafer thin and whose own qualifications appear to be founded merely from attending someone else's seminar.

In this book, on the way to illustrating what you should be doing and how to achieve certain trading goals with specific options strategies, I also highlight what you *shouldn't* be doing. Don't worry; I'll make it crystal clear so you'll know which is which!

My own credentials come from three main sources:

- An initial academic background with options through my Finance MBA

- Trading in the field what must now be thousands of trades

- Developing my own software suite and building the engine several hundred times, covering over 60 different options strategies

During my journey in this field, I've discovered that the best options masters out there were either highly respected floor traders or those with a part-academic/part-software development aspect to their curriculum vitae. Engineers often make great options traders provided they can resist the temptation to over-analyze!

Advantages of Trading Options

So why are options so appealing, and why should you invest your time learning about them? In a world of many alternatives, what makes options so special that they're becoming more and more popular as a trading vehicle, particularly in the U.S., the world's largest financial market place?

Well, there is no nutshell answer other than "flexibility," but what do we really mean by *flexibility* in the context of options? The answer comes in multiple forms. Following are the main advantages of trading options. Options enable us to

- **Control more assets for less money.**

  Consider the implications of this, and it becomes obvious how phenomenal this single characteristic of traded options is. Here's the way it works for equity (share) options: One option contract represents 100 shares of stock and is only a fraction of the cost of what you'd pay for the equivalent number of shares.

  For example, ACME stock is priced at $38.40 on 25 May 2005.

  A call option to *buy* ACME shares might be priced at 3.80. Because one contract represents 100 shares, you can buy one ACME call contract for

$380.00 [100 × 3.80]. The alternative would be to buy 100 shares of the stock for a total sum of $3,840. So in this example you can buy ACME call options for around 10% of the stock price in order to control $3,840 of ACME stock until the appropriate expiration date of the option.

Call options are always cheaper than the underlying asset and put options usually are.[1] Options are often more volatile than their underlying instruments, therefore traders get "more bang for their buck" or more action. Clearly this can also be perceived as being riskier, but in the right hands, it can also be safer and more conservative. Options will give you far greater flexibility in your trading and even give you the ability to make profit when you don't know the direction in which the stock will move. I cover this in detail during the course of this book.

● **Trade with "leverage."**

This is a variation of the same theme in the first point. When we calculate a return on an investment, the numerator is the numerical return, and the denominator is the amount invested. If the amount invested is lower, then our percentage return will rise. Because our cost basis is proportionately lower with options (as witnessed here), the position becomes much more sensitive to the underlying stock's price movements, so our percentage returns can be so much greater.

Here's an example: ACME stock rises from $38.40 to $42.40. This is a rise of $4 or just over 10%. The corresponding call option premium rises from 3.80 to 7.60. Do you see how a mere 10% move in the stock has helped to cause a 100% rise in the option premium? That's leverage! Now of course, leverage can affect us both ways, either in our favor or against us. It's our job to make the right decisions so that leverage works *for* us.

● **Trade for income.**

We can structure options strategies specifically for the purpose of generating income on a regular basis. As far as I'm aware, options are the only financial instrument we can use for this. I cover income strategies in Chapter 7, "The Practical Way to Trade Volatility."

---

[1] An exception would be when a stock price has made a massive fall. The higher strike puts will have a high intrinsic value. For example, consider a stock that falls from $20.00 to $5.00 on a bad earnings report. The $20 strike puts will have an intrinsic value of $15.00.

- **Profit from declining stocks.**

  One of the most important trades you'll ever make is when you profit from a stock that has fallen in price. If you only ever consider buying stocks, then you're bound to be looking at the stock market with an upward bias. Your analysis is therefore compromised by your desire to only see reasons for a stock to rise. Once you start making money from declining stocks as well, then you can simply look at the markets as a mechanism for making money, without a predetermined bias.

  With options, we can trade puts and calls to ensure we can make money if the stock goes up, down, or sideways, giving us ultimate flexibility. Even investors with wide-ranging equity portfolios can efficiently implement protective measures in the event of a severe market downturn.

- **Profit from volatility and protect against other factors.**

  Different options strategies protect us or enable us to benefit from factors such as time decay, volatility, lack of volatility, and so on.

- **Reduce or eliminate risk.**

  Options allow you to substantially reduce your risk of trading, and in certain rare cases, you can even eliminate risk altogether, albeit with the trade-off of very limited profit potential.

So with all the different benefits of options, why would traders *not* be curious to learn more about them? Well, for a start, options are reasonably complex instruments. Once you're over that hurdle, however, they become more and more fascinating.

Given that options can be a challenge, I've found it highly effective to convert the subject material into pictures so we can *see* what a strategy looks like. My style is designed to be user-friendly, particularly in a visual sense. I have discovered that this approach makes everything fit into place, and my students have found it the fastest way to learn. For more education visit www.optioneasy.com where there is free dynamic content where I extend logic even faster and further than in a book format.

Options give traders added flexibility, potentially much greater gains for a given movement in the stock price, and protection against risk. On the flip side, used in the wrong way, options can lead traders to serious losses. In this book you learn how to trade strategies safely and how to adhere to the simple rules governing those strategies.

Risk Profile Charts

Pictures are used to explain virtually every concept in this book. By using visual tools, your learning experience will be accelerated in two ways. First, you won't have to stare at continuous lines of text throughout the book. I love books with pictures and tables because they break up the monotony of straight reading. Second, you'll find with a bit of time that the pictures are incredibly intuitive and that you can learn at a pace that you would never have imagined possible.

Let's now look at a risk profile chart and why I use them.

A *risk profile chart* shows your profit/loss position for each trade. It differs from a standard price/time chart that you'll view to monitor stock prices. Typically we're used to seeing time along the x-axis and price up and down the y-axis. With risk profiles we move the price to the x-axis, and we have our profit/loss on the y-axis.

There are four steps to creating a risk profile chart:

Step 1: Y-axis for profit/loss position

Step 2: X-axis for stock price range

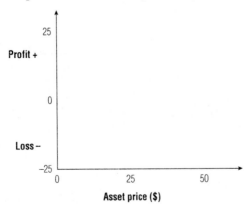

Step 3: Breakeven line

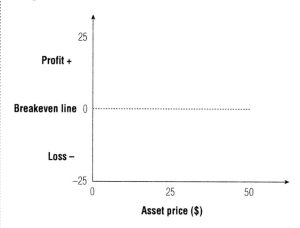

Step 4: Risk profile line

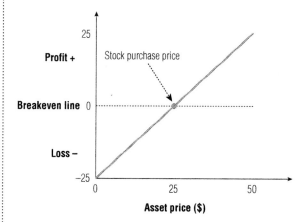

The previous chart shows your risk profile for buying a stock. As the stock price rises above your purchase price (along the x-axis), you move into profit. Your risk is limited to the amount you paid, as is your breakeven point, and your potential reward is uncapped as the stock rises.

What about if you short a stock? Well, in this case the *opposite* occurs. Here as the stock price rises above the price you shorted at, your short position shows a loss, which can be unlimited as the stock continues to rise. Your risk is therefore uncapped as the stock rises, and your potential reward is limited to the price you shorted at, as is your breakeven point.

Figure 1.3   Short stock risk profile

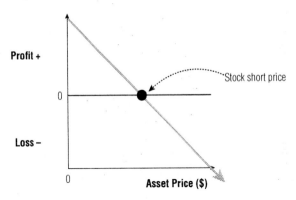

Now we know what buying and shorting a stock looks like, let's see what option risk profiles look like.

The four basic strategies are:

- Long call
- Short call
- Long put
- Short put

A few points before we construct the drawings. From the definition of an option, we already know that options expire and that the time value portion of the premium decays as the expiration date nears. What this means is that we'd like to own options that aren't about to expire in order to give ourselves a chance of making money without being hammered by time decay.

The Rule of the Opposites tells us, however, that if time decay hurts option buyers, then it must *help* option sellers. We'll see later that time decay increases exponentially during the last month to expiration. Therefore we typically don't want to buy those short-dated (front month) options. Instead, we'd rather short them.

With reference to these four strategies, we would buy calls and puts with at least three months (or more) left to expiration, looking for the options to increase in value during that time without the ravages of time decay. By contrast, we would short calls and puts with a month or less to expiration, thereby gaining short-term income as the option (hopefully) declines in value or expires worthless.

Long Call Risk Profile

Let's say we buy a call for a premium of $7.50.

Stock price	$56.00
Call premium	7.50
Strike price	50.00
Time to expiration	2 months

Figure 1.4   Long call risk profile

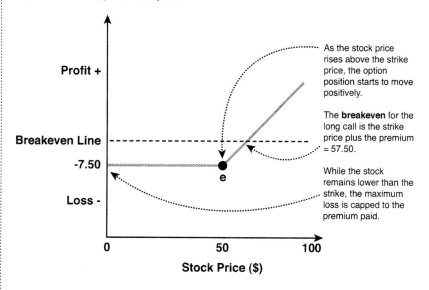

Remember that buying a call gives you the *right*, not the obligation to buy the stock. You would exercise that right if the stock price exceeds the strike price at expiration.

Your risk when you buy an option is capped to what you paid (hence the horizontal line in the loss zone), and your reward is potentially unlimited (hence the upward sloping diagonal line).

Short Call Risk Profile

The Rule of the Opposites tells us that the opposite of buying a call must be shorting a call.

This is reflected in the risk profile. The call *writer* is therefore taking the opposite position to the call buyer.

This time we're going to short a call for a premium of $7.50.

Stock price	$56.00
Call premium	7.50
Strike price	50.00
Time to expiration	2 months

Figure 1.5   Short call risk profile

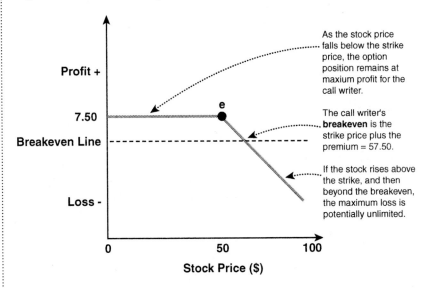

Remember that shorting a call gives you the potential *obligation* to *sell* the stock if you're exercised. With a short call you would only be exercised if the stock price exceeds the strike price.

Your reward when you sell an option is capped to what you received (hence the horizontal line in the profit zone), and your risk is potentially unlimited (hence the downward sloping diagonal line). So here you have a position where you are potentially obligated to do something and you have uncapped risk potential. Your obligation would be to sell the stock at the strike price. But in order to sell it at that price, you'd also have to buy it at the market price, which may now be substantially higher than the strike price. Not an ideal scenario.

Long Put Risk Profile

The Rule of the Opposites also tells us that the opposite of buying a call must be buying a put.

This is reflected in the risk profile, but it's different from shorting a call. The put buyer is taking the opposite position of the call buyer. So here we'll buy a put option for a premium of $7.50.

Stock price	$46.00
Call premium	7.50
Strike price	50.00
Time to expiration	2 months

Figure 1.6 Long put risk profile

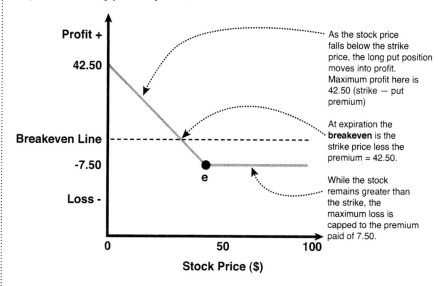

Remember that buying the put gives you the *right*, not the obligation, to sell the stock. With puts you would exercise that right if the stock price is below the strike price at expiration.

Your risk when you buy an option is capped to what you paid (hence the horizontal line in the loss zone), and your reward is potentially unlimited until the stock reaches zero, at which point your profit is capped at the strike price less the premium you paid, that is 50.00 − 7.50 = 42.50.

Short Put Risk Profile

So the other opposite of buying a put must be *selling* a put. Here, we'll short a put option to receive a premium of $7.50.

Stock price	$46.00
Call premium	7.50
Strike price	50.00
Time to expiration	2 months

Figure 1.7   Short put risk profile

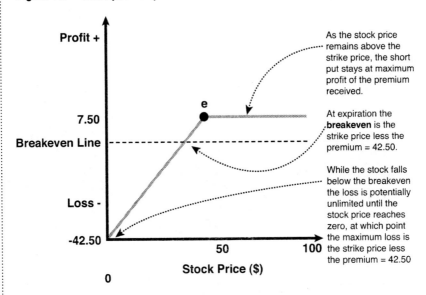

Remember that shorting a put gives you the potential *obligation* to *buy* the stock if you're exercised. With a short put you would only be exercised if the stock price is less than the strike price. If you were exercised you would have to buy the stock at the strike price.

Your reward when you sell an option is capped to what you received (hence the horizontal line in the profit zone), and your risk is potentially unlimited until the stock reaches zero, at which point your loss is capped at the strike price less the premium we received, which would be 50.00 − 7.50 = 42.50.

The Four Basic Risk Profiles Summarized

These are the four charts you need to remember. Even if you just remember the long call option risk profile, you should now be able to construct the other three basic option positions. Once you're comfortable with these and the logic behind them, you'll be ready to look at multi-leg strategies with ease.

Imagine there is a horizontal or vertical mirror separating each of the risk profiles and see how each strategy is the opposite of the one on the other side of the mirror.

Figure 1.8   The four basic option risk profiles

The four basic options risk profiles

Imagine the dotted lines are mirrors and see how each strategy is the opposite of the one on the other side of the mirror.

Buying a call

- belief that stock will rise (bullish outlook)
- risk limited to premium paid
- unlimited maximum reward

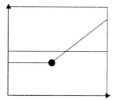

Buying a put

- belief that stock will fall (bearish outlook)
- risk limited to premium paid
- unlimited maximum reward up to the strike price
- less the premium paid

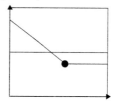

Writing a call

- belief that stock will fall (bearish outlook)
- maximum reward limited to premium received
- risk potentially unlimited (as stock price rises)
- can be combined with another position to limit the risk

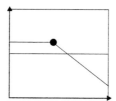

Writing a put

- belief that stock will rise (bullish outlook)
- maximum risk is the strike price less the premium received. We can think of this as either being "unlimited" until the stock reaches zero, or "limited" to the [strike price – premium] formula.
- maximum reward limited to the premium received
- can be combined with another position to limit the risk

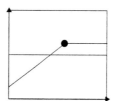

Options in the Marketplace

Let's now look at options in the context of the marketplace and real numbers.

Option Contracts

Stock options are traded in contracts (or lots), not as individual derivative units. Each contract represents 100 shares of the underlying stock.[2]

When you see a U.S. equity call option price of, say, $2.45, you will have to pay $2.45 × 100 for just one contract. A single contract is the minimum amount you can trade, and for U.S. equity options, one contract represents 100 individual shares. In other words, by paying $245.00 you now have the right to buy 100 shares of the stock at whatever strike price you were trading. This is important when considering multi-leg orders, which combine the trading of shares together with options in order to create a new risk profile.

Expiration Dates

Every option has an expiration date, which is usually specified as a month. U.S. equity, index, and Treasury/interest-rate options expire on the Saturday following the third Friday in the expiration month. Trading in the options ceases on that Friday, but the owner can actually exercise the options on the final Saturday.

Strike Prices

Generally, U.S. equity option strike prices start at $5 and then go in $2.50 increments; once they hit $25, they go in $5 increments; at $200 they convert to $10 increments. Anomalies can occur, however, due to stock splits and mergers.

Option Ticker Symbols

Individual options have ticker symbols just like individual stocks do. The symbol identifies the underlying stock, the expiration month, the strike price, and the type of option. It's unlikely you'll ever construct these for yourself, but it's useful to understand the composition of an option ticker nevertheless.

---

[2] For the purpose of this book, I focus on U.S. stock options.

The option ticker is identified by a series of letters. They appear in the order of "root," the expiration month, and strike price. The expiration month letter also identifies whether the option is a call or a put.

The first letter or group of letters (up to three) identifies the underlying stock and is called the root. It doesn't have to be the same as the stock symbol. Microsoft has the stock symbol of MSFT. But because that's more than three letters, a root symbol is devised by the standardizing authority, and a group of three letters is used. MSQ is the primary root for Microsoft options. There can be others under certain conditions, but for now let's keep it simple. The root for Microsoft is MSQ.

The next-to-last letter in an option symbol indicates the expiration month. If the option is a call, then the first half of the alphabet is used. If the option is a put, then the second half of the alphabet is used. Table 1.4 illustrates these codes.

Table 1.4   Expiration Month Codes

	Jan	Feb	Mar	Apr	May	Jun	Jul	Aug	Sep	Oct	Nov	Dec
Calls	A	B	C	D	E	F	G	H	I	J	K	L
Puts	M	N	O	P	Q	R	S	T	U	V	W	X

The last letter of the option symbol indicates the strike price. Again there are codes to decipher the strike price, as shown in Table 1.5.

Table 1.5   Strike Price Codes

A	B	C	D	E	F	G	H	I	J	K	L	M
5	10	15	20	25	30	35	40	45	50	55	60	65
105	110	115	120	125	130	135	140	145	150	155	160	165
205	210	215	220	225	230	235	240	245	250	255	260	265
305	310	315	320	325	330	335	340	345	350	355	360	365

Table 1.5   continued

N	O	P	Q	R	S	T	U	V	W	X	Y	Z
70	75	80	85	90	95	100	7.5	12.5	17.5	22.5	27.5	32.5
170	175	180	185	190	195	200	37.5	42.5	47.5	52.5	57.5	62.5
270	275	280	285	290	295	300	67.5	72.5	77.5	82.5	87.5	92.5
370	375	380	385	390	395	400	97.5	102.5	107.5	112.5	117.5	122.5

By using this information, we can decipher the option symbol MSQAF:

● The MSQ is the root identifying Microsoft, the "A" is for the month of January, and it is a call option.

● The last letter "F" tells us the option is for the $30.00 strike price.

The designation of letters is more complex for long-term options, known as LEAPS (Long-Term Equity Anticipation Securities). Because expiration months may extend out two years or more, alternative symbols are used in the root to distinguish one expiration month from another. Don't worry about remembering or memorizing all the codes. They are readily available and easily obtained when you need them, and most traders working online simply click the applicable option rather than try to figure out the configuration of letters.

Open Interest

Open interest represents the total number of option contracts currently open and is a measure of liquidity in a particular options class. In other words, open interest is a figure that reflects the number of contracts that have been traded but that have not yet been exercised or liquidated by an offsetting trade.

When you trade an option, you may in fact be creating a new option contract. Both buying and selling options will increase the open interest figure, providing the action opens a position. Conversely, buying or selling to close a position will cause open interest to fall. If one side is opening a buy position and the counterparty to the trade is selling his existing bought position, then the open interest will not change.

Looking at the open interest, there is no way of knowing whether the options were bought or sold. However, the figure can be compared with the volume of contracts traded on a given day. When the daily volume exceeds the existing open interest, it suggests that trading in that option was unusually high.

Open interest also indicates the liquidity of an option. When options have high open interest, it means they have a large number of buyers and sellers, and an active secondary market will increase the odds of getting an order filled at a decent price. Generally speaking, the larger the open interest, the easier it will be to trade that option at a reasonable bid-ask spread. But even when disparity exists between the number of buyers and sellers, every option trade entered as a market order will be executed. The Options Clearing Corporation (OCC) ensures an orderly market by acting as seller to each buyer and as buyer to each seller.

Placing Your Trade

The detailed process of placing your trades will depend on your brokerage's practices, but the majority of firms have similar basic components. Here are a few of the major types of orders you'll be making with your online broker.

Market Order

This type of order authorizes your broker to buy or sell stock or options at the best price in the market. Some brokers will be better at doing this than others according to how they route your orders.

Limit Order

This is where you try to get the best value for your order by specifying the price at which you're prepared to buy at some predetermined lower price and sell at some predetermined higher price. With stocks or futures this can be relevant to support or resistance levels. So with limit orders on a stock it could mean

- only *buy* if share falls to a certain target price or lower or
- only *sell* if share rises to a certain price or higher.

Limits are recommended with options, particularly for spreads and combination trades. The reason for this is that the bid-ask spread prices can fluctuate dramatically, and more often not in your favor, so it's better to specify the price at which you'd like to have your order filled.

Contingent Orders

Typically I enter *contingent* orders. This is where the order specifies the precise trigger requirements in order for my trade to be executed. You can combine the contingent order with a limit order. So for example, your order might be like this: *Buy 10 contracts of ACME January 2009 55 strike calls @ 7.30 limit if AMCE last price hits $55.35 or higher.*

So you would only buy the ten contracts at a limit price of 7.30 if the stock trades to $55.35 or higher. In this case the trade is triggered by two separate events. First the stock has to trade to $55.35 or higher, and second, the ACME calls must be at 7.30 or lower. Only then are the criteria met for the trade to be executed. Assuming the trade is filled at 7.30, your trade will actually cost 7.30 x 10 contracts x 100 shares = $7,300. The equivalent share trade would be buying 1,000 shares of ACME at around $55.35 making a total price tag of $55,350. We can agree that $7,300 is much friendlier.

With the limit order in place, if ACME calls are trading above 7.30, you won't get a fill even if the ACME stock has touched or gone through $55.35.

We can also apply contingent orders to stop and limit orders. We can even enter "one cancels other" or OCO orders, which I address later.

Sell Stop Loss

This is where you sell your existing position if the price falls below a specified price. The sell stop is placed below the current price, preferably just below a support area of the underlying asset price. If the stock price rises, you can adjust your stop upwards at any time. You can also place a stop loss when trading options. The stop loss can be contingent on the underlying stock price, the actual option premium, or both.

Sell Stop to Open

This is an order creating a short position. You would do this where you want to take advantage of a falling stock, shorting it as it falls through support.

Buy Stop to Open

This order generates a buy once the stock has reached or exceeded a certain level on its way upwards. This is the opposite of a limit order where you buy below a specified price. A buy stop is appropriate where you expect the price to rise up beyond a resistance level.

Buy Stop Loss

This is an order to buy-to-close your open short position if the stock rises above a specified level. The buy stop is placed above the current price, preferably just above a resistance area if we're talking about stocks. If the stock price falls, you can adjust your stop downwards at any time. You can also place a buy stop loss when trading options. The stop loss can be contingent on the underlying stock price, the actual option premium, or both.

Buy Stop Limit to Open

This order is triggered as the price rises through resistance but you only want to enter your order at a specified price. The buy stop limit will protect you against trading an upward gap or spike that is now trading above the breakout point.

Buy Stop Limit and Stop Loss

This is an extension of the buy stop limit order but includes an "if done" provision specifying that if the buy stop is executed, it triggers a stop loss order at the level you set.

Good till Cancelled (GTC)

This order is valid until you cancel it or until it is filled. For example, a limit order GTC means you authorize your broker to buy at a particular price or lower, today or any time in the future where the price is at that particular level, until you have bought the requisite number of shares or contracts.

Day Only

The order will be cancelled if it is not filled by the end of the trading day on which the order is placed. This is a good ploy because it encourages the floor traders to deal. If they don't fill the order by the end of the day, they won't get their commission, so there is an incentive for floor traders to put this type of trade nearer to the top of their list.

Week Only

The order will be cancelled if it is not filled by the end of the week.

Fill or Kill

The fill or kill order has maximum priority. If it isn't filled immediately, the order is cancelled. This order is bound to capture the attention of the floor trader, but if it's a limit order, then you need to make it realistic.

All or None

Either the entire order is filled or none of it. This is not generally a good idea given that many trades aren't filled all at once anyway because there has to be a buyer or seller on the other side, and most of the time they won't be specifically dealing in the same lot sizes as your order.

Other Market Considerations

Always have a stop in mind when you make a trade
This point is discussed in more detail in Chapters 10 and 11. It is vital to know where you will exit a position, whether it is a profitable situation or otherwise. Some people don't like to actually place stops with their brokers. This can be risky, so at the very least you must have one firmly in your mind, and you must act on it if the stop level has been breached. Also you must always have in your mind when you are likely to want to take profits, and you must act on that too if and when the situation occurs.

I talk about where to place your stops later in the book, but I recommend that when trading options, you base your stops on the stock price, not the option prices unless you are creating combination spreads or day-trading options.

Whipsaws

A whipsaw occurs when a price changes direction rapidly and violently twice or more in quick succession; in intra-day trading terms, this can happen in just a few ticks. The danger is that the whipsaw may trigger your stop loss by a few ticks before the stock continues in the direction you envisaged—but without you on the profit-ride! Whipsaws happen and are part of the trading game. What do you do about them? Well, if you get caught by one, just accept it as part of your trading costs. If you're getting whipsawed over and over again, you'll need to examine why. Could it be because your stops are too tight? Or could it be because of the types of stocks you're trading?

Learning Points

In this chapter you've learned what options are, how they're valued, and how they're traded in the markets. You've learned about risk profiles and how they relate to the position you're trading through the use of options. You've also learned about the main advantages of trading options, the components that make up an options premium, and the main types of orders you can place in the markets.

In the next chapter I show you how you can use certain chart patterns (trends and flags) to help you improve the timing of your trades.

chapter 2

Trends and Flags

This chapter is focused on a couple of chart patterns that work consistently, whether in the context of trading volatility or otherwise simply as devices for improving your timing in the markets.

Before we get into the chart patterns themselves, we must understand something even more deep-rooted. The key to consistent trading is good psychology.

- One of the keys to good psychology is having a trading plan. Trading without a plan is tantamount to amateur gambling.

- The key to a good trading plan is a clear set of rules.

- The key to a clear set of rules is an easily definable chart pattern that identifies clear areas of support and resistance for entry, exit, stop placement, and profit management.

- If you're clear about all that and can stick to the rules, then you'll win—pure and simple. I've trained people with no experience whatsoever, and they're now "boringly" consistent traders who understand the virtue of being patient and take only the prime opportunities on offer.

So let's review our requirements for finding a tradable chart pattern. It must provide us with easily identifiable areas of

- Support
- Resistance

For:

- Entry
- Stop placement
- Profit management

These are all critical elements. If you only trade when you have these elements in place, your trading results will soar in the right direction, whether you're trading options, stocks, or futures.

A Common Mistake

Have you ever traded a stock where you were in a winning position? Have you seen your paper profits start to increase as the stock rose in your favor? What did you do? Did you have a plan for taking profits, or did you stay in too long? *Did you stay in too long?* Did you stay in as the stock started to fall? Did you stay in until your profits were all wiped out and you then had a loss-making situation? Did your winner end up being a loser?

Most people who have invested in the markets have been through this type of situation…on multiple occasions.

Why is it that traders stay in a position too long? Why is it that traders don't take their profits when the signs are that the stock is about to reverse?

Well, I can only go by the countless interviews I've conducted with traders and investors, plus my own early experiences. The fact is that most people don't have a consistent method of identifying suitable candidate stocks regularly in the first place! So when they suddenly find themselves in a winning situation, they tend to hang on too long, as if it's the only opportunity they're ever going to find. Does that ring a bell? Because if you did know how to find good opportunities on a regular basis, then you wouldn't need to hang around in an existing position if all the signs said "sell."

There's another key, one that I've already alluded to. That is to have a clearly defined *trading plan*. Most traders have no idea what a trading plan is. They go to seminars and read books, but they are never taught how to enter or exit their trades. A trading plan outlines your entry and exit points so you know exactly what to do in any circumstance ahead of time. In other words, every trade has a business plan attached to it.

So we need to address two disciplines in this chapter:

1. How to find stocks
2. How to create a trading plan

Benefits of this Method

To clarify why the methodology you're about to learn is so important, here are some compelling reasons to make this a serious part of your trading routine:

● Not letting a winning position turn into a losing one.

● Gaining confidence to seek out and find new opportunities.

● Exercising discipline in your trading plan methodology.

● Specializing your trading based on proven chart patterns.

● Avoiding confusion with this simplified method.

● Only entering into trades when the trend is proven and confirmed by the pattern.

When people have attended my workshops, they leave knowing how to create a trading plan, which is exactly what we're going to accomplish here in the next few pages.

The typical problems faced by traders include

● Overwhelming amounts of information

● Complexity of trading methods

● Lack of confidence in finding new opportunities

● Lack of discipline owing to complexity and lack of confidence

● Poor timing of trades

● Time constraints to learn about and then implement trades

Every trader needs to create a proper trading plan and specialize in a proven chart pattern within the overall context of a trend. By following the method, you'll discover that time no longer is a constraint. You won't be overwhelmed because the trading plan is simple to execute, thereby helping your timing. Your confidence will increase as you start finding opportunities with ease.

The first step is to identify what types of stocks we're looking to trade.

Trending Stocks

We've all heard the expression "the trend is your friend." Well, although it's a little hackneyed now, the basic premise is true. Trading in the direction of the trend is the most consistently profitable method I've seen. The trick is how to identify that a trend is actually in place. Trends can vary in time from minutes on a tick chart to years on a monthly chart.

What Is a Trend?

A trend can be defined as follows:

- **Uptrend**
  An uptrend can be described as a sequence of higher lows in conjunction with higher highs.

- **Downtrend**
  A downtrend can be described as a sequence of lower highs in conjunction with lower lows.

Some people define an uptrend as the point when the closing price is above the moving average (of a specific period), and a downtrend is when the closing price is below the specific moving average. I don't use moving averages of price movement to define trend, nor to source trending stocks. There are inherent challenges with only using moving averages, which I discuss next.

In my workshops I ask my students how they unearth trending stocks, and the two most common answers I hear relate to moving averages and fundamental filters. From those two answers I already know that the person concerned doesn't find trending stocks purely because moving averages and fundamental filters generally don't lead to trending stocks!

So first things first, let's look at some trending stocks and clarify why they're trending (Figure 2.1).

Figure 2.1 An uptrending stock

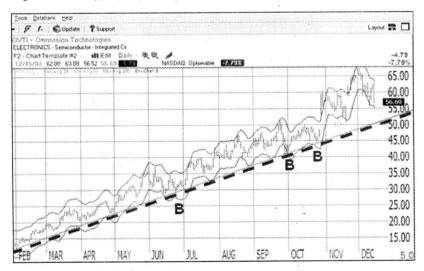

TC2000®.com. Courtesy of Worden Brothers Inc.

As you can see, the stock is rising and appears to keep bouncing off the imaginary trendline at the points B. This trendline is providing *support* for the stock. Typically we expect volume to rise as the price hits the trendline and bounces off it, confirming the supporting action. Notice that with an uptrend, we draw the trendline to join up the *lows*.

Sooner or later the uptrend has to be broken, and the stock will retrace downward. The beauty of using a trendline is that when the price breaks through it, we can define the trend as being over for the time being.

So far so good. Let's now look at a downtrending stock (Figure 2.2).

Figure 2.2 A downtrending stock

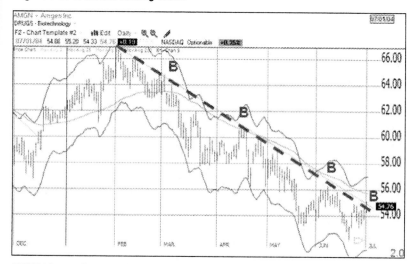

TC2000®.com. Courtesy of Worden Brothers Inc.

Here is the opposite scenario. The stock is falling and appears to keep bouncing off the imaginary trendline at the points B. This trendline is providing *resistance* for the stock. Typically we expect volume to rise as the price hits the trendline and bounces off it, confirming the resistance action. Notice that with a downtrend, we draw the trendline to join up the *highs*.

Sooner or later the downtrend has to be broken, and the stock will retrace upward. By using a trendline we know that when the price breaks through it, we can define the trend as being over.

If this sounds easy, the reason is because it *is*! If you're looking for something more complex, then I'll show you moving averages and why they're more difficult for defining trends. You want your interpretations of trend to be made easily because it helps your decision-making process when it comes to actual trading. If your interpretation of a chart isn't clear, your trading will be equally as unclear, which will only lead to inconsistent, bad, and unsuccessful trading.

The Challenge with Moving Averages

Moving averages are the most widely known and used technical indicators. A moving average is simply the average closing price of a period of bars on a price chart. On a daily chart, a 20-period moving average is the average of the last 20 days' prices. Moving averages are useful for the way in which they smooth price action, and they are perceived by many to be good indicators of trend. The challenge, however, is in getting the settings correct, and those may change from stock to stock as different stocks will trend with different smoothness and different timescales.

The most popular way of using moving averages is to have one short term and one longer term. When the short moving average rises up through the longer term moving average, this is a bullish signal. When the short term moving averages fall down through the longer term moving average, this is seen as a bearish sign.

The problem is that this moving average crossover method is only relevant with trending stocks. And if we can't readily find or identify trending stocks, then there's no merit in it whatsoever. The other problem with it is that by the time the short Moving Average (MA crosses the longer MA, the stock price may well have plummeted or rocketed ahead of time. In other words, a moving average is a *lagging indicator*, and if the lag is too long, then the stock moves ahead without you. If the lag is too short, then there are no smoothing benefits to using the moving averages at all.

So what if the stock is rangebound or zig-zagging all over the place? Well, then moving averages aren't going to be any use to you.

The chart in Figure 2.3 uses moving average crossovers, and the sell signal occurs a full $40.00 below the high of the stock. That's not exactly very efficient, and in the meantime the stock has been up and down in vicious swings that would send us diving for the Pepto-Bismol. Admittedly the 10-week and 40-week moving average settings here are too slow and therefore inappropriate. However, it's just as easy to get the moving average settings too fast, which then makes them equally as inappropriate.

Figure 2.3 Moving averages example

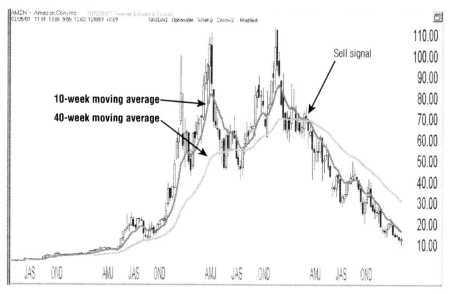

TC2000®.com. Courtesy of Worden Brothers Inc.

So moving averages are best used in the context of trending stocks. In the next example (Figure 2.4) we see how confusing the signals become when the stock is rangebound.

Figure 2.4 Moving averages double crossovers

TC2000®.com. Courtesy of Worden Brothers Inc.

Each "D" stands for "Double Crossover," whereby the moving average crossovers send a long and short signal (or short then long signal) in quick succession, resulting in losses to your account. If this happens continually, then your accounts can be eroded pretty fast! Do you now see how moving average crossovers could be something of a challenge if not calibrated correctly in each case?

Notice in Figure 2.5 that we're back into a trending situation. This time the trend is down, there are fewer double crossovers, and the position is a little clearer. But even here, (a) you still have those confusing double crossovers, and (b) you still need to understand how to *find* trending stocks.

Figure 2.5 Moving averages of a trending stock

TC2000®.com. Courtesy of Worden Brothers Inc.

Trendlines

The easiest way to *identify* a trend is by creating a trendline for the price action. Trendlines are far more reliable and simpler to use than moving averages.

● With an uptrend, the easiest way to trade is to wait for the trendline to be hit and the price bar to bounce upward off it, continuing the uptrend.

● With a downtrend, the easiest way to trade is to wait for the trendline to be hit and the price bar to bounce downward off it, continuing the downtrend.

A break of the trendline, particularly with rising volume, may signify the end of that trend.

Figure 2.6 Trendlines

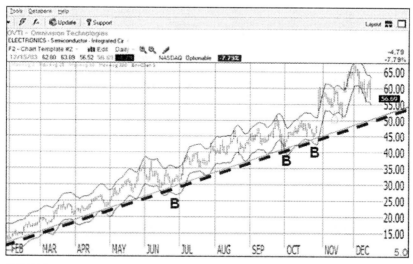

TC2000®.com. Courtesy of Worden Brothers Inc.

If the trendline is broken, particularly with an increase in trading volume, then you know the trend is over, and you can go and find another stock that meets your trending criteria. The advantage is that you exit almost immediately and the rule is very straightforward. If you were using a moving average, you might have to wait several more days until the lines cross over, and by that time you could be sitting on significant losses.

Trending stocks tend to move in steps. These steps involve thrusting moves followed by consolidation. These moves can be referred to as steps or in some cases, *flags*. A flag is distinguished by the significant thrusting move prior to the flag forming.

Consolidating Chart Patterns

My favorite chart pattern is the flag. This occurs after a thrusting surge (the flagpole) then consolidates to form the actual flag. The thrust can occur in either an upward (bullish) or downward (bearish) direction. A flag occurs during a persistent and dominant trend and temporarily interrupts that trend before it resumes.

The flag itself consists of the price pattern rebounding off two parallel interim trendlines before breaking out in the direction of the dominant trend.

Bull Flag

With bull flags, our entry is a *buy* order, and our stop loss is a *sell* order. We anticipate a rising stock price.

Figure 2.7 Bull flag

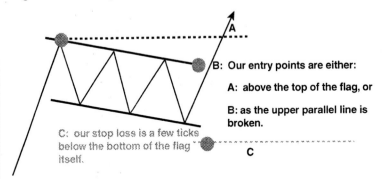

B: Our entry points are either:

A: above the top of the flag, or

B: as the upper parallel line is broken.

C: our stop loss is a few ticks below the bottom of the flag itself.

So here we can see that we have the makings of a trading plan, and you enter your buy order at either point A or B.

Point A is at the level of the top of the flag. This is the most conservative entry point because it is where the price is making new highs. You must make sure that volume is increasing as the new high is made. Increasing volume means there is conviction behind the move, which makes it more likely to be sustainable.

Point B is where the price breaks out of the flag itself. This is more aggressive than Point A and again requires increasing trading volume to demonstrate conviction in the move.

If the entry is activated, then you need a stop loss. Point C is the level where, if you were already in the trade, you'd exit with a small loss.

This is your basic trading plan for a bull flag within the context of an upward trend.

Bear Flag

With bear flags, our entry is a sell (short) order, and our stop loss is a buy order to close the position. We anticipate a falling stock price.

Figure 2.8 Bear flag

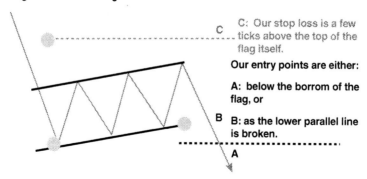

C: Our stop loss is a few ticks above the top of the flag itself.

Our entry points are either:

A: below the borrom of the flag, or

B: as the lower parallel line is broken.

We enter our sell (short) order at either point A or B.

Point A is at the level of the bottom of the flag. As such it is the most conservative entry point because it is where the price is making new lows. You must make sure that volume is increasing as the new low is made. Increasing volume means there is conviction behind the move, which makes it more likely to be sustainable.

Point B is where the price breaks out of the flag itself. This is more aggressive than Point A and again requires increasing trading volume to demonstrate conviction in the move.

If the entry is activated, then you need a stop loss. Point C is the level where, if you were already in the trade, you'd exit with a small loss.

This is your basic trading plan for a bear flag within the context of a downward trend. You can see examples of both a bull and bear flag in Figures 2.9 and 2.10.

Figure 2.9 Bull flag chart

TC2000®.com. Courtesy of Worden Brothers Inc.

The chart in Figure 2.9 is actually a *cup and handle* pattern. These manifest themselves as flags at the end of a bowl pattern or right around a double top. If they break to the upside, two areas of resistance are broken, the flag itself and the previous high.

Figure 2.10 Bear flag chart

TC2000®.com. Courtesy of Worden Brothers Inc.

Flags Within the Context of a Trend

Now, what if I said to you, how about finding flags within the context of a trend? That means you can play the flag, knowing that the trend is backing you up. Now we're beginning to add some backbone to our trading plan.

All we have to do is draw a trendline to see if the flag is forming within the context of a trend.

In the previous two examples you could see that this is the case. The bull flag is within the context of a two-month uptrend, and the bear flag is within the context of a one-month downtrend.

Figure 2.11 Bull flag resolved to the upside

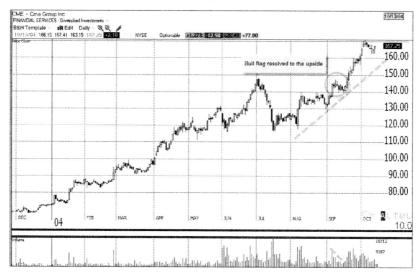

TC2000®.com. Courtesy of Worden Brothers Inc.

Figure 2.12 Bear flag resolved to the downside

TC2000®.com. Courtesy of Worden Brothers Inc.

I haven't drawn the trendlines in at the precise angles in these charts, but if they are broken by the stock price action, then you would exit the long (bull flag) or short (bear flag) positions. Similarly, to enter into the long stock position, the price would need to rise above the top of the bull flag or break up through the upper flag trendline.

To enter the short stock position, the price would need to fall below the bottom of the bear flag or break down through the lower flag trendline.

Can you see how you can make simple rules regarding the trend and flag patterns in order to create a cohesive trading plan?

When a stock is trending, it typically does so in steps...or flags. So by identifying trending stocks, we're going to find flags too. Not all flags are in long-established trends. For example, take a look at this fantastic bull flag in Figure 2.13 that I found as the stock was emerging from a downtrend.

Figure 2.13 Bull flag in context of downtrend

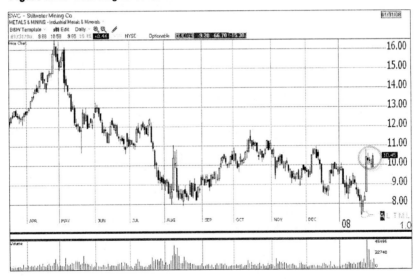

TC2000®.com. Courtesy of Worden Brothers Inc.

As you can see in Figure 2.14, the stock doubled in one month after breaking out from the bull flag pattern. Furthermore, by simply drawing a trendline as the stock rises, you could manage your trade and exit with a huge profit once that trendline was broken.

Figure 2.14 Bull flag breakout from downtrend

TC2000®.com. Courtesy of Worden Brothers Inc.

Managing Your Profits

Stop losses are easy to understand and in the context of flag patterns, easy to identify and enter. However, one of the major difficulties traders have is how to manage profits. There are two areas of importance:

1. Taking partial profits or scaling out
2. Letting the rest run

You've probably heard things like "cut your losses and let your profits run." That's all well and good, but you must have a mechanism to do it. Flag patterns give you such a mechanism.

The One to One (1:1) Theory

If you intra-day trade the indices such as the S&P e-minis, then you may be aware of a pattern occurring that is known as an "equal drive" or 1:1. Supposedly the pattern originates from Elliott Wave and Gann theory, but having studied them in depth for several years, I'd stay away from them both in order to save yourself from going round in circles and getting very frustrated!

Let me save you some time right here and now. Counter to the Gann and Elliott theory, there is no pre-ordained destiny for the markets whatsoever. There are three factors that affect a stock price:

- Technical analysis (of which chart patterns, Gann, Elliott, Fibonacci, and a myriad of other techniques may be *part*)

- Fundamental analysis (the study of corporate and economic financial information)

- News (international, national, industrial, corporate, political, economic, and financial)

When news is at the fore, all the other techniques pretty much go out the window until the market returns to normal and stops over-reacting either out of panic or greed. This is why black-box trading systems never work brilliantly all the time. To be consistently successful, you need to factor in the human element for which the catalyst is a news event such as an earnings report, an economic data release, an election, or a surprise of any kind.

Back to 1:1s. The concept involved here is that a stock makes an "impulse" move in the direction of the dominant trend and then retraces before making another move in the direction of the trend.

The *theory* is that the second impulse move will keep going until it reaches the magnitude of the previous impulse move. Does this always happen? No, of course not, but we're using the theory *not* to help us enter our trades, but to help us *manage our profits*.

Figure 2.15 1:1 bullish

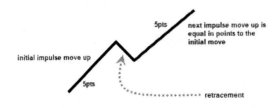

Figure 2.16 1:1 bearish

It's also feasible that the retracements themselves can make 1:1 moves, but you don't need to look at those for the purposes of managing your profits. So the question is how does the 1:1 theory help you manage your profits? Well, if we assume that the first impulse move occurs before the flag pattern, then we can project a target for afterwards if the stock price breaks out of that flag pattern in the direction of the trend.

For example, take that chart of SWC again from Figure 2.14. We can see that the second impulse move is very similar to the first move before consolidating again into the second flag pattern.

Figure 2.17 SWC 1:1 move

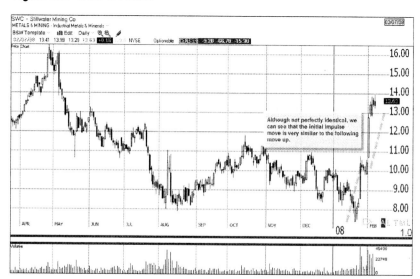

TC2000®.com. Courtesy of Worden Brothers Inc.

Of course, who's to say how long this would continue? For our purposes we can use the theory to identify a target at which to take partial profits. The question is—at what point on the chart would you take partial profits? In my experience about 50% of the initial impulse move is a sound place to take some money off the table while letting the rest run with the trendline serving as a trailing stop.

Figure 2.18 Setting profit target using 1:1

TC2000®.com. Courtesy of Worden Brothers Inc.

The trade is entered above the high of the first bull flag. The initial stop placement is just below the flag bottom.

As the stock price rises and we take partial profits, we can move our initial stop up to where we entered the trade and manage the remaining profits using a trendline.

Figure 2.19 Managing your profits by adjusting the initial sell stop loss

TC2000®.com. Courtesy of Worden Brothers Inc.

It's important to note that you do have discretion over the trendline and how steep you want to make it. In the case of SWC, it's clear that the stock is making another bull flag pattern, so you may want to give it a bit more room to form the pattern and move further to the upside by adjusting the trendline and making it a bit shallower. With SWC it's quite feasible that you could have ridden this stock all the way to $20, almost doubling your money in just over one month.

Figure 2.20 Managing your bull flag profits by using a trendline

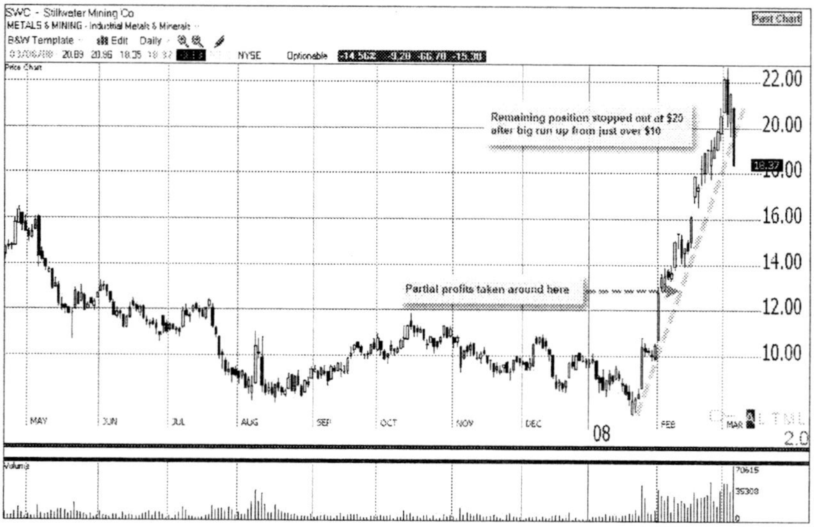

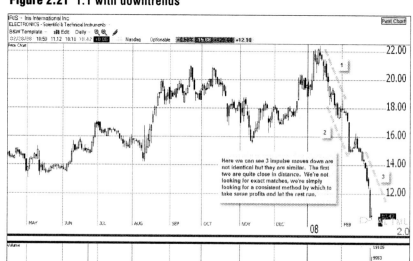

TC2000®.com. Courtesy of Worden Brothers Inc.

The same works exactly in reverse for bear flags.

Figure 2.21 1:1 with downtrends

TC2000®.com. Courtesy of Worden Brothers Inc.

As with the bull flags, we don't know how long the next impulse move will be, but our objective is not to try to predict the future. It's to employ a method to take partial profits and let the rest run in an organized and controlled way. Please don't fall into the trap of trying to predict the future. You'd be doomed to fail, sentencing yourself to a life's work that sends you round and round in circles. I've been there, so be warned!

You're going to look to take partial profits when the new impulse move reaches 50% of the previous one. You let the rest run with the downward trendline serving as your trailing stop.

Figure 2.22 Managing your bear flag profits

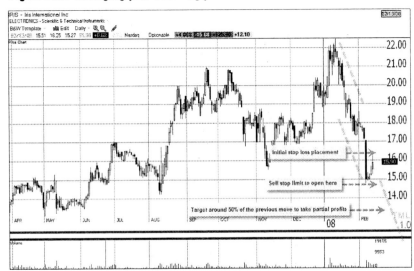

TC2000®.com. Courtesy of Worden Brothers Inc.

In this example we're assuming that we see the trade on February 13. We place a sell stop limit to open at just under $15.00 (the low of the flag). Our initial stop loss is just over $16.00 (the top of the flag area), and we set our first target for partial profits at around $13.50, which represents a downward move of around $1.50, which is around 50% of the previous impulse moves downward.

Figure 2.23 Managing your profits by adjusting the initial buy stop loss

TC2000®.com. Courtesy of Worden Brothers Inc.

As the stock price falls in your favor, you can move the initial stop down to where your entry order was so that you put yourself in a no-lose position; in other words, "moving your stop to breakeven."

Figure 2.24 Using a trendline to exit a profitable trade

TC2000®.com. Courtesy of Worden Brothers Inc.

We can see here how we took partial profits at the 50% mark (around $1.50 down from our entry point, making our first target around $13.50 as our initial trade entry was just below $15.00). The remainder of our position is stopped out at a profit as the stock bounces up and hits our trendline at around $12.00.

Rounded Tops and Flag Failures

What happens when a flag pattern doesn't do what it's supposed to do? There are two things that can happen:

a. The flag forms, breaks out, triggers your trade, and then immediately comes back and stops you out for a small loss.

b. The flag forms but doesn't break out, and your trade isn't triggered.

Case (a) is pretty straightforward. You know that you're not guaranteed a profit from the outset, but you can contain your risk to just a small amount.

Case (b) is interesting in that you can't make a loss in such a scenario. Remember you're entering a stop order to enter the trade. Therefore, if it isn't triggered, you cannot make a loss.

Let's take two examples of the same stock, BWLD. On October 2, the stock is forming a perfect bull flag, as shown in Figure 2.25.

Figure 2.25 BWLD bull flag (i)

TC2000®.com. Courtesy of Worden Brothers Inc.

So far so good. It resolves itself to the upside, and you're in profit, having been triggered into the trade at around $38.90. On October 10, another bull flag starts to form. So if you missed the first one on October 2, you have another chance here on October 10, provided the high of the flag is exceeded, preferably with rising volume.

Figure 2.26 BWLD bull flag (ii)

TC2000®.com. Courtesy of Worden Brothers Inc.

The top of the flag is $42.12, so if the stock reaches, say $42.25 with rising volume, then we'd like to be in the trade. However, take a look at Figure 2.27 to what happens next.

Figure 2.27 BWLD rounded top

TC2000®.com. Courtesy of Worden Brothers Inc.

It never gets going and forms a rounded top pattern. Your order is never executed, and so you neither make nor lose money. This is one of the key benefits about flag patterns. Often when they don't work or are not going to work, you don't lose anything at all.

Let's now look at an example of a bear flag that doesn't get going. Using BWLD again, the bear flag is perfectly formed on March 14, but you should also notice that it's a double bottom, so that would give you a warning sign. If the stock breaks the previous low in January, then that's a stronger signal than merely breaking the low of the current flag.

Figure 2.28 BWLD bear flag

TC2000®.com. Courtesy of Worden Brothers Inc.

In order to be triggered into the short trade, your choice is that either the stock breaks below the current flag low, say around $19.50 (as the actual flag low is $19.63), or it has to break below the January low of $18.25.

Figure 2.29 shows what happens next.

The stock gaps up, the trade isn't triggered, and yet you don't lose anything. That's a great result when what you anticipated doesn't materialize. Although this isn't perfectly formed in this particular example, just as we can get rounded tops from bull flags, we can also get rounded bottoms from failed bear flags.

Isn't it great that you can be wrong and still not lose anything?

51

Figure 2.29 BWLD rounded bottom

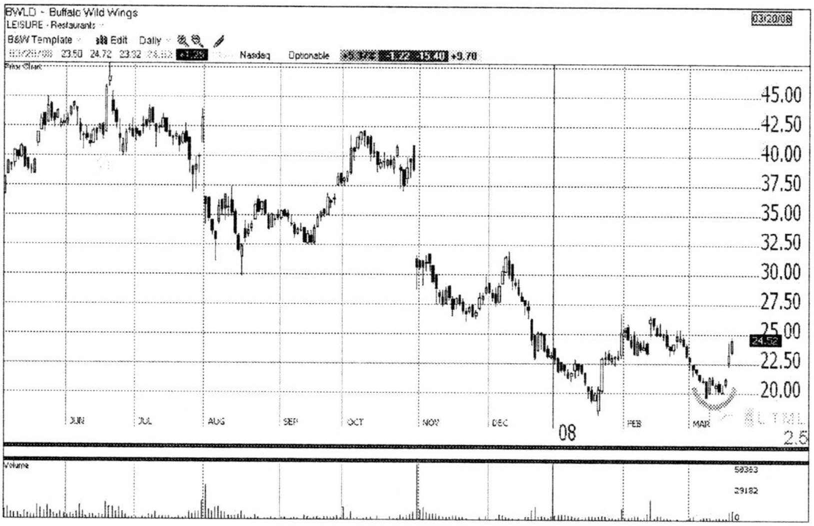

TC2000®.com. Courtesy of Worden Brothers Inc.

Cup and Handle—Two Patterns in One

The cup and handle pattern is one of the most prized chart patterns out there. A few years ago I figured out why this is so: It's because it comprises two bullish chart patterns in one. The first is a "bowl" or cup. The second part of a cup and handle is a...you guessed it...a flag. Both individual patterns are bullish. Both together are very bullish.

Take a look at Figures 2.30-2.33, and you'll see exactly what I mean. It's important to appreciate that cup and handle patterns come in all sorts of shapes, sizes, and timeframes.

● If the flag forms above the first lip of the cup, you trade it in the same way that you trade a bull flag by entering your buy stop order just above the flag area.

● If the flag forms below the first lip of the cup, you either trade it as a flag, or you enter your stop order above the first lip of the cup. In other words, you only get filled when both resistances have been cleared by the stock, preferably with rising volume.

All of the following charts resolved to the upside.

With ARTC in Figure 2.30, the handle (flag) formed its tops just above the first lip of the cup. This is a bonus as you can simply trade it as a flag pattern but with the added bonus that it is in fact a cup and handle and therefore a more powerful pattern.

Figure 2.30 ARTC cup and handle

TC2000®.com. Courtesy of Worden Brothers Inc.

With CTRP, again the handle forms above the first lip of the cup. Notice how this pattern is literally only a month in duration, starting in mid-November and becoming ready to trade in mid-December.

Figure 2.31 CTRP cup and handle

TC2000®.com. Courtesy of Worden Brothers Inc.

CTV is slightly messier, and the handle forms below the first lip of the cup. This is not nearly as easy to trade as the previous two charts.

Figure 2.32 CTV cup and handle

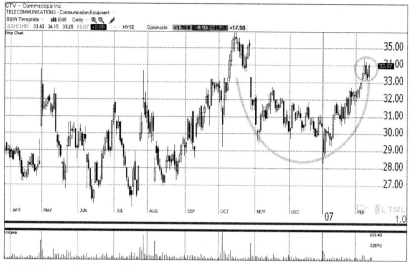

TC2000®.com. Courtesy of Worden Brothers Inc.

This last example, CYNO, has a very lopsided cup, which lasts for two months before forming an elongated handle—but it is still highly tradable.

Figure 2.33 CYNO cup and handle

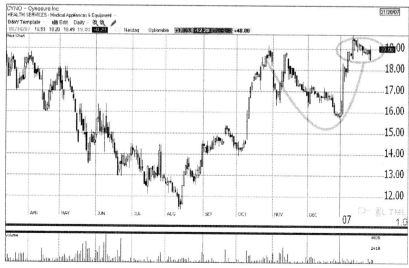

TC2000®.com. Courtesy of Worden Brothers Inc.

The opposite of a cup and handle has no official name but is identical in reverse.

Figure 2.34 BGP reverse cup and handle

TC2000®.com. Courtesy of Worden Brothers Inc.

You treat the reverse cup and handle exactly the same as the cup and handle, except it's in reverse.

● If the bear flag forms below the first low of the upside-down cup, you trade it in the same way that you trade a bear flag by entering your sell stop order just below the flag area.

● If the bear flag forms above the first low of the cup, you either trade it as a bear flag or you enter your sell short stop order below the first low of the upside-down cup. In other words, you only get filled when both support areas have been breached by the stock, preferably with rising volume.

In Figure 2.34, the bear flag formed just above the first low of the pattern. If you wanted to trade this, you'd be safer to wait until the first low of the upside-down cup was breached. Just a few days later the chart formed another bear flag just below the first low of the upside-down cup, providing an opportunity to trade it as a straightforward bear flag.

Figure 2.35 BGP bear flag after cup and handle

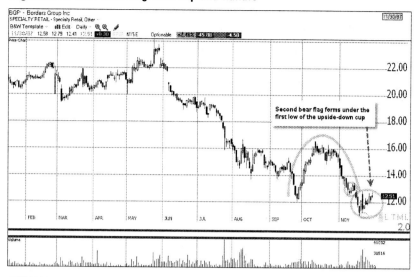

TC2000®.com. Courtesy of Worden Brothers Inc.

Finding Flag Patterns

One of the keys to consistent trading is being able to find what you're looking for. Over the years I've developed sophisticated algorithms to find fantastic flag patterns with ease. Along the way, I've also found some simpler formulae that can do a reasonable job of finding decent consolidating patterns. You can find the basic formula by logging into www.volatilemarketsmadeeasy.com/formula.

Learning Points

Now you know why I hunt trending stocks that form flag patterns. If you want to be consistent with your trading, then most of the time you'll do better by trading in the direction of the trend. The key is how to find trending stocks and flag patterns at will. The problem many people have with trading a winning position is that they're scared they won't find one ever again. So they stay in too long and eventually end up forfeiting their profits. Does that sound at all familiar?

When the markets are generally trending down, there are likely to be fewer uptrending stocks and vice versa. Typically, whatever the general trend of the market, you will want to trade in the same direction until the trendline is broken. By trading in this way, you're being responsive to a potential change in direction, but you're not trading so tight that you'd be whipsawed out of a profitable position.

You've also learned in this chapter how easy it is to enter and manage trades with these patterns. That's the whole reason why I use them. My trading psychology is always crystal clear, and there's no room to maneuver and kid myself. For that reason alone, trading in this way is invaluable to me—and can be for you too. The bonus with these patterns is that they often experience explosive moves in the direction of the trend. Your trade is only triggered when the flag pattern is breached in the direction of the prevailing dominant trend. So if there is a reversal, you're not triggered into the trade, and if you're not in the trade to begin with, you can't lose money. This is another great reason to trade these patterns.

chapter 3

Options and the Greeks

In this chapter I give you a basic overview of what is known as the *Greeks* and set the basic foundations that you'll need for the strategy chapters ahead.

The Greeks are sensitivities to options risk characteristics, the names taken from actual Greek letters. To understand why options have sensitivities to various factors, let's go back to the original definition of an option:

● The right, not the obligation

● To buy or sell an asset

● At a fixed price

● Before a predetermined date

Remember the seven factors that affect an option's premium:

1. Type of option (call or put)

2. The underlying stock price

3. The option strike price

4. The option expiration date

5. The stock price's volatility

6. The risk free rate of interest

7. Dividends paid

If these factors affect the pricing of an option, it stands to reason that option premiums must be sensitive to them. We can distill this further by highlighting the following sensitivities:

Table 3.1 Option definition and sensitivities

Factor affecting option premium	Sensitivity of option to...
Underlying stock price →	**Speed of the stock price movement**
Expiration date →	**Time decay**
Volatility of underlying asset →	**Volatility of the stock**
Risk free rate of interest →	**Interest rates**

Each sensitivity has a corresponding "Greek" as follows:

Table 3.2 Option sensitivities and Greeks

Sensitivity of option to...	Greek
Speed of underlying asset price movement → →	**Delta** **Gamma***
Time decay →	**Theta**
Volatility →	**Vega**
Interest rates →	**Rho**

*Gamma measures the option sensitivity to Delta, which we discuss in this chapter.

Tables 3.3 and 3.4 explain and summarize the Greeks:

Table 3.3 Greeks descriptions

Greek		Description
Delta	Δ	Change in option price relative to change in underlying asset price (i.e., *speed*). You can see this as the effect (on the option position) of a $1 increase in the stock price.
Gamma	Γ	Rate of change of the option delta relative to change in underlying asset price (i.e., *acceleration*).
Theta	Θ	Change in option price relative to change in time left to expiration (i.e., *time decay*). The rate of time decay is often expressed in dollars per day.
Vega	K	Change in option price relative to the change in the asset's volatility (i.e., *historical volatility*). We can see this as the effect (on the option position) of a 1% increase in volatility.
Rho	P	Change in option price relative to changes in the risk-free interest rate (i.e., *interest rates*). We can see this as the effect (on the option position) of a 1% increase in interest rates.

Table 3.4 Greeks definitions

Greek	Definition	Comment
Delta	Delta is a measure of the option's sensitivity to change in the stock price (i.e., speed). *A positive delta means that the option's position will become more valuable as the stock price rises. A negative delta means that the options value will increase as the stock price falls.*	The delta ratio is also known as the hedge ratio. We can view delta as the probability of an option expiring In the Money (ITM). An At the Money (ATM) option will have a 50:50 chance of expiring ITM. For a call this means a delta of 0.5, and for a put this means a delta of -0.5 (because the put will rise as the stock falls and vice versa). An option premium should never move faster than the underlying stock price in dollar for dollar terms; therefore, the delta will never exceed 1 or -1 per contract. When making calculations for combination positions, if we say one share of stock has a delta of 1, then 100 shares of stock has a delta of 100. One ATM call option contract will therefore have a delta of 50 (0.5 x 100), and one ATM put will have a delta of -50 (-0.5 x 100).
Gamma	Gamma is a measure of the option's sensitivity to delta relative to the underlying stock price. If delta can be viewed as the option's sensitivity to the speed, then gamma can be viewed as the option's sensitivity to acceleration. *Gamma is positive for long call and long put positions and has the same value for equivalent ATM calls and puts. A low gamma means that large shifts in the stock price will be required to be beneficial to the option position while a high gamma signifies that even small shifts in the stock price will be beneficial to the options position.*	We can view gamma as the rate of change of delta, i.e., the curvature of delta risk. We can also interpret gamma as the odds of a change in the option position. The odds of a change in delta will be highest where there is a turning point in the risk profile chart, i.e., at a strike price. So for a long call or put, gamma will peak ATM. The strike prices are where the action is to be had because this is the area where delta is on a knife edge and will change if the stock moves one way or the other (ITM or Out of the Money [OTM]).

Table 3.4 Greeks definitions (continued)

Greek	Definition	Comment
Theta	Theta measures the sensitivity of the option price relative to change in time left to expiration. *For long options positions, theta is usually negative, signifying that time decay is hurting the long option position and that the passage of time will reduce the value of that long position.* For combination options trades, theta can be positive, showing that time decay can help the spread position, particularly if the position is currently in profit.*	Time decay is fastest during the last 30 days until expiration and when option is ATM. Time decay hurts option buyers and helps option sellers.
Vega	Vega is the measure of the option sensitivity relative to the change in the stock's volatility. *Vega is always positive for long options positions and is identical for equivalent ATM calls and puts. A high positive vega signifies that small increases in volatility will be helpful to the option position, while a low vega signifies that high volatility will be required to augment the option's position.*	Historical volatility relates to the volatility of the underlying stock, and implied volatility relates to the volatility implied within the market traded option premium.
Rho	Rho measures the sensitivity of the option price relative to changes in the risk-free interest rate. *Higher interest rates will be beneficial to calls and detrimental to puts. Also, the longer the time to expiration, the greater value (positive or negative) rho will have, given that interest rates need time to bite.*	In a low interest rate environment rho has the least impact on options positions than any of the other Greeks.
Zeta	Zeta measures the percentage change in option price per 1% change in implied volatility.	A 10% increase in implied volatility can in some cases double the option premium.

*The one exception to the rule being with deep ITM put options.

Let's go through each Greek in more detail to make sense of all this.

Delta Δ

The basics:

- The option delta is the rate of change of the option price compared with the price movement of the underlying asset price. In other words, delta measures the speed of the option price movement as compared with movement of the underlying asset.

$$\text{Delta} = \frac{\text{rate of change in option price}}{\text{rate of change of underlying asset price}}$$

- You can think of delta as being the probability of the option expiring ITM. As a general rule, ATM calls have deltas of 0.5. Therefore, for every $1.00 the stock moves, the call will move at approximately $0.50, that is, half the dollar-move of the underlying stock. Inevitably, as the stock price moves away from the ATM position, the delta value will change too, away from 0.5.

- Because U.S. stock options contracts represent 100 shares, the delta value of an ATM call option is represented as 50 instead of 0.5. One individual share has a delta of one. 100 shares have a delta of 100. Because a contract represents 100 shares, [100 x 0.5 = 50].

- A delta of +/- 50 is like saying the option has a 50% chance of expiring ITM. This makes complete sense because ATM options have a 50% chance of expiring in or out of the money.

- ATM = +/− 50 deltas. That is, it moves at half the speed of the underlying asset.

- ATM calls have a delta of 0.5, meaning that for every 1 point the stock rises, the option will increase by 0.5 points.

- ATM puts have a delta of -0.5 meaning that for every 1 point the stock falls, the option price will increase by 0.5 points.
    - If you buy an ATM call, then you have a delta of 0.5.
    - If you sell an ATM call, then you have a delta of -0.5.
    - If you buy an ATM put, then you have a delta of -0.5.
    - If you sell an ATM put, then you have a delta of 0.5.

- All bought calls have a positive delta.

- All sold calls have a negative delta.

- All bought puts have a negative delta.

- All sold puts have a positive delta.

Example

If you buy 100 shares of ACME (+100 deltas), you would need to buy two ATM puts (-50 deltas each) for a delta *neutral position* where the total delta would be roughly zero.

Example

Let's say you want to buy 10 contracts of $100 strike price calls as follows:

- Days to expiration: 8
- Stock price: $96.50
- Historical (stock) volatility: 45%
- Call premium: $1.40
- Call delta: 0.32

If you buy 10 contracts at 1.40, your net debit is 10 x 100 x 1.40 = $1,400. If the stock instantly rises by $1.00, the call would be expected to move by approximately 32%, which translates to a total move of $448 to a total position value of $1,848. So you can see that a quick 1% move in the stock translates here to a 32% rise in the option premium. If the stock falls by $1.00 (or around 1%) the option position drops by around $340 to $1,060.

We know that delta will be roughly 0.5 with ATM calls. We also know that delta will approach 1 as the call gets further ITM. And we know that delta will decline towards zero the further OTM the option becomes. In other words, as the stock price moves, the option delta will also fluctuate. Taking the first scenario where the stock rose by $1.00 to $97.50, the delta also moved from 0.32 to 0.38. As the stock approaches $100, the delta will climb toward 0.50, so it's a constantly moving target.

Another point worth noting is that delta will diminish as the stock approaches the expiration date. This is particularly evident with OTM options. Take the same call option but with only three days left to expiration. The stock remains at the original $96.50, but the new delta has plunged to 0.23. A $1.00 move in the stock price will now only translate to a $0.23 move in the option position, but, again, remember that delta will move as the stock price moves— delta is not linear. Rather it moves dynamically with price and time. It's also worth noting that the 230 shares is the equivalent to a 10 contract call position with a delta of 0.23. This is important for advanced traders who will adjust their positions frequently in order to achieve a constantly balanced delta neutral position.

Why Does Speed Matter?

Delta is important because it is an indication of the leverage we have in a position.

Imagine buying 100 shares of stock. Each $1.00 your stock rises, you make $100 x $1.00 = $100. Each $1.00 your stock falls, you lose $100.

How about if by purchasing calls you could now make $200 when your stock rises by $1.00? This would also mean that you could lose $200 for every point the stock falls. Let's say you bought the stock at $40.00. To buy 100 shares costs you $4,000. Compare that to buying the equivalent in call options: One deep ITM call contract costs you, say $12.00, for which you'll have to pay a total of $1,200 (12 x 1 x 100).

Because the option is deep ITM, let's say that your delta is 1, that is, for every one point the stock moves, the call option you've bought also moves by 1 point. If the stock rises to $45...

● Your shares will increase by $5.00 per share, and you'll make $500 profit, or 12.5% on the $4,000 investment.

● Your options will increase by $5.00, and you'll make $500 profit, or 42% on the $1,200 investment.

So far so good, but what would have happened if the market went against you and the stock had actually fallen from $40 to $35?

● Your shares would have decreased by $5.00 per share, and you would have lost $500, a loss of 12.5%. From the $4,000 you started with, you would have had then had $3,500.

● Your options would have decreased by $5.00 and would have lost $500, a loss of over 42%. From the $1,200 you started with, you would have only had $700.

Can you now see why we might want to do something about the speed of the option's price movements depending on our outlook and why we might want to offset (or hedge) delta?

Just as you always want enough time to be right when you buy an option, you also want to make sure that modest swings in the stock price aren't causing uncomfortably wild downside movements in your options position. This is why you want to hedge delta or in other words, slow down the speed of the percentage movement of your position. From here it's possible, with active management of your positions, to create delta neutral positions that you adjust from time to time as the stock price fluctuates by taking incremental profits and fine-tuning the position back to delta neutral when it gets too far out of kilter. This is known as...

Delta Neutral Trading

Delta neutral trading is a method of trading whereby the delta on your multi-legged trade is equal to *zero*. The idea is that this conveys a "hedged" position, whereby the risk is reduced because your position speed is slowed down.

Delta neutral traders do this on the basis that they can continually make profitable adjustments to their trade as the asset price fluctuates. The adjustments (usually selling part of the profitable side) bring the spread trade back to a delta neutral position (that is, where the sum of the deltas for that position equal zero), while continually capitalizing on the profitable side of the trade as the stock fluctuates up and down. This can also be known as *gamma trading*.

A popular technique is to make the profitable adjustments back to delta neutral when the underlying asset has moved by 10–20% in either direction.

Delta neutral does *not* mean risk-free. As you've already seen, delta is *not* linear and will fluctuate with time and as the stock price moves.

Leverage and Gearing

Options have high leverage because a small percentage move in the underlying asset can mean a very high percentage move from the corresponding options.

Let's look at an idealized example that emphasizes delta in the context of leverage.

ACME Co. has a stock price of $20.00. You decide to buy a call option with strike price (e) of $25.00. The call option costs you $1.00. (Remember that an option has two parts to its value: time value and intrinsic value.)

In this example, until the stock price of ACME rises beyond $25, there will be no intrinsic value because the strike price is $25.00. So now let's assume that there is no change to the time value portion. If the ACME stock price now rises to $30, what is the intrinsic value of the option?

Answer: $30 − $25 = $5.00.

Therefore, the value of the call premium must be at least $5.00.

Conclusion: ACME's stock price has risen from $20 to $30, an increase of 50%. And the option premium has risen from $1 to $5, an increase of 500%.

This is what I mean by leverage—the ability to generate greater percentage returns with lower cost.

Of course we know from before that leverage works the other way too. If ACME's stock price moves back down to $20 from $30, this is a decrease of 33%. If the option premium moves from $5 back down to $1, this is a far greater percentage decrease than 33%.

Delta Neutral Trading for Hedging

What you have just seen is the phenomenon of delta. When a call option moves ITM, the delta increases. So the higher the delta, the faster the option price is moving as compared with the stock price and the greater the probability the call has of being ITM at expiration. OTM options have lower (and slower) deltas reflecting their lesser probability of expiring ITM. Remember, an ATM call will have a delta of roughly 0.5. Buying OTM options in order to slow down a positive delta is not a satisfactory tactic because of OTM options' low probability of expiring ITM.

In order to slow down your delta, you can combine stock and option legs and create combination or "spread" trades. These trades are intended to reduce risk of exposure to fast moving delta by bringing the delta value close to zero. By doing this you are not exposed to such wild swings on the downside, while also keeping your probability of success high. You make your profits by incrementally adjusting the position back to delta neutral. Sometimes further cash investment in a position is required in order to balance it back to delta neutral, though preferably the adjustments are made by selling portions of the profitable side of the spread.

Delta neutral does not mean zero risk. Delta neutral trading is sometimes talked about as some sort of nirvana. This is not the case, although it should be pointed out that it can significantly reduce risk in certain scenarios and with particular strategies but is mainly useful for the professionals only who can trade inside the normal bid-ask spread.

Example

Consider a simple six-month call option where the stock price is $69 and the $70 strike call premium is $9.80. We're going to examine the call risk profile in the context of its delta profile.

Figure 3.1 Long call risk profile

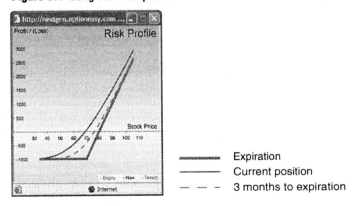

Expiration
Current position
3 months to expiration

Figure 3.2 Long call delta

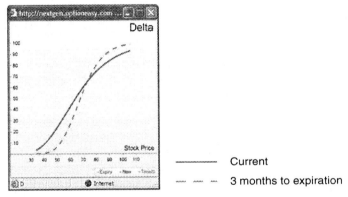

Current
3 months to expiration

*Note on the charts, the "current" line has six months to expiration while the dotted lines have three months to expiration.

Now if you cast your eyes vertically on the two charts in Figures 3.1 and 3.2 as they appear on the page, notice how delta changes as the stock price moves. As we go toward the right side of the charts, delta rises as the stock price rises. In other words, delta peaks at 100 as the stock gets deep ITM.

Also notice how the three-month (shorter time to expiration) delta curve is steeper than the longer expiration delta curve. This tells us that delta is more sensitive the shorter the term left to expiration. As the stock declines to OTM, the shorter term delta line declines more rapidly.

One idea would be to try and slow down delta to near zero while at the same time retaining bullish objectives within the trade. To accomplish this we could sell a call option with a different strike price or expiration date. When we buy a call our delta will be positive. To bring it back toward delta neutral we can either buy a put option (which has a negative delta) or sell a call option (a sold call creates a negative delta) to counterbalance the long call positive delta.

Other Points to Remember

- Delta neutral still requires you to manage time decay. You'll see this later when we look at straddles, strangles, and other strategies.

- Longer-term options will tend to have smoother deltas than shorter-term options, as seen in the previous section.

- The position delta is also known as the "hedge ratio."

- Delta is principally affected by time left to expiration and price of the underlying asset relative to the strike price.

- With calls, delta increases as the underlying asset price increases. As the stock rises, the long call value will also rise; therefore, long call deltas are always positive. When you sell a naked call, the position has a negative delta. (A sold option is described as naked when there is no other position in place to protect the short position from a potentially unlimited loss.)

- With puts, as the stock price rises, the put will fall in value and vice versa. Long put delta is therefore negative. When you sell a naked put, the position has a positive delta.

Table 3.5 provides a summary of the delta outlook for a variety of positions:

Table 3.5 Delta position summary

Position	Delta (+ or -)	Comment
Buy 100 shares	+100	One share has a delta of +1.
Sell 50 shares	-50	Selling 1 share gives a -1 delta.
Buy call	+	A long call always has a positive delta. As the stock price rises, so does the call premium. As the stock price falls, so does the call premium.
Buy ITM call	+	An ITM call will have a higher positive delta than an ATM or OTM call.
Deep ITM call	+100 (maximum)	One deep ITM call will move roughly 1 for 1 with the underlying stock. It can never move faster than the underlying stock. Where you see numbers higher than this, it's because there must be more than one contract being traded.
Deep OTM call	0	Deep OTM calls will have deltas of almost zero, reflecting that they have very little chance of expiring ITM.
Buy ATM call	+50	One contract represents 100 shares. 100 x 0.5 = +50
Sell ATM call	-50	One contract represents 100 shares. 100 x -0.5 = -50
Sell call	-	A short call always has a negative delta.

Position	Delta (+ or -)	Comment
Buy put	-	A long put always has a negative delta. As the stock price rises, the put premium will fall. As the stock price falls, the put premium will rise. This inverse relationship results in a negative delta.
Buy ATM put	-50	One contract represents 100 shares. 100 x -0.5 = -50
Sell ATM put	+50	One contract represents 100 shares. 100 x 0.5 = +50 Notice a short put has a positive delta.
Sell put	+	Short put always has a positive delta.
Deep ITM put	-100 (maximum)	One deep ITM put will move inversely roughly 1 for 1 against the underlying stock.
Deep OTM put	0	Deep OTM puts will have deltas of almost zero, reflecting that they have very little chance of expiring ITM.
ATM straddle (Chapter 4)	0	The ATM call delta of +50 will be countered by the ATM put delta of -50.
ATM strangle (Chapter 4)	0	The OTM positive call delta will be countered by the OTM negative put delta.
Call ratio backspreads (Chapter 5)	–	Virtually all positive.
Diagonal calls (Chapter 6)	+	Mainly positive but with a twist when deep ITM as the stock rises well beyond the strike price. At the most positive when ATM.

Example of Diagonal Call Spread

ACME is currently trading at $50 per share. We create a diagonal call spread as follows:

Buy a six-month 40 strike call and sell a one-month 55 strike call at the same time. Notice the different strikes and expiration dates.

- Buy 10 x 40c   Delta =   1 x 100 x 0.8   =   +80
- Sell 10 x 55c   Delta =   1 x 100 x (–0.30)   =   -30
- Hedge ratio (delta) =   +50

So we've created a positive delta, though this will change as we approach the short call's expiration date and as the stock price fluctuates up and down.

Delta with Puts

Let's say we have a stock price of $69, and the $70 strike six-month put option is at $8.60.

Figure 3.3 Long put risk profile

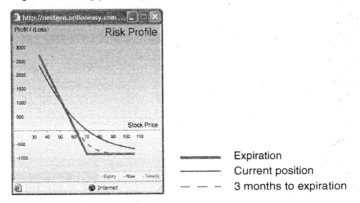

—————— Expiration
---------------- Current position
-- --- --- 3 months to expiration

Figure 3.4 Long put delta

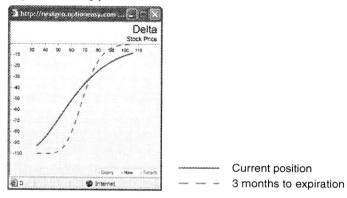

—————— Current position
— — — 3 months to expiration

*Note on the charts, the "current" line has six months to expiration while the dotted lines have three months to expiration.

Notice how the long put delta looks identical to the long call delta profile. Then look closer, and you'll see the difference is, of course, that the long put delta is negative.

Figure 3.4a Delta summary

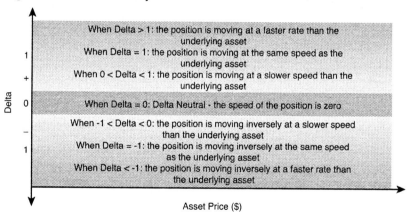

Gamma Γ

Gamma is the rate of change of delta measured against the rate of change in the underlying asset. In simple terms, gamma is the speed of delta, or the "speed of speed." The speed of speed is more commonly known as *acceleration*.

$$Gamma = \frac{rate\ of\ change\ of\ delta}{rate\ of\ change\ of\ underlying\ asset\ price}$$

Gamma is significant because it helps us measure risk, particularly for delta neutral trades. Gamma effectively shows us how quickly the odds are changing of the option expiring ITM. The option gamma tells us how quickly delta will change and therefore how quickly we should adjust our position in advance of this.

Table 3.6 summarizes how gamma behaves.

Table 3.6 Gamma summary

ATM	Gamma tends to be high when the option is near the money (NTM). When the option is NTM, it means that the delta is highly sensitive to changes in the stock price. In other words the **odds** of the option changing from being OTM to ITM or vice versa are high when the option is NTM. This of course makes perfect sense, and therefore it is logical that ATM options have high gammas.
ITM	When options are deep ITM, delta is close to 1 and in itself is not particularly sensitive to changes in the underlying asset price. Therefore, the gamma of deep ITM options is low.
OTM	Similarly, gamma is low for deep OTM options.
In general	The gamma for puts and calls is always identical and can be positive (for longs) or negative (for shorts).

Mathematically speaking, gamma is the second derivative of delta. So if delta is a measure of speed, gamma is a measure of acceleration. Unlike the other Greeks, gamma is not a measure of the option price versus another parameter, but rather a measure of how delta moves against changes in the stock price. To this end, the gamma for calls and puts is identical, and gamma can be positive or negative.

Gamma tends to be high when an option is near the money. A high gamma simply means that delta is highly sensitive to changes in the stock price around its current level (Kolb, 1997).

Some traders like to hedge their gamma positions so that that the delta will not spiral out of control (remember, gamma is a measure of acceleration, so if the acceleration is contained, then the speed, delta, will more or less remain constant). Of course, it is also possible to hedge both gamma and delta simultaneously. The gamma of NTM calls and puts rises as they get closer to expiration. For deep ITM or deep OTM options, gamma will veer to zero as the expiration date approaches.

Remember the long call delta chart in Figure 3.2, and you'll see how the delta curve of a bought call becomes steeper when the call is ATM, and as the call becomes ITM and then deep ITM, the delta continues to increase but at a reduced rate until it gets to 1. This gives us a huge clue as to how the gamma of the same trade will behave, for example, gamma will also decline as the call gets deep ITM (see Figure 3.5).

Figure 3.5 Long call gamma

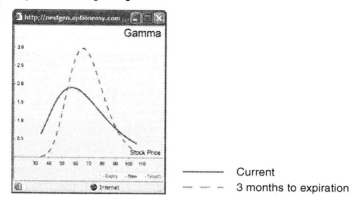

———————— Current

----- ---- --- 3 months to expiration

We see how the long call gamma decelerates at its fastest when the stock price is above the $70 strike area and continues to decline as the stock price rises and the option moves further ITM. Around this deep ITM area, the option is moving 1 to 1 with the stock price, that is, with a delta of 1. As the stock price rises, delta will continue to max out at 1. If the stock falls from this deep ITM area, it will have to do so with a real big move in order for the delta to start to fall, so again we can see that gamma would be virtually zero because delta is pretty constant when the option is deep ITM.

Similarly, gamma is extremely low when the stock price is deep OTM, to the left of the chart, where delta is virtually zero. Around this deep OTM area, modest moves in the stock price aren't going to affect the option much—as it's still so deep OTM, and the odds of expiring ITM will continue to be remote (that is, near to zero, and delta is constant around that zero area).

It's worth noting that delta neutral does not necessarily mean gamma neutral and vice versa—we see this in the strategy chapters later on.

Figure 3.6 Long put gamma

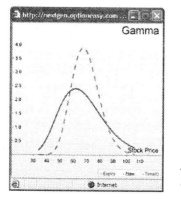

———————— Current

----- ---- --- 3 months to expiration

As you can see, gamma for puts and calls is identical, as you'd expect from a second derivative.

To conclude this section on gamma:

● Gamma measures how sensitive delta is to changes in the stock price.

● Gamma tells us how quickly the delta will change and how quickly we should adjust our position.

● Gamma is significant because it helps the trader measure risk, particularly for delta neutral traders.

● Gamma tends to be large when the option is NTM. This means that the delta is highly sensitive around the ATM areas to even small changes in the stock price.

● When options are deep ITM, the delta will be close to 1 for calls and -1 for puts and will not be too sensitive itself to changes in the underlying asset price. Therefore, the gamma of deep ITM options will be low.

● Similarly, gamma will be low for deep OTM (or DOTM) options.

● The gamma of a put and a call is always identical and can be positive or negative.

Table 3.7 Gamma position summary

Stock price	Delta	Gamma
ATM	Calls → around 0.5 Puts → around -0.5	High
NTM	Calls → around 0.5 Puts → around -0.5	High
Deep ITM	Calls → around 1 Puts → around -1	Low
Deep OTM	Calls → low, near 0 Puts → low, near 0	Low

Figure 3.6a Gamma summary

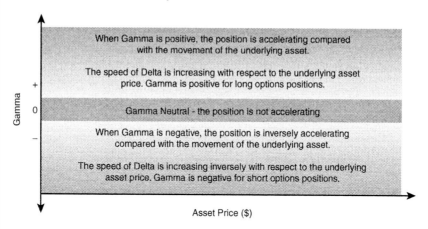

When Gamma is positive, the position is accelerating compared with the movement of the underlying asset.

The speed of Delta is increasing with respect to the underlying asset price. Gamma is positive for long options positions.

Gamma Neutral - the position is not accelerating

When Gamma is negative, the position is inversely accelerating compared with the movement of the underlying asset.

The speed of Delta is increasing inversely with respect to the underlying asset price. Gamma is negative for short options positions.

Asset Price ($)

Theta Θ

Theta is a measure of how time decay affects the option premium. When you buy an option, time decay will hurt the position. So theta is nearly always negative for long options.[1] This makes sense because time decay erodes the option value as time to expiration diminishes.

Example of Time Decay

Let's say you pay me $1.00 for an OTM option with 10 days until expiration.

With each day that passes, let's assume the option loses $0.10 of time value (please note this is just an illustration; in practice time decay is not linear).

So assuming there is no movement in the underlying stock price, the option value will behave as shown in Table 3.8:

---

[1] Theta can be positive for deep ITM puts in certain scenarios: When a stock price reaches zero it cannot move any lower, and the put cannot get any more valuable. Therefore a short time to expiration can mean the realization of profit more quickly, hence the slightly counterintuitive positive theta in such cases.

Table 3.8 Time decay

Day	Option Value	Buyer Profit	Seller Profit
Day 0	$1.00		
Day 1	$0.90	(0.10)	+ 0.10
Day 2	$0.80	(0.20)	+ 0.20
Day 3	$0.70	(0.30)	+ 0.30
Day 4	$0.60	(0.40)	+ 0.40
Day 5	$0.70	(0.50)	+ 0.50
...			
Day 10	$0.00	(1.00)	+1.00

Time decay has helped me (the seller) and hurt you (the buyer). So the lesson is never buy OTM options with less than 1 month to expiration unless it forms part of a multi-legged combination trade.

The negative value of theta tells us that as the expiration date approaches, time decay increases and the option value decreases. With options, time decay increases exponentially during the last month before expiration. Put another way, time value decreases exponentially during the expiration month.

So how can we mitigate time decay?

1. **Sell off any owned ATM or OTM options with 30 days left to expiration**—Time decay accelerates at its fastest during the last 30 days to expiration. Remember that OTM and ATM options have no intrinsic value, so they must be made up purely of time value. Because we know that time value decreases exponentially during the final month before expiration, it makes sense to dispose of these options.

2. **Sell options you don't own as an adjustment to existing trades**—We're not creating naked positions here. The sold option would be complementary to your existing play (for example, diagonal spreads).

3. **Buy short-term deep ITM options**—A deep ITM put or deep ITM call will have lots of intrinsic value and relatively little time value. Deep ITM options can have tiny amounts of time value as a proportion of the entire option premium because the option is so deep ITM.

It's useful to examine each of these points in a bit more detail.

1. **Sell off OTM or ATM options with less than 30 days to expiration.**
   Figure 3.7 perfectly illustrates how theta decay works with options. Notice how the slope falls off at its steepest during the last 30 days, demonstrating how time decay accelerates exponentially during those last 30 days until expiration.

Figure 3.7 Theta decay

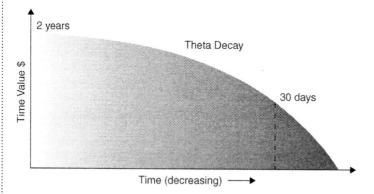

2. **Sell options you don't own as an adjustment to existing trades.**
   This is not the same as selling options naked and exposing yourself to unlimited risk. Of course there are people who do successfully sell OTM options every month and collect a decent premium. However, if the market suddenly jolts against them and they get exercised, then an entire year of profits or more can be wiped out (and more) in literally one day. Although there are some high-probability mathematical techniques of naked options selling, if your capital can be wiped out that fast when you're not looking, then that's simply not a sensible way to go about your business unless you're exceedingly experienced and your time exposure to the risk is a very narrow window.

3. **Buy short-term deep ITM options.**
   You can mitigate the effects of time decay by buying deep ITM options because intrinsic value is vastly outweighing time value. If there is little to no time value in the option (as compared with intrinsic value and as a percentage of the entire premium), then your risk exposure to time decay is, by definition, little to none.

Figure 3.8 Time value for deep ITM options

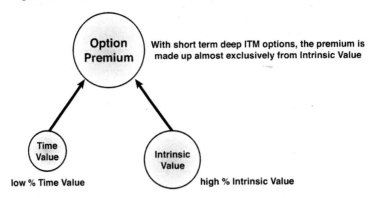

If you look at the options series in Table 3.9, you'll see that the stock price is currently $42.10. There are only 18 days left to October expiration and just over six weeks left till the November expiration.

Question: How much time value and intrinsic value is there for the following options? For our purposes here, look at the Ask:

Remember that

● Call intrinsic value = stock price – strike price

● Call time value = call premium – intrinsic value

● Intrinsic value minimum = zero

Now fill Table 3.9.

Table 3.9 Calculating intrinsic and time value

Call Option	Last ($)	Intrinsic Value	Time Value
Oct 12.5	30.20	42.10 – 12.50 = **29.60**	30.20 – 29.60 = **0.60**
Oct 15	27.80		
Oct 17.5	25.30		
Oct 20	22.80		
Oct 22.5	20.30		
Oct 25	18.00		
Oct 40	5.50		

Call option	Last ($)	Intrinsic Value	Time Value
Nov 20	23.20		
Nov 22.5	20.90		
Nov 25	18.70		
Nov 40	8.20		

See Table 3.10 for the answers (notice the percentage of the entire option premium, which is taken up by intrinsic or time value as the option gets nearer to ATM) .

Table 3.10 Intrinsic and time value

Call Option	Last ($)	Intrinsic Value		Time Value	
Oct 12.5	30.20	29.60	98%	0.60	2%
Oct 15	27.80	27.10	97.5%	0.70	2.5%
Oct 17.5	25.30	24.60	97%	0.70	3%
Oct 20	22.80	22.10	97%	0.70	3%
Oct 22.5	20.30	19.60	96.5%	0.70	3.5%
Oct 25	18.00	17.10	95%	0.90	5%
Oct 40	5.50	2.10	**38%**	3.40	**62%**
Nov 20	23.20	22.10	95%	1.10	5%
Nov 22.5	20.90	19.60	93.8%	1.30	6.2%
Nov 25	18.70	17.10	91.5%	1.60	8.5%
Nov 40	8.20	2.10	**25.6%**	6.10	**74.4%**

Do you see how deep ITM options premiums have lots of intrinsic value and little time value, thus reducing the exposure to time decay? Conversely, ATM and OTM option premiums are exclusively made up of time value.

Staying with our simple call option where the stock price is $69 and the $70 strike call is priced at $9.80, let's look at the theta with six months left till expiration and compare it with the position of theta with only one month left to expiration (see Figure 3.9).

Figure 3.9 Long call theta

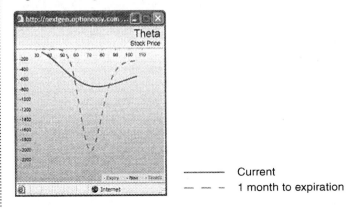

——————— Current

— — — — 1 month to expiration

Notice how both theta lines are negative, illustrating that time decay harms a long call position. Also notice how the line depicting only one month to expiration extends lower than the longer term line. This illustrates the greater severity of time decay when there is less time to expiration, particularly in the final month. Finally, be aware that theta reaches its lowest at around the strike price.

Exactly the same applies to puts.

Figure 3.10 Long put theta

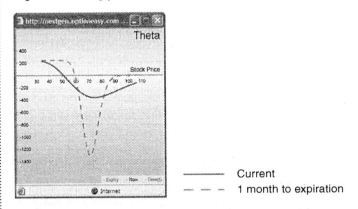

——————— Current

— — — — 1 month to expiration

We know that time decay hurts long option positions. The Rule of the Opposites from Chapter 1, "Introduction to Options," suggests that time decay must therefore help short option positions.

Figure 3.11 Short call theta

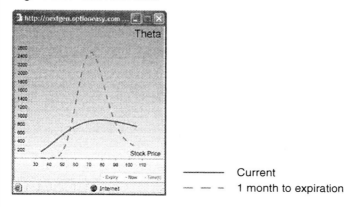

————————— Current

--- --- -- 1 month to expiration

As we can see, the lines are now in positive territory, illustrating that time decay is helping the short position. The shorter time left until expiration, the more time decay will help the short position.

Figure 3.12 Short put theta

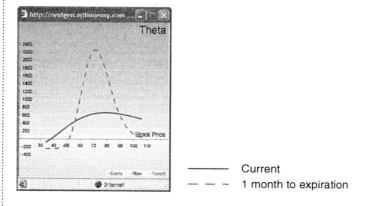

————————— Current

--- --- -- 1 month to expiration

In summary, when theta is positive, time decay is helping the position. When theta is negative, time decay is hurting the position. When we buy options, theta is negative, indicating that time decay hurts our long option position. This makes sense as an option is a wasting asset. When you write (sell) options, you would expect the opposite to be the case, which of course it is. When you write an option, its value will decline as the expiration date approaches.

If time decay is harmful to your long option positions, then it stands to reason that it will be helpful to your short option positions. You can see this by way of simple graphical representation in that now the theta lines are positive, showing that theta decay is helpful to a short option position.

Figure 3.13 Theta summary

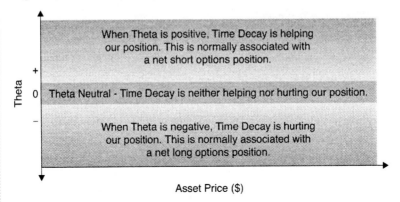

Asset Price ($)

Vega K

Remember the seven factors that influence an option's price:

1. The type of option (call or put)

2. The stock price

3. The strike price

4. The expiration date

5. **Volatility**—implied and historical

6. Risk-free interest rate

7. Dividends paid

Volatility is an indication of how a security's price is moving and is a measure of risk. If a stock price fluctuates all over the place in wild swings, you'd find it uncomfortable because you wouldn't have a clue what it was going to do next, and it would feel risky. On the other hand if a stock price remains static all the time, then you might get a bit frustrated seeing your money not growing.

Increasing volatility is illustrated by wider, faster price fluctuations. This translates into greater uncertainty and greater risk. The greater the volatility and risk, the more expensive options premiums become.

Volatility is calculated by measuring the standard deviation of closing prices expressed as an annualized percentage figure. Volatility is not directional. If a stock is priced at $50 and has volatility of 20%, then we expect the stock to trade in the range of $40–$60 for the next year.

Vega measures an option position's sensitivity to the stock's volatility. The stock's volatility is known as *historical volatility*.

There are two categories of volatility: historical and implied.

- **Historical volatility**
  Derived from the standard deviation of the stock price movement over a known period of time.
- **Implied volatility**
  Derived from the market price of the option itself.

Of the seven variables that affect an option's premium, six of these variables are known with certainty:

- Stock price
- Strike price
- Type of option
- Time to expiration
- Interest rates
- Dividends

The final variable can be considered not to be known with certainty and is the *expected volatility* of the stock going forward.

Implied Volatility

There are numerous mathematical models for calculating the *theoretical* value of an option. I stress the word theoretical because the theoretical price is *not* the market price of the option premium. Sometimes the theoretical price will be the same as the market price; sometimes they'll be different—there's no magic rule.

- The theoretical option price uses historical volatility of the stock to calculate the theoretical value of an option. So all the seven factors go into the pot, and we emerge with a theoretical option price.
- The market price of an option premium has a volatility figure implied within it. Therefore we reverse the theoretical option price model in order to find out what the implied figure for volatility was within the market traded option premium. So we mix the six other factors (not volatility) using actual market option price to calculate the implied volatility figure implicit within option premium traded.

Theoretical Option Pricing

As ever, the clearest way of explaining this is by way of diagrams.

Figure 3.14 Calculating the theoretical option value

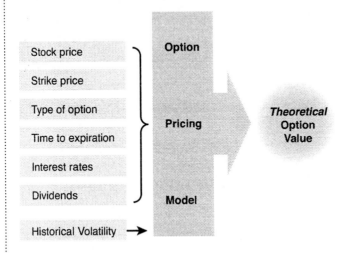

Figure 3.15 Calculating the implied volatility

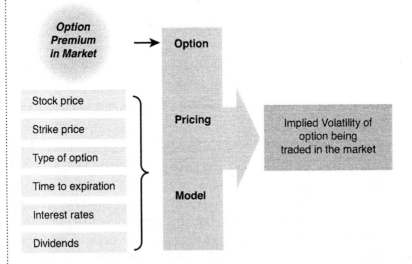

This implied volatility figure is expressed as an annualized percentage and, working back from the option premium itself, is a figure that is "implied" from the market traded premium itself.

So to recap, historical volatility is the annualized standard deviation of past price movements of the stock. We use historical volatility as a reference figure for calculating what the fair value of the option should be, given the stock's historical volatility. In the real world, option premiums frequently trade away from their fair values, adopting trading ranges driven more by demand and supply in the cut and thrust of market activity.

- **Historical volatility**
  Underlying stock volatility over a period of time, for example the past 20 trading days. Expressed as an annual percentage figure reflecting the standard deviation of the stock closing price.

- **Implied volatility**
  The volatility derived from the *option's* traded market price using an option pricing model. Expressed as an annual percentage figure.

There are also a number of different methodologies available for options pricing models, each with their associated merits. I typically use the Black-Scholes Options Pricing Model. In the marketplace the value assigned to an option is determined by market forces combined with floor specialists' implementation of a pricing model, such as Black-Scholes.

This often creates inconsistencies between the fair value of an option and the actual premium of the option in the marketplace. As we know, the option fair value is mathematically derived from the pricing model using historical volatility as the figure for volatility. The inconsistency emerges when the market price differs from the fair value, which is a common occurrence. Of all the seven factors that influence the option price, the only one that could be subject to debate is volatility.

Although historical volatility itself is fixed (with respect to whatever time period we're assigning to it, say, 20 trading days), the choice of time frame can be arbitrary and doesn't necessarily fit with the time left to the option's expiration.

The discretion between the option's market value and its fair value is interpreted as an anomaly of volatility (it simply cannot be any of the other six factors). Implied volatility is a calculated figure arising from the market price.

Example

Consider AAPL on January 19, 2008. The stock was at $161.36, and the April 160 strike calls and puts were priced at $18.90 and $16.15, respectively. April was almost exactly three months away.

Table 3.11 AAPL example

Option	3-month Expiration	Option Premium	Historical Volatility*	Implied Volatility	Fair Value
Call strike $160	April 2008	$18.90	48.7% *	55.3%	$16.83
Put strike $160	April 2008	$16.15	48.7% *	54.9%	$14.20

* 1-month historical volatility figure used

If the options were priced in the market according to the historical volatility, the call would be worth $16.83, and the put would be priced at $14.20. Are you overpaying here for these options?[2] Well, that would depend on whether implied volatility is usually at a discount or premium to historical volatility with this particular stock, as well as a number of other factors.

In extremely volatile market conditions, you are going to experience higher implied volatilities. What if you used the last two-week figure for historical volatility (55.9%)? In other words, calculate historical volatility using the last two weeks' price data?

Table 3.12 AAPL example using 2-week historical volatility figures

Option	3-month Expiration	Option Premium	Historical Volatility*	Implied Volatility	Fair Value
Call strike $160	April 2008	$18.90	55.9% *	55.3%	$19.10
Put strike $160	April 2008	$16.15	55.9% *	54.9%	$16.47

*2 week historical volatility figure used

Using this data, it would seem to suggest that the option premiums are well priced, perhaps even quite a good value. We know the current market has been increasing in volatility, and it is currently earnings season as well. The success of any trade will be partly dependent on the accuracy of your opinion of future volatility. If volatility in the markets continues to rise, then buying these options will be rewarded by higher premiums, provided the implied volatility of the options follows suit. If volatility falls, buying these options may be a bad move as the premiums would be crushed as the markets settle back down.

[2.] The higher the implied volatility, the higher the option premium will be and vice versa. If implied volatility is substantially lower than historical volatility, there could be an argument to suggest good value in the option price itself, particularly in a volatile market such as January 2008.

So far this example has involved AAPL's three-month options. Let's now look at AAPL's front month options, that is, the February options.

Table 3.13 AAPL example using front month expiration

Option	1-month Expiration	Option Premium	Historical Volatility*	Implied Volatility	Fair Value
Call strike $160	Feb 2008	$12.80	48.7% *	67.5%	$9.49
Put strike $160	Feb 2008	$10.80	48.7% *	65.6%	$7.82

*1-month historical volatility figure used

In Table 3.13 we can see there's a more substantial degree of implied volatility (around 66% average) to the one-month historical volatility of 48.7% for the February expiration options compared with the April expirations. This kind of discrepancy will often be the case.

If we now use the last two week figure for historical volatility, what would our fair values be?

Table 3.14 AAPL example using front month expiration and 2-week historical volatility figures

Option	1-month Expiration	Option Premium	Historical Volatility*	Implied Volatility	Fair Value
Call strike $160	Feb 2008	$12.80	55.9% *	67.5%	$10.75
Put strike $160	Feb 2008	$10.80	55.9% *	65.6%	$9.09

** 2 week historical volatility figure used

As expected, in Table 3.14 we can see that the fair values are still considerably below the respective premiums in the market place because the two-week historical volatility of 55.9% is still well below the implied volatility of the option premiums in the marketplace (65.6% and 67.5%, respectively). Of course, when you plug in 55.9% to the option pricing model, the fair values are going to be lower than the real premiums that are illustrating implied volatilities of 65.6% and 67.5%.

Each stock will have different characteristics in the relationship between implied and historical volatility of their options chains. Just like you have to familiarize yourself with a stock's personality, you should also familiarize yourself with its options and the established relationship between its historical and implied volatility.

For now, just remember that historical volatility is derived from the underlying asset's price movement, and implied volatility is derived from the actual market premium of the option itself, as discussed in Table 3.15.

Table 3.15 Historical and implied volatility

Volatility	Based on
Historical	● Stock price volatility over a period of time, for example, the past 20 trading days. ● Expressed as a percentage reflecting the average annual range (i.e. standard deviation).
Implied	● The volatility derived from the option's traded market price using an option pricing model. Expressed as a percentage and based on the perception of where market will be in the future. ● This is the volatility figure derived from a pricing model such as Black-Scholes.

In terms of trading, if you can recognize how implied and historical volatility relate to each other with a specific stock, you can also identify powerful ways to trade the options. At the time of writing I am creating software to do just that very task for me. The idea is to identify stocks where there are anomalies between the option premiums and the stock price. More specifically, you should look for anomalies of implied volatility and historical volatility both against each other and against their own histories.

For example, where I can spot a flag pattern on a stock where I'm anticipating a breakout, if the implied volatility has calmed down compared with itself and the actual stock price (which must have by way of the formation of the consolidating flag pattern itself), then I may sense an opportunity to buy options. If earnings are within a couple of weeks too, and the stock has a tendency to make big moves during earnings season, then I'll be doubly excited and may look to trade a straddle (much more about that in Chapter 4, "Straddles and Strangles").

The traditionally taught view of volatility is overly simplistic and involves a straightforward relationship between implied and historical volatility. The incomplete theory would state something like, "If implied volatility is greater than historical volatility, then the options premiums are expensive; and if implied volatility is less than historical volatility, then the options are good value." This is far too simplistic and could even be dangerous.

The reality is that some stocks' options always trade at a discount and some at a premium to their fair values. This is part of the stocks' option chain characteristics. Some stocks' options will trade consistently at par to their fair values. You have to identify which is doing which.

Volatility swings are often likened to the "rubber band effect" where if the rubber band is stretched too tight in one direction or too loose in the other, it will generally revert back to its most natural position most of the time (see Figure 3.16). So if implied volatility is generally around 40% for a stock, but for a period of time it plummets to 20%, could it be possible that the options prices might be good value? Or, using the same example, say implied volatility vaults up to 60%—could the options perhaps be overvalued? Over the medium to long term, implied volatility does tend to veer toward its own average, but this will depend on the consistency of the historical volatility of the underlying stock.

Figure 3.16 Implied volatility relative to itself

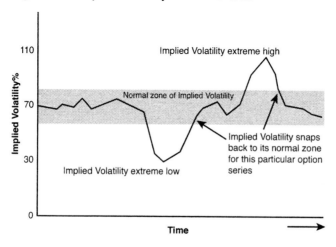

It's preached quite a bit in seminars, but it's dangerous to simply look to buy options with low implied volatility compared with the historical volatility of the stock. The perception is that the options are cheap or undervalued and therefore must represent a good trade. But that simply won't ring true much of the time. For a start, option premiums often have implied volatilities inconsistent with the historical volatility of the stock. Second, just because an option is cheap today doesn't mean it'll be expensive tomorrow. So the rationale for that tactic is flawed. Far more relevant is to examine the history of implied volatility against itself and observe if current options prices are trading away from their own averages.

Similarly, some traders look to sell options with high implied volatility compared with the historical volatility of the stock. Again, this is a flawed approach.

Vega is identical and positive for long calls and puts. Higher volatility increases the option premium. When vega is positive, it suggests that increasing volatility is helping our position. When vega is negative, it suggests that increasing volatility is harmful to our position.

Example

Let's take AAPL again on January 18, 2008. The stock price was $161.36, and the July 2008 (6-month) $160 strike calls and puts were priced at $26.15 and $22.05, respectively.

Figure 3.17 Long call vega

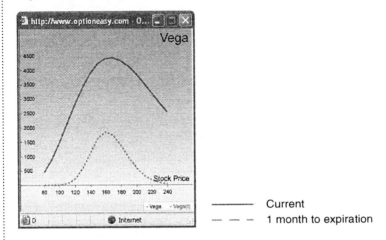

——————— Current

~~ ~~ ~~ 1 month to expiration

Figure 3.18 Long put vega

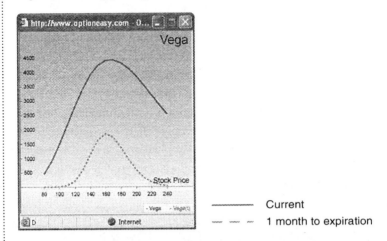

——————— Current

~~ ~~ ~~ 1 month to expiration

As you can see in Figures 3.17 and 3.18, vega is identical for the calls and puts. Notice how it increases around the strike price and also how vega is vastly reduced where there is less time to expiration. This is because there is less time for increased volatility to make an impact on the time value component of the option's premium.

Figure 3.19 Vega summary

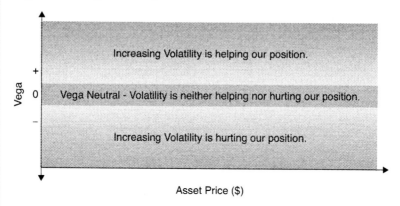

Rho P

In a low interest rate environment, rho is the least significant of the five main Greeks. Rho is positive for call options on underlying stocks. Higher interest rates will lead to increased call premiums. With interest rates at low levels, the sensitivity is not nearly as pronounced as with the other Greeks.

● Call rho is always positive, meaning that higher interest rates will increase the call premium (see Figure 3.20).

● Put rho is always negative, meaning that higher interest rates will cause the put premium to decline (see Figure 3.21).

Figure 3.20 Long call rho

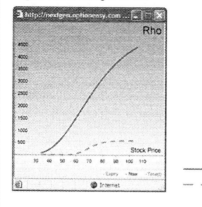

——————— Current
~~~ ~~~ ~~~ 1 month to expiration

Figure 3.21 Long put rho

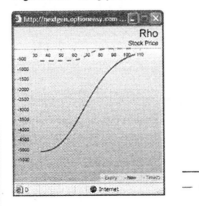

-------------------- Current

----- ---- ---- 1 month to expiration

Learning Points

In this chapter you've seen that the Greeks are sensitivities of option positions to the components of an options pricing model, as summarized in Table 3.16.

Table 3.16 Greeks summary

Delta	The speed of the option price over the speed of the underlying asset price. Can also be viewed as the probability of an option expiring ITM.
Gamma	Sensitivity of delta relative to the underlying asset price movement. Can also be viewed as the odds of a change in delta.
Theta	Option price sensitivity to time decay. When theta is positive, time decay is helping the position. When theta is negative, time decay is hurting the position.
Vega	Option price sensitivity to the underlying stock price *volatility*. When vega is positive, volatility is helping the position. When vega is negative, volatility is hurting the position.
Rho	Option price sensitivity to *interest rates*. When rho is positive, increasing interest rates are helping the position. When rho is negative, increasing interest rates are hurting the position.

Now you know the factors that affect the pricing of options, you can start to devise specific strategies to mitigate the impact of the important sensitivities and even take advantage of them, particularly delta, theta, and vega.

chapter 4

Straddles and Strangles

The straddle is one of the best known strategies in the options universe; however, it is also one of the most misunderstood and mistraded. Its attraction is that you can make a fast, significant profit without having to have any bias for the direction in which the stock price moves.

We're looking for increased volatility but only once we're in the trade. My preference is for that increasing volatility to be decisive in one direction or the other, but we're not biased either way from the outset. In other words if volatility is forcing the stock upward, then we'd prefer the stock to continue rising, and if it's forcing the stock downward, then we'd prefer the stock to continue falling.

Inevitably if the stock rises, the call's intrinsic value will rise, and we'd expect the put premium to decline. Similarly if the stock falls, the put's intrinsic value will rise, and the call's overall value is likely to decline. The exception to the rule is if the losing option's implied volatility were to rise significantly, the benefit of this can counterbalance even the fact that the option is drifting further out of the money. In an ideal world we want the trade to profit from both the options' implied volatilities rising *and* from the winning side's intrinsic value rising by more than the other side's overall decline.

The straddle is a fantastic strategy, but beyond all the hype, there are some serious niceties to being able to trade it with consistency, and there are several different ways of doing this with different time frames. In this chapter I detail the most conservative ways of trading straddles.

The good news is that when you get it right, the straddle is a low risk—high reward strategy. In this chapter you learn about the straddle and its closely related strategy, the strangle.

Straddles

The (long) straddle involves two steps:

Step 1:   Buy ATM strike puts.

Step 2:   Buy ATM strike calls with the same expiration date.

The straddle can expose you to significant time decay (if executed poorly) because you are long ATM calls and puts which have no intrinsic value. However, it needn't be a high-risk strategy, even if the anticipated volatile price action doesn't materialize.

Figure 4.1 Straddle components

Buy put   **Buy call**   **Straddle**

The risk profile of a straddle is shown in Table 4.1.

Table 4.1 Straddle risk profile

Maximum risk	Net debit of the spread (i.e., what you pay)
Maximum reward	Unlimited to the upside Limited to the strike price less the premium paid for both options to the downside
Breakeven on the downside (at expiration)	Strike price *less* net debit
Breakeven on the upside (at expiration)	Strike price *plus* net debit
Maximum risk on net debit or net credit	100% risk on net debit

Strike Price Position and Trade Bias

As you can see, the strategy has two breakeven points, one below and one above the strike price. The call and put share the same strike price, which should be as near to the money (i.e., as close to the current stock price) as possible. It's not always possible to trade a straddle when the stock price is nailed on a strike price, so one side is bound to be slightly skewed in favor and vice versa.

Example

- Stock price = $47.00
- Nearest and cheapest strike price = $45.00.

Assuming 50% implied volatility:

- Call = 5.30 (this includes $2.00 of intrinsic value)
- Put = 3.00 (this has no intrinsic value)

Notice how the call premium is more than the put premium. This is because the call is slightly in the money and the put is slightly OTM. Remember for calls the intrinsic value is [stock price – strike price]. Here that equation is positive, signifying that the call is ITM. If the call is ITM, then the Rule of the Opposites (from Chapter 1, "Introduction to Options") reminds us that the put must therefore be OTM.

What happens if the stock quickly rises to $55.00?

- The call must be worth at least $10.00 plus time value.
- The put must still have zero intrinsic value and significantly less time value than before because it's further OTM. Time value is a function of time, volatility, and hope value. A significantly OTM option will have very little hope value (and a low delta too) as there's little perceived chance of it expiring ITM.

Assuming that the implied volatility of the options has remained the same (at 50%), the call will then be worth around 11.30 and the put around 1.00. The straddle is theoretically worth 12.30, a 48% increase on a stock that moved only 17% (or $8.00) and you took both sides.

Let's now assume the stock fell by $9.00 to $38.00 and see how much profit you make this time.

Assuming the implied volatilities remain at 50% the put is now worth 7.90 and the call is worth 1.20. That's a theoretical straddle value of $9.10, which represents a profit of only 10%. So when the stock rose by $9.00 your profit was 48%, and when the stock fell by $9.00 your profit was only 10%. How could this be? Well, the answer is simple. The call was slightly ITM, and the put was slightly OTM. When this happens, because you pay more for the ITM option, you have a natural preference for the ITM option to be the winner. Here the ITM option was the call, so you want the call to win—that is, you want the stock to rise even though you're, strictly speaking, trading a direction-neutral strategy.

The reasons for this are as follows:

a. If the option you paid more for (i.e., the ITM option) wins, then the option you paid less for (the OTM option) has less to lose.

b. The delta of the ITM option will be higher and therefore will move faster as it becomes further ITM, whereas the OTM option will lose its value at a slightly slower rate because it had a lower delta to start with.

In the example just given, you paid less for the put so you would lose less with it than you would for the call. And because the calls were ITM, the call delta was higher than the put delta, meaning the calls would rise at a faster rate than the puts would fall.

If we study this in the opposite direction, let's assume the original stock price was $43.00 and examine our 45.00 strike straddle. Note here that from the outset the put is now ITM, and the call is OTM.

With implied volatilities at 50% the call is worth 3.05, and the put is worth 4.75, totaling $7.80.

● When the stock rises $9.00 to $52.00, the call is worth 8.85, and the put is worth 1.55, making a total theoretical straddle value of $9.40, an increase of 20.50%.

● When the stock falls $9.00 to $34.00, the call is worth 0.45, and the put is worth 11.15, making a total of almost 49%.

So when the stock rose by $9.00, your profit was only 20.5% this time, and when the stock fell by $9.00, your profit was 49%. Here the put was slightly ITM, and the call was slightly OTM. Because of this, you'd benefit more from the stock falling. The reasons are identical to the previous example, but here the put had a higher delta, and you paid more for the put in the first place.

Before we move on to discuss all the other factors that affect straddles, we must outline the strangle.

Strangles

Essentially the strangle is identical to the straddle, except that the put has a lower strike, the call has a higher strike, and the stock price is typically in between, preferable equidistant between the two.

The (long) strangle involves two steps:

Step 1:   Buy OTM strike puts.

Step 2:   Buy OTM strike calls with the same expiration date.

The strangle can expose us to significant time decay because we are long OTM calls and puts, which have no intrinsic value. Because of this, the strangle is cheaper than the straddle where the calls and puts are ATM.[1] The other significant difference is that the risk profile has two turning points, one for each of the strikes. The rules are virtually the same for both strategies, though typically I won't look at a strangle unless the straddle looks like a good value or if the stock price is too far from a strike price, meaning the straddle cannot be considered.

The components of a strangle are shown in Figure 4.2.

Figure 4.2 Strangle components

Buy OTM put   Buy OTM call   Strangle

The risk profile of a strangle is shown in Table 4.2:

Table 4.2 Strangle risk profile

Maximum risk	Net debit of the spread (i.e. what you pay)
Maximum reward	Unlimited to the upside. Limited to the put strike less the premium paid for both options to the downside
Breakeven on the downside (at expiration)	Lower (put) strike price *less* net debit
Breakeven on the upside (at expiration)	Higher (call) strike price *plus* net debit
Maximum risk on net debit or net credit	100% risk on net debit

Again, this strategy has two breakeven points, one below and one above the strike price. From the outset, the put strike is typically below the stock price, and the call strike is typically above the current stock price. In order to have direction neutrality from the outset of the trade, preferably both put and call strikes are equidistant from the stock price when the trade is initiated. In most cases strangles will have wider breakevens to straddles, and this is something we need to compare thoroughly when assessing whether to take the straddle, strangle, or both. I take you through some real examples later in the chapter.

---

[1] Remember, ATM options also have no intrinsic value but will have significantly more hope value than OTM options because an ATM option is only a penny from being just ITM and therefore has a much greater chance of expiring ITM.

Factors Affecting Straddles and Strangles

Aside from the positioning of the strike prices in relation to the stock price, there are many other factors that will affect the outcome of the straddle and strangle. I am talking mainly about straddles in the chapter, but the same effects apply to strangles unless specified otherwise.

Factors that will affect volatility trades include

- Volatility—implied and historical
- News events such as earnings reports
- Time decay
- Straddle cost
- Stock chart patterns
- Breakeven points

These factors are interlinked and are not mutually exclusive.

Volatility

The key to successfully trading straddles and strangles is understanding volatility. The ideal scenario is to buy low implied volatility options, which then explode, making your option premiums more valuable.

Consider our ATM straddle with just over two months to expiration and with the stock at $45.00.

If volatility is 40%, then the call is theoretically worth 3.30, and the put is worth 3.00.

With nothing else changing apart from volatility increasing to 50%, the call will grow to 4.10 and the put to 3.80. Those are increases of 24% and 26%, respectively. So even without the stock moving at all, if we can find an opportunity where implied volatilities are likely to rise, then we're going to be very happy. The key is to find the opportunities where implied volatility is low and likely to rise after we've entered our long position.

To illustrate the point, let's examine Tables 4.3 and 4.4 with an OTM call option with only a short time left to expiration.

Table 4.3 OTM Call

Stock price	$43.00
Strike	45.00
Days to expiration	10

Table 4.4 Implied Volatility Effect on OTM Call Premium

Volatility	Call premium
30%	0.25
40%	0.48
50%	0.74
60%	1.01

As we can see, we've doubled the volatility from 30% to 60%, and our call premium has quadrupled. This is hugely significant. Now let's repeat the exercise but for ATM and ITM calls (Table 4.5).

Table 4.5 Implied Volatility Effect on OTM, ATM, and ITM Calls

Volatility	Stock = $43.00 45 strike OTM call		Stock = $45.00 45 strike ATM call		Stock = $47.00 45 strike ITM call	
30%	0.25		0.96		2.31	
40%	0.48		1.27		2.55	
50%	0.74		1.58		2.82	
60%	**1.01**	**(+300%)**	**1.89**	**(+96.9%)**	**3.11**	**(+34.6%)**

Notice how the most affected options are the OTMs in percentage terms. A doubling of volatility quadruples the OTMs but only increases the ITMs by 34.6%. There are logical reasons for this, one being that the ITM option here contains $2.00 of intrinsic value. At 30% volatility the time value portion of the ITM call is 0.31 compared with 0.25 for the OTM call and 0.96 for the ATM call (which contains no intrinsic value either but is right on the cusp). Because volatility is the unknown quantity that makes up time value, we can see that around the strike price the options are hugely sensitive to volatility. This tallies with the vega analysis in Chapter 3, "Options and the Greeks."

Figure 4.3 Long call vega

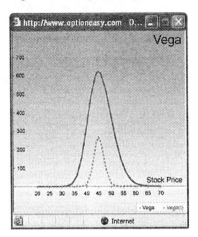

—————— Current (3 months to expiration)

.... 1 month to expiration

Notice how the vega chart peaks at the strike price. That's showing us where the sensitivity is. Seeing this, you might ask why buy ATM options? Well, the answer is straightforward. If you buy the OTMs you run a greater risk of our options both expiring OTM and worthless. If you buy ITM calls and puts, you create a "Guts" trade that would be prohibitively expensive. Also the losing side of the trade would deteriorate too quickly because each option's delta is high at the trade initiation as they're both ITM.

In theory the optimum scenario would be to buy the OTMs (i.e., the strangle), and the stock price subsequently explodes in one direction and keeps going. The base cost of the strangle is lower than the straddle, so once one of the options gets ITM, if the stock keeps moving, the winning option will climb at an ever greater percentage rate in line with the increasing delta until the delta of the winning option leg reaches 1. If only trading could be like that all the time!

Straddles Versus Strangles

The decision of whether to take the straddle, strangle or both, is a function of the following:

a. Cost of the trade

b. Breakevens

c. Expected stock price behavior

d. Expected volatility of both the stock and the options

Let's break these down:

a. **Cost of the trade**

The lower the cost of the trade, the less the stock price movement is required to make the trade profitable. Also the lower the cost of the trade, the lower the implied volatility has been in buying the options and the less they can decline by, at least in theory. I tend not to pay more than around 10% or so for straddles with less than two months to expiration. I don't like to go much over 15% for straddles with between two to three months to expiration and 20% for straddles with between three and four months to expiration. These figures are simply a guideline I like to keep, and while it's not particularly scientific, it does tend to keep me out of trouble, particularly from rapidly declining implied volatility that may occur after entering a trade.

During bearish market phases stocks can be highly volatile, which is reflected both in stock price action and the options premiums because of higher implied volatilities. During these market phases there tends to be fewer of the sort of trades I like, so I simply have to stay away from them until things return to a semblance of normalcy. The worst thing you can do is to "chase" the opportunity like a desperate gambler. My game-plan is to buy low volatility and sell higher. It isn't to buy high volatility and hope it'll get higher still. I should emphasize that what I've just described is completely different from buying a stock that is reaching new highs—that's something I'm always okay with as it breaks out of a consolidation pattern, as we discussed in Chapter 2, "Trends and Flags."

b. **Breakevens**

The expiration breakeven point of the trade is something of a moot point in terms of the fact that we never hold on to expiration anyway. However, we still pay close attention to it as it gives us a guide to how our breakevens will behave even before expiration.

Breakeven Example

NICE is trading at $40.05 on November 2, 2007. Let's look at the February 40.00 straddle and then the 35–45 strike strangle and see how they compare purely in terms of breakevens at expiration. Remember we wouldn't hold the trade to expiration, but we'd still use the calculation as part of our analysis to compare the straddle with the strangle.

● For the straddle, the 40 strike puts are trading at 2.65–2.95, and the calls are at 3.30–3.60. If we buy at the ask, then our trade cost is 6.55.

● For the strangle, the 35 strike puts are trading at 0.90–1.10, and the 45 strike calls are at 1.35–1.55. If we buy at the ask, then our trade cost is 2.65.

Table 4.6 Breakeven example

	Calls	Puts	Cost	Breakeven down	Breakeven up
Straddle	3.60	2.95	6.55	[40 - 6.55] = 33.45	[40 + 6.55] = 46.55
Strangle	1.55	1.10	2.65	[35 - 2.65] = 32.35	[45 + 2.65] = 47.65

The strangle breakevens are both 1.10 wider than the straddle breakevens. That means if you kept the trades open until expiration the stock would have to move an extra 1.10 either way in order for the strangle to breakeven as compared with the straddle. Although you'd never hang on to expiration anyway, it gives you a rough guide as to the relative probability of the strangle's likelihood to break even compared with the straddle. The wider apart the breakevens are, the less probability the trade will break even, and vice versa.

In this case if your analysis strongly indicates that that stock is going to make a massive move, then I wouldn't be put off by a difference of only 1.10 on either side with the stock price around $40.00. Typically I look for the strangle to be around half the cost of the straddle with the breakevens not too far away from the straddle breakevens. In this example I'm okay with the strangle as a complementary trade to the straddle, based purely on the breakeven criteria.

c. **Expected stock price behavior**

As suggested earlier, the expectation of stock price behavior is a major factor in comparing the straddle with the strangle. While the strangle is cheaper because of the OTM options, the breakevens, as we just saw, are typically slightly wider. This means that the probability of profit is lower. Also the potential *percentage* loss is greater with the strangle because both options are starting OTM. The trade could expire with the stock in between the strikes, and so both options are still OTM. With a straddle, it's more likely that one of the options will be ITM and the other OTM, but it's highly unlikely that the stock will end up on the single strike at expiration, leaving both call and put with no intrinsic value.

Because the strangle has a lower base cost than the straddle, the potential *percentage* gain is also greater than the straddle. A 100% gain in the straddle can mean a 300% gain in a good-value strangle—I should know because I've done it! That happy scenario is facilitated by a massive move in the stock. In my experience these massive moves have often been predicated by spectacular looking flag patterns about one week before the earnings announcement. The strangle has greater leverage than the straddle because of the lower base cost. If the stock doesn't move, the strangle will lose a bigger percentage, but if the stock moves big-time, the strangle can make a far greater percentage profit.

When I'm anticipating a mega move in the stock, I try to have a strangle on it, sometimes in isolation and sometimes together with the straddle—that's just a personal quirk due to my past experience. There are times where the stock moves enough to make the straddle profitable (owing to the tighter breakevens), but the strangle doesn't quite get there, so at least I'm hedged to an extent in that my straddle pays for the strangle in such circumstances.

d. **Expected volatility of both the stock and the options**

On a similar theme, in order to consider the strangle, I also like to have evidence that the expected volatility of both the stock and the options will increase after I've put on my trade. In terms of the stock itself, I like to see well-formed flag patterns with a good flag pole followed by a few days of shorter ranged bars. The hope is that this consolidation will be followed by a resumption of increased volatility, hopefully in a decisive manner one way or the other. In other words I want the stock to explode up or down and then keep going in that direction.

The implied volatility of the options is more complex. There are scenarios where the stock is consolidating yet the implied volatility of the options is increasing. This seems counter-intuitive, and it is. Surely if the stock price is consolidating and the historical volatility is decreasing, the implied volatility of the options should follow suit. Not necessarily…otherwise this would all be too easy. It's not uncommon for implied volatility to rise sharply say in few days before an earnings announcement. This occurs as a result of an anticipated increase in volatility from the earnings announcement, and therefore option premiums rise to compensate the option sellers for the increased risk of being exercised because of a major move.

Remember, option sellers have unlimited risk. Implied volatilities can also rise prior to a news announcement simply because the sellers know they can get away with driving up the premiums; such will be the demand in the lead up to earnings. The trick is, of course, is to avoid such options because after the earnings report the implied volatilities (and therefore the premiums) can come crashing down, crunching all those who are long. This can be devastating to straddle and strangle buyers if the stock didn't make a move.

Therefore, I like to find opportunities where implied volatilities haven't yet started to make the pre-earnings rise. My program finds the following criteria for me before I undertake my discretionary analysis:

- Stocks with earnings approaching.
- Flag patterns.
- Straddle cost as a proportion of the stock price range over a similar time period as the time to expiration.
- Straddle cost compared with the stock price.
- Implied volatility not having ramped up pre-earnings.
- Reasonably priced options in terms of implied volatility, i.e., the implied volatility of the ATM options being not significantly greater than its average over other relevant time periods. For this I'll compare implied volatility readings on a chart from previous earnings cycles as well as standard monthly, bi-monthly, and quarterly comparisons.

News Events

Earnings reports and other corporate news announcements have a huge impact on volatility trades. We can target a news event as our catalyst for a big move, but we need to ensure that implied volatility hasn't risen too far by the time we place the trade.

Ideally you enter the trade before any implied volatility spike occurs. There's no hard and fast rule as to when pre-earnings or other pre-news-event implied volatility spikes will occur, but typically it will be noticeable the week before the event. That requires placing the straddle well before this; however, this means you may be in the trade for a week or so longer, so time decay could be a factor unless you give yourself sufficient time until expiration. In the event that the stock price moves strongly after the news event, you don't want time decay ruining your trade, so it's better to look at options with two to four months to expiration, but preferably three.

One popular strategy is to buy the straddle well in advance of earnings, say one month beforehand, and then sell it after the implied volatility spike (assuming it happens) but before the earnings announcement, thereby avoiding any risk of a post earnings implied volatility collapse. This is a smart strategy, but in order to execute it properly you must be able to find the opportunities based on past and present implied volatility patterns. This is a formidable task unless you have access to software that can easily reduce the study to a relatively small list of stocks.

Time Decay

Time decay is the enemy of the long volatility trader. We already know that time decay increases exponentially during the final month before expiration, and you don't want to own straddles during that final month. Therefore, look for option expirations where (a) your planned exit is timed well before the start of the final month and (b) where time decay wouldn't be a huge factor between the time you place the trade and the planned exit date.

Straddle Cost

Of course, the lower the cost of the straddle, the lower the risk, the tighter the breakevens, the greater the probability of profit, the greater potential percentage profit, and so on. However, don't think that going for cheap front month straddles is the answer...it's not. The "front month" is the nearest expiration month. This time period can range from four weeks to a single day. Either way, the front month is subject to the most extreme ravages of time decay, and that's no good for long volatility traders.

Stock Chart Patterns

We're spending plenty of time on chart patterns such as flags, cup and handles, and double tops and bottoms for good reason. Before entering into a volatility trade, you want to see a fairly neat looking chart with an easily identifiable chart pattern. This neatness can often represent the calm before the storm of volatility that may ensue after you're in the trade. Ideally you want to see evidence in the past that the stock can make a sharp move in either direction. Again, it's all about buying low and selling high and obeying the criteria that conform.

Let's look at two charts and see which is "prettier" (Figure 4.3a or 4.3b). The object of the exercise is to see which chart is easier on the eye and from which you could identify a chart pattern and form a trading plan.

Figure 4.3a Chart A

TC2000®.com. Courtesy of Worden Brothers Inc.

Figure 4.3b Chart B

TC2000®.com. Courtesy of Worden Brothers Inc.

It shouldn't be too difficult to notice that chart A is much prettier; the bars are steady with the occasional big jump. We can see that it tends to move in steps and flags and it's currently forming a consolidation pattern, which we like. In the following three weeks (after the chart) APOL jumped to a peak of $65, an increase of 25%.

Chart B in Figure 4.3b is messy. There is no discernable trend, there is no discernable pattern, and the bars are highly inconsistent in terms of their length. This is what I would call an ugly chart! For me I cannot find a way of putting together a trading plan for this chart.

Breakeven Points

We analyzed breakeven points earlier when comparing a straddle with a strangle. With a straddle the lower breakeven point is [strike price - straddle cost], and the upper breakeven is [strike price + straddle cost]. These calculations are made for the breakeven at *expiration*. But you don't hold onto straddles to expiration, so how are they useful to us? Well, we use them as a guide.

Let's say that we liked the look of APOL on June 25, 2007. The August 50 strike straddle was priced at 5.30 at the ask. So it costs roughly 10% for the straddle with two months left to expiration...that's okay. The breakevens were therefore 44.70 and 55.30. With just under two months to expiration and earnings coming in a few days, even though you wouldn't hold to expiration, what was the likelihood of APOL moving $5.30 either up or down in the following seven to eight weeks? Well, given the fact that earnings was looming and in April we'd seen a five dollar move in only a few days, my assessment was that there was a fair chance it could move fast and furiously after earnings. A repeat of the April performance would have you in big profit instantly, which is exactly what happened. On June 29, the same straddle was worth 9.10 at the bid. That's a 72% increase in just a few days when the stock moved by only 16% to $58.00.

Now that we've highlighted the major factors we need to analyze, we now go through an example in detail of how to assess a candidate trading opportunity from start to finish.

Example

Let's go back to NICE as our trading example. It has several borderline aspects to it, which makes it a great example to use in order to refine our trading discretion. See the chart in Figure 4.4.

Figure 4.4 NICE Chart

TC2000®.com. Courtesy of Worden Brothers Inc.

The chart shows a rather protracted bull flag, which wouldn't normally inspire me. However, earnings are due in a few days, and it's also struggling to get to about $40.00, which is a double top from May. This is not just a flag, but a cup and handle too, albeit quite a long-term one. The stock has proved that it can make big jumps, and the previous earnings reports in August and May show that earnings can be a catalyst to increasing volatility with this stock. Note that the August earnings dovetailed with the first news of the sub-prime mortgage crisis that was about to unfold, so that particular earnings report was especially volatile. For November you would be expecting more of the same, with either a clear breakout above $40.00 or more likely the confirmation of a double top. I also like the fact that the stock price is nailed right on a strike price, which ensures the trade isn't biased in a directional sense (see Figure 4.5).

Figure 4.5 NICE option chains

Symbol	Prev. Close		Current Close		High	Low	Volume		
NICE	39.17		40.85		40.29	39.17	163476		

		Calls						Puts				
Symbol	Last	Bid	Ask	Vol	OpInt	Strike	Symbol	Last	Bid	Ask	Vol	OpInt
						2008-5 May						
2008EQJEG	7.3	7.5	7.9		6	35	2008EQJQG	1.9	1.65	1.95	94	40
2008EQJEH	4.7	4.6	4.9	71	30	40	2008EQJQH	3.6	3.5	3.9	240	95
2008EQJEI	2.45	2.45	2.7	118	49	45	2008EQJQI	6.8	6.5	6.9	21	55
						2008-2 Feb						
2008EQJBE	14.8	15.2	15.7		55	25	2008EQJNE	0.6		0.15		20
2008EQJBF	10.3	10.3	11		152	30	2008EQJNF	0.8	0.15	0.35		45
2008EQJBG	5.9	6.1	6.5		87	35	2008EQJNG	1.95	0.9	1.1		75
2008EQJBH	3.3	3.3	3.6	86	250	40	2008EQJNH	2.95	2.65	2.95	63	3
2008EQJBI	1.55	1.55	1.55	4	20	45	2008EQJNI	5.8	5.7	6.1		10

(a) Straddle   Buy February 2008 $40 strike put @ $2.95 and

Buy February 2008 $40 strike call @ $3.60

This particular straddle in Table 4.7 is just about acceptable in terms of price relative to the stock price. At a cost of 6.55, the straddle is just over 16% of the stock price, and there is just over three months to expiration. We'll be hoping to get out of this one in the next two weeks, with earnings scheduled for November 6.

Table 4.7 NICE straddle example

	November 2 Straddle (a)
You pay (net debit)	6.55 *
**Maximum risk ** **	6.55
Maximum risk with one month to expiration	c. 4.50 (68% of the trade on the assumption that the stock price historical volatility remains at an all-time low 16.5%) c. 2.75 (42% of the trade if the stock's historical volatility rises to 30%)
Maximum reward	Unlimited if the stock rises. 33.45 if the stock were to fall to zero
Breakeven (downside) at expiration	$33.45
Breakeven (upside) at expiration	$46.55
Maximum risk on net debit	100%
Call implied volatility	39.41%
Put implied volatility	37.11%

* one contract would mean [6.55 x 1 x 100] = **$655**

** if you held to expiration (which, of course, you wouldn't)

Can we tell if this would be a good trade? Well, without the benefit of hindsight, it's impossible to say. However, there are a few things in its favor and a few things against it (at least in theory), as discussed in Table 4.8.

Table 4.8 NICE straddle—for and against

For	Against
The stock price is nailed on a strike price—this leads to efficiency and a delta neutral starting point.	Implied volatility is significantly greater than the historical volatility. The option premiums haven't declined in line with the almost month-long stock price consolidation.
Flag pattern and cup and handle pattern in the stock.	The stock price has shown no willingness to move for some time.
Earnings approaching in just a few days.	The approach of earnings could have driven up the options premiums (we check on this later).
Previous two earnings seasons have witnessed good moves in the stock.	If the stock doesn't move then the position could lose significantly, up to 68% up to the final month before expiration.
The straddle is a good value as a percentage of the stock price (though this isn't the only factor you should consider). Crudely speaking, with less than two months to expiration the straddle shouldn't cost much more than around 10% of the stock price—between two and three months not much more than 15% and for straddles with three to months to expiration, 20%. These are only rough guidelines and will be more difficult to find where the markets are sinking and displaying high volatility.	The straddle is pricey when compared with the range of the stock price high and low over the past three months. A good rule of thumb is that the straddle cost should not be more than 50% of the difference between the stock's high and low for the same period as the time to expiration. So a three-month stock range of say $10 should be accompanied only by a three-month straddle costing four less than 5.00. Similarly a two-month stock range of $8.00 is compatible with a two-month straddle costing less than 4.00. In the case of NICE the three-month price range is $11.00 (40.52 - 29.52), whereas this straddle is 6.55, representing 59% of the range, which is slightly on the high side. There's not enough open interest in the February expirations yet (this really stops the trade from the outset). The bid-ask spread on the options is very high—in fact over 10% (this is another killer blow).

November 2 NICE Straddle Risk Profile

You can see in Figure 4.6 how the risk profile migrates toward the expiration curve. The thinner solid line is the risk profile on the trade date itself with over three months left to expiration. The dotted line assumes there is one month left to expiration. The thick pointed V shape line is the risk profile at expiration. Of course you never hold on to expiration, but the diagram helps you see how the risk profile changes over time and migrates to the expiration profile. As time goes by, your risk increases, so you don't want to hang on too long, and you typically want a decent amount of time to make the trade work for you.

Figure 4.6 NICE straddle risk profile

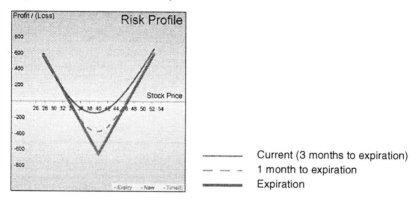

Current (3 months to expiration)
1 month to expiration
Expiration

November 2 NICE Straddle Delta Profile

As shown in Figure 4.7, when the stock price goes down a significant amount, the position assumes a delta of -1, and if the stock price moves up a significant amount, the position assumes a delta of +1. In other words the position will move one to one with the stock only when either the put or the call is deep ITM. In the event that that stock declines by a significant amount, the position delta will increase *inversely*, ultimately to its maximum of -1 (per contract) if the downward stock price movement is sufficiently dramatic. The -1 signifies that as the stock falls by a dollar, the position will gain by a dollar at that point. Conversely if the stock gains sufficiently, the +1 delta signifies that as the stock increases in price, as will the straddle position, by way of the calls being profitable.

Figure 4.7 NICE straddle delta

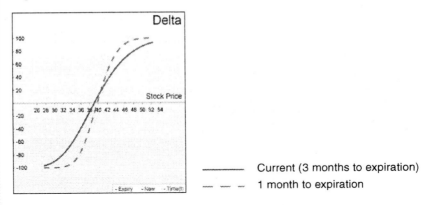

Current (3 months to expiration)
1 month to expiration

November 2 NICE Straddle Gamma Profile

In Figure 4.8, gamma shows just where our sensitivity is. Around the strike price area gamma is peaking, showing that delta is highly sensitive in this area. With the stock price significantly far from the strike price, gamma is virtually neutral, signifying that the position is so far ITM (with the stock either up or down) and that small changes in the stock price aren't going to have a big effect on the position's speed. The big changes in the position's speed occur near the strike price.

Figure 4.8 NICE straddle gamma

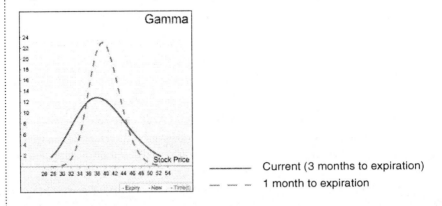

Current (3 months to expiration)
1 month to expiration

November 2 NICE Straddle Theta Profile

Theta shows in Figure 4.9 that time decay is hurting our position here. The dotted line only has one month to expiration, whereas the solid line has over three months to expiration. We can see how the dotted line is more damaging because there is less time to expiration.

Figure 4.9 NICE theta profile

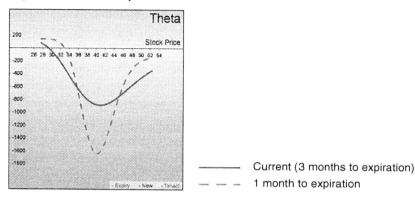

——————— Current (3 months to expiration)

~~~ ~~~ ~~~ 1 month to expiration

November 2 NICE Straddle Vega Profile

Vega shows that volatility is helping our position here (see Figure 4.10). The dotted line only has one month to expiration, whereas the solid line has over three months to expiration. We can see how the dotted line is less helpful because it has less time remaining to help us.

Figure 4.10 NICE vega profile

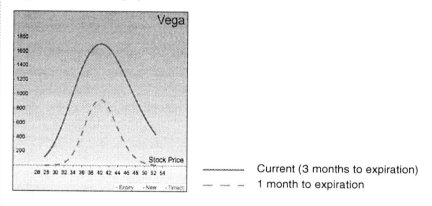

——————— Current (3 months to expiration)

~~~ ~~~ ~~~ 1 month to expiration

On balance only, the chart pattern and the previous price history after earnings announcements bring serious encouragement to this trade. It's disappointing that the options premiums are so high in volatility compared with the stock. It does look like this stock is likely to move with the news...the question is how much and will it be enough? The killer blow, however, is the fact that there's so little open interest for the February expirations, and the bid-ask spread is so wide. Liquidity is clearly an issue here. However, this is still a good example to use because it flatters to deceive. It's borderline in several ways, and this gives insight into the trader's dilemma with these borderline opportunities. If market conditions presented only a few decent opportunities, then this would be an even greater temptation. If good-looking opportunities were plentiful, this frankly wouldn't show on the radar.

Rising Implied Volatility Pre-earnings

There's something else we must consider in this example. So far we've seen the price data for this stock on November 2. However, being only a few days before earnings, there's a significant possibility that the implied volatilities of the options could have risen in the past week or two as floor traders (specialists) anticipate greater volatility and greater trading activity because of the impending earnings news. Let's see what the option prices were on October 23, more than a week prior and before the anticipation of earnings should have taken any effect.

Figure 4.11 NICE options chain

NICE SYSTEMS LTD											
Symbol	Prev. Close		Current Close		High	Low	Volume				
NICE	39.84		39.94		40.52	39.65	238854				
		Calls						Puts			
Symbol	Last	Bid	Ask	Vol	OpInt	Strike	Symbol	Last	Bid	Ask	Vol	OpInt
						2008-5 May						
2008EQJEG	7.3	7.2	7.5		6	35	2008EQJQG	1.45	1.45	1.6	10	40
2008EQJEH	3.6	4.2	4.6		30	40	2008EQJQH	4.3	3.2	3.5		95
2008EQJEI	2.3	2.25	2.45	2	43	45	2008EQJQI	6.6	6.3	6.6		55
						2008-2 Feb						
2008EQJBE	13.3	15.2	15.9		57	25	2008EQJNE	0.6		0.2		20
2008EQJBF	10.3	10.5	11.1		152	30	2008EQJNF	0.8	0.15	0.35		45
2008EQJBG	6.7	6.2	6.7		80	35	2008EQJNG	1.1	0.8	1		35
2008EQJBH	3	3	3.4		259	40	2008EQJNH	5	2.4	2.75		3
2008EQJBI	1.25	1.2	1.35		20	45	2008EQJNI	5.8	5.7	5.9	10	

As you can see in Figure 4.11, eight trading days earlier the same straddle was only 6.15 (the calls were at 3.40, the puts were at 2.75, and the stock price was virtually the same at 39.94). That's a 0.50 difference in the straddle cost—very high under the circumstances. Despite time decay and the fact that the stock price has remained static between the two dates, the option premiums actually rose between October 23 and November 2. This is almost certainly due to the fact that the stock has demonstrated great volatility in the past with earnings announcements. The specialists priced up the options accordingly, reflecting the extra risk they carried when they sold these options to traders. Remember, the specialists are there to make a market. If they're selling options, then they're exposed (though typically they'll be hedged by having other positions) and need to be compensated for that risk of increasing volatility, so they drive up the premiums, thereby pushing up the implied volatilities. Remember, as option sellers they will be affected adversely by future volatility. The option buyers are helped by future volatility. The key is to buy before that volatility kicks in. Table 4.9 compares both trades.

Table 4.9 NICE straddle comparison

	November Straddle 2 (a)	October Straddle 23 (b)
You pay (net debit)	6.55	6.15
Maximum risk	6.55	6.15
Maximum risk with one month to expiration (estimated)	c. 4.50 (68% of the trade on the assumption that the stock price historical volatility remains at an all time low 16.5%) c. 2.75 (42% of the trade if the stock's historical volatility rises to 30%)	c. 4.50 (73% of the trade on the assumption that the stock price historical volatility remains at an all time low 16.5%) c. 3.50 (57% of the trade if the stock's historical volatility rises to 30%)
Maximum reward	Unlimited if the stock rises. 33.45 if the stock falls to zero.	Unlimited if the stock rises. 33.85 if the stock falls to zero.
Breakeven (downside) at expiration	$33.45	$33.85
Breakeven (upside) at expiration	$46.55	$46.15
Maximum risk on net debit	100%	100%
Call implied volatility	39.41%	35.22%
Put implied volatility	37.11%	33.45%

There are several factors to take note of in analyzing the information in the table:

● The October straddle has significantly lower implied volatility than the November straddle. This cannot be due to increasing volatility of the stock price action as it has in fact continued to consolidate. The reason must be because earnings are that much closer, just four days away from the November 2 trade date. This is a crucial factor to be aware of when trading straddles and strangles.

Be aware of the option price history and whether or not the specialists are ramping up the implied volatilities and therefore the option premiums. Part of the success of trading straddles is ensuring you pay as little for them as possible, while not being overexposed to the contingent risks such as time decay. In this particular example there is the possibility that the November 2 trade is overpriced.

- The maximum risk with one month left to expiration is unusually high in this example. There are two reasons for this. First, we're more than three months out from the start of each of the trades, meaning that two months of time decay would have set in by then. Secondly, the implied volatility of both straddles is far greater than the current historical volatilities of the stock.

  As of November 2, the stock volatility for one month of data was around 16.50%, demonstrating how the stock price had consolidated. The two-month volatility was only 22% and the three month 25%, still well below the implied volatilities priced into the options premiums. As of October 23 the corresponding historical volatilities for the stock were 20%, 23%, and 27%. Think about that. The stock volatility was greater on October 23, yet the straddle cost was cheaper—and we still have to remember that the October 23 straddle would have had eight days' more time value too! This is proof of the "earnings effect" that you need to be aware of when trading straddles.

  Is it necessarily a bad thing that the implied volatilities of the options are far greater than the historical volatility of the stock price? No because we're anticipating a surge in stock price volatility, which hopefully will take us beyond the implied volatility that we've paid for in the options. But it's not the ideal start, particularly here where there's a pretty large discrepancy between the two. Note also that the October 23 straddle has worse figures for the maximum risk with one month left to expiration. This is mainly because the trade will be exposed to the same time decay as that for the November 2 trade, but the denominator (cost) is lower (6.15 versus 6.55), so as a percentage the potential time decay will be a little more severe. That said, the October 23 trade will still be far better because you'll pay less, and you won't be holding onto the trade that long anyway.

- The breakevens are closer and therefore better for the October 23 straddle. Remember, the straddle can make us unlimited profits if the stock rises—as the stock can rise infinitely. To the downside, the stock can only fall as far as zero, so the puts can only rise as high as the strike price, from which we then subtract the cost of our trade to work out the downside breakeven. The closer the breakevens are, the better because it means the stock has to move fewer points to get there.

- If there's a surge in the stock price's volatility, then the option values will almost certainly rise as well. In this case we're going to also need a big move in one direction or another to make the trade work. Seeing as we're right at a double top / cup and handle, I'd say the chances are good for a big move.

Bid-Ask Spread

Just a quick word on the bid-ask spread. We've been assuming that we only buy at the ask and sell at the bid. This is not so in real life. In practice we always try to get a fill somewhere in between, both on the way in and on the way out. This isn't always easy, particularly where there's a lack of liquidity like there is with this February options chain. There are times when it's more appropriate to get a quick fill, in which case you may place a limit order on at the ask, but most of the time it's worth chipping away at it and trying to sneak in between the spread. In recent times the CBOE has initiated its "penny pilot program," which can be found at www.cboe.com/penny/default.aspx. Here you can find some blue chip stocks offering penny bid-ask spreads, which certainly helps.

So we've now discussed a number of factors that we must be aware of prior to entering a straddle. Before we look at how the trade panned out, let's remind ourselves, by taking a look at Table 4.10, of all the factors we know about so far.

Table 4.10 Factors affecting our trade

News events	Earnings announcements and major economic news announcements such as FOMC meetings, inflation reports, non-farm payrolls, employment figures, interest rate changes, etc. can all affect stock prices, particularly if they spring a surprise.
Stock chart pattern	A consolidation pattern is preferable, suggesting an imminent breakout and increase in volatility to follow. If it's a cup and handle, then so much the better. We don't want the breakout to have started because volatility will already have begun to rise in the option prices, particularly if the initial stock price breakout is to the downside. Also double tops and bottoms are useful before they resolve one way or the other.
Volatility	Implied and historical. Ideally we buy options with low implied volatility compared with both itself and with the historical volatility of the stock. Seeing how the implied volatility crept up in the week before earnings, you could see the effect this could have on how much you have to pay for a trade.
Time decay	Time decay is the other major enemy of long straddle trades. We insure against it by (a) picking options with two to three months to expiration and (b) by closing our position well in advance of that time, at least one month before expiration, to avoid the most damaging effects of time decay. Remember the straddle risk profile drawing earlier where the curve migrates towards the expiration line as time progresses.
Straddle cost	Compared with stock price and stock price range. In effect these can be used as a crude approximation of implied versus historical volatility.
Breakeven points	Although we never hang on to expiration, how likely is it that the stock could trade through the breakeven points by expiration?

Table 4.10 Factors affecting our trade (continued)

The bid-ask spread	A 10% bid-ask spread is too high. The tighter the better. Always try to get inside the bid-ask spread with a limit order anyway. If the straddle cost is 5.95–6.55 (as it was on November 2), try to get in between the two at around 6.25. If you don't get filled, you can always adjust your limit order toward the ask.
Open interest	Over 100 is preferable if you're trading a small number of contracts. If you want to play with decent numbers, then we'd look for more, even about 500 if we're trading big lot sizes.
Greeks	We know that vega will be positive, illustrating how volatility helps us once we're in the trade. Conversely, theta will be negative because we are long options, and time decay hurts our position. Delta will be neutral around the strike price, with our position gaining speed as the stock moves well away from the money. Gamma peaks around the strike price, indicating a change in delta in that stock price range. We talk about this later, how a straddle can be adjusted, bit by bit, to a delta neutral position by selling profitable portions, piece by piece, as the stock price fluctuates back and forth.

Okay, so now we're ready to see what happened to NICE.

Figure 4.12 NICE chart after earnings

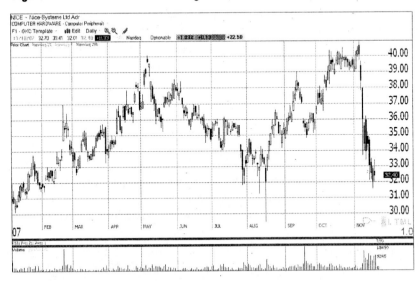

TC2000®.com. Courtesy of Worden Brothers Inc.

That's a pretty impressive move in Figure 4.12, wouldn't you say? Earnings were known later on November 6, with their full impact starting to be felt on November 7. From there the stock barely looked back until it hit the August closing lows around $32.00. This is a logical point of exit (at least of the puts), and you would have remained in the trade until at least this time. The question is, how do you manage a straddle trade like this? Well, in much the same way as you do with flags. Once the breakout occurs, we should be able to draw a trendline, which determines whether we stay in or get out.

Here, the trendline can barely even form, due to the steepness of the descent. Your exit point is determined here by a function of time (you don't want to wait too long; otherwise time decay will start to be a factor) and by the fact that the stock price is hitting the August closing lows, which could herald a double bottom.

Figure 4.13 NICE post earnings options chain

NICE SYSTEMS LTD										
Symbol	**Prev. Close**		**Current Close**		**High**	**Low**	**Volume**			
NICE	32.7		32.4		33.41	32.81	1166593			

Calls							Puts				
Symbol	**Last**	**Bid**	**Ask**	**Vol**	**OpInt**	**Strike**	**Symbol**	**Last**	**Bid**	**Ask**	**Vol**	**OpInt**
2008-5 May											
2008EQJEF	5.3	5.2	5.5		45	30	2008EQJQF	0.7	2.15	2.55		1
2008EQJEG	3.3	2.85	3.2	17	47	33	2008EQJQG	1.95	4.8	5.3		123
2008EQJEH	1.45	1.5	1.7		276	40	2008EQJQH	6.9	8.4	8.9		212
2008EQJEI	0.85	0.65	0.9		153	44	2008EQJQI	6.8	12.6	13.3		66
2008-2 Feb											
2008EQJBE	13.8	7.7	8.2		56	25	2008EQJNE	0.6	0.25	0.5		20
2008EQJBF	4	4	4.3	1	163	30	2008EQJNF	0.8	1.4	1.55		55
2008EQJBG	1.55	1.6	1.8	68	174	35	2008EQJNG	3.6	3.9	4.3	2	95
2008EQJBH	0.65	0.55	0.8	26	592	40	2008EQJNH	3.2	7.8	8.3		39
2008EQJBI	0.4	0.15	0.4		157	45	2008EQJNI	12.5	12.5	13.1		20

TC2000®.com. Courtesy of Worden Brothers Inc.

At this point on November 19 (see Figure 4.13), the straddle is now worth 8.35 at the bid (the call is at 0.55, and the put is 7.80), a net profit of 27.5% on the November 2 straddle and 35.8% on the October 23 straddle. Not bad for a matter of days and not even having picked a direction.

Figure 4.14 NICE post earnings with trendline

So despite this not having been a picture perfect opportunity, it performed pretty well, largely because of the $8.00 price drop from $40.00 to $32.00 (see Figure 4.14).

Let's see what the historical and implied volatility of the options is now. Well, the stock volatility on November 19 has jumped up to around 30% for the 1-month, 2-month, and 3-month historical volatilities. The call at 0.55 has an implied volatility of 39.71%, and the put at 7.80 has an implied volatility of 39.46%. This represents a slight increase from the October 23 trade but no increase from the November 2 trade. However, it's important to note that these figures on November 19 are the *bid* figures because we're now selling to close the trades. The corresponding November 19 ask figures of 0.80 and 8.30 have respective implied volatilities of 45.37% and 50.31%, which is a significant increase from both the October 23 and November 2 trade entry dates. Of course we can't sell at the ask; however, we can see that the difference between the two dates is actually quite marked, but a wide bid-ask spread can seriously damage an otherwise good trade. Such are the realities of trading. We must be aware of all these factors, and we should also pay attention to commissions too, though these don't have the impact of the early days of online trading.

Managing the Trade with a Trendline to Maximize Profit

As you've seen, you can use a trendline to manage your trade. The idea is that once the stock has made its decisive move, you want to stay in until it starts to retrace heavily against the new move. The easiest way to achieve this is to draw a trendline. You can always adjust the trendline if you believe the stock is pausing or forming a new flag before making another move in the same direction, so it's not a precise science, per se. In the example of NICE, the trendline was very steep, so there was scope to soften it as there was no suggestion of a big upward retracement on the horizon.

If we take a look at the chart (see Figure 4.14) again, you can see that the stock consolidated around the $32–33 level. You could have made the decision to remain in the trade unless the stock hit $34.00 in order to give the stock a chance to make another big fall. Now all this would had to have been assessed in the context of the option premium movements. You have to remember that the stock had already made a big move down. Any consolidation from this point may adversely affect the implied volatilities by driving them downward, thereby reducing your profit when you sell to close the trade. Not only that but you don't really want to hang around much longer than two weeks after the earnings report.

Looking at what actually transpired in the chart, if you hadn't exited on November 19, the logical place for the trendline to be drawn would have been from the peak on November 6 to the end of the consolidation period at the end of November. The stock then drops again before gapping back up on December 10, whereupon you'd be stopped out with the stock at around $31.24.

Figure 4.15 NICE chart with trendline

TC2000®.com. Courtesy of Worden Brothers Inc.

The problem with waiting so long is time decay. However, there was plenty of time left until the February expiration, and because of the additional downward move, the 40 strike straddle at the bid was worth 8.90 on December 10. This compares favorably with the 8.35 value on November 19 when the stock was around $32.40.

Figure 4.16 NICE options chain on November 19

Symbol	Prev. Close		Current Close		High	Low	Volume			
NICE	31.47		31.24		31.86	31.14	1083593			

	Calls							Puts				
Symbol	Last	Bid	Ask	Vol	OpInt	Strike	Symbol	Last	Bid	Ask	Vol	OpInt
						2008-5 May						
2008EQJEF	4.6	4.2	4.5	19	737	30	2008EQJQF	2.55	2.25	2.75	5	611
2008EQJEG	2.3	2.1	2.6	6	127	35	2008EQJQG	6.1	5.1	5.5		257
2008EQJEH	0.7	1.05	1.35		326	40	2008EQJQH	6.9	8.9	9.5		212
2008EQJEI	0.85	0.4	0.7		153	45	2008EQJQI	6.8	13.4	14.1		45
						2008-2 Feb						
2008EQJBE	5	6.6	7.2		64	25	2008EQJNE	0.4	0.25	0.45		31
2008EQJBF	3.6	2.9	3.3	5	174	30	2008EQJNF	1.35	1.4	1.65	1	74
2008EQJBG	1.05	0.9	1.1	44	263	35	2008EQJNG	4.3	4.3	4.7	13	249
2008EQJBH	0.2	0.3	0.45		575	40	2008EQJNH	10.1	8.6	9		44
2008EQJBI	0.4		0.2		157	45	2008EQJNI	12.5	13.4	14		

Interestingly, the implied volatilities of the call and put on December 10 were 43.04% and 33.41% respectively at the bid, with the puts actually being quoted at less than their intrinsic value. As an experienced trader you would have spotted that and not accepted anything below the intrinsic value for the ITM puts. At the ask, the implied volatilities were 48.28% and 49.86% for the call and put, respectively. That's a huge discrepancy for the puts in particular, and the answer would be to place your limit order in between the bid-ask spread as you should at least get the intrinsic value of 8.76 for the puts alone.

Time Stops

Typically you'll use a time stop in with a straddle trade. You should also be monitoring the implied volatility behavior pretty closely. In the case of NICE, we were wrong to exit on November 19 because a few weeks later we could have got more for the trade—but hindsight is a wonderful thing. I'm typically out of the trade within two weeks after earnings unless there's a clear case of the stock continuing its post-earnings move in easily identifiable steps and flags. In such cases the flags should be tight and only last a few days before making the next move, thereby allowing a breach of the trendline stop out of the trade. This of course is provided that there's sufficient time left to expiration and we're nowhere near the final month.

Now let's look at the strangles for NICE and compare them with the straddles we've just analyzed.

NICE Strangles

We already know the basic setup of this stock as it was leading up to the earnings report on November 6. Let's compare the 35–45 February expiration strangle on November 2 with the equivalent on October 23 and see how they performed, assuming we exit the trades on November 19 compared with December 10. Remembering the October 23 straddle performed better than the November 2 straddle, we'd expect the October 23 strangle to perform better too. Figures 4.17 and 4.18 show the option chains on the relevant trade dates.

Figure 4.17 November 2

Figure 4.18 October 23 series

Table 4.11 NICE strangle comparison

	November Strangle 2 (c)	October Strangle 23 (d)
You pay (net debit)	2.65	2.35
Maximum risk	2.65	2.35
Maximum reward	Unlimited if the stock rises. 32.35 if the stock falls to zero.	Unlimited if the stock rises. 32.65 if the stock falls to zero.
Breakeven (downside) at expiration	$32.35	$32.65
Breakeven (upside) at expiration	$47.65	$47.35
Maximum risk on net debit	100%	100%
Call implied volatility	36.66%	32.87%
Put implied volatility	38.44%	34.99%

We can see again in Table 4.11 that the October 23 options had around 4% less implied volatility and were actually cheaper than the November 2 equivalents, even though they had more time left to expiration. Let's compare the strangle implied volatilities here with the 40 strike straddle equivalents (Table 4.12).

Table 4.12 NICE 40 strike straddle implied volatility comparison

	November Straddle 2 (a)	October Straddle 23 (b)
Call implied volatility	39.41%	35.22%
Put implied volatility	37.11%	33.45%

As expected the October 23 implied volatilities are roughly in line with each other and are a few percentage points below the November 2 implied volatilities.

Before we complete our comparison analysis of these strangles, let's look at the October 23 risk and Greek profiles for our full understanding of the strangle strategy.

October 23, NICE Strangle Risk Profile

As with the straddle, we can see how the strangle risk profile migrates toward the expiration curve over time in Figure 4.19. The thinner solid line is the risk profile on the trade date itself with over three months left to expiration. The dotted line assumes there is one month left to expiration. The thick solid line is the risk profile at expiration. Of course we never hold on to expiration, but the diagram helps us see how the risk profile changes over time and migrates to the expiration profile. As time goes by, our risk increases, so we don't want to hang on too long, and we typically want a decent amount of time to make the trade work for us.

Figure 4.19 NICE strangle risk profile

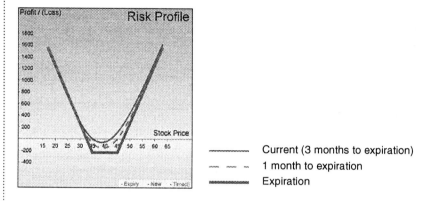

———— Current (3 months to expiration)
~~~ ~~~ ~~~ 1 month to expiration
▬▬▬▬▬ Expiration

October 23, NICE Strangle Delta Profile

We can see here in Figure 4.20 that when the stock price goes down a significant amount, the position assumes a delta of -1, and when the stock price goes up a significant amount, the position assumes a delta of +1. In other words the position will move one to one with the stock only when one side (call or put) is deep ITM.

Figure 4.20 NICE delta profile

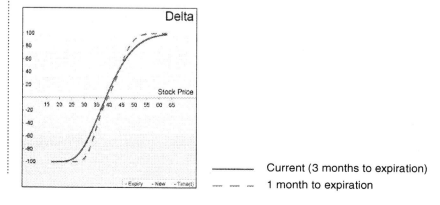

———— Current (3 months to expiration)
~~~ ~~~ ~~~ 1 month to expiration

October 23, NICE Strangle Gamma Profile

Gamma is showing in Figure 4.21 that the sensitivity of the position is found near the strike prices. Away from the strike price, gamma declines to virtually neutral, signifying that the position is so far ITM either with the calls or the puts that small changes in the stock price aren't going to have a big effect on the position. The big changes are occurring around the strike price.

Figure 4.21 NICE gamma profile

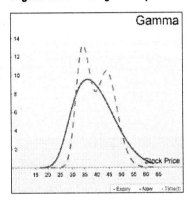

——————— Current (3 months to expiration)

— — — —— —— 1 month to expiration

October 23, NICE Strangle Theta Profile

Theta is showing that time decay is hurting the position here (Figure 4.22). The dotted line only has one month to expiration, whereas the solid line has over three months to expiration. We can see how the dotted line is more damaging because there is less time to expiration.

Figure 4.22 NICE theta profile

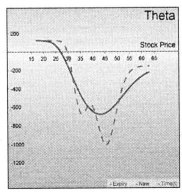

——————— Current (3 months to expiration)

— — — —— —— 1 month to expiration

October 23, NICE Strangle Vega Profile

Vega is showing that volatility is helping the position here (Figure 4.23). The dotted line only has one month to expiration, whereas the solid line has over three months to expiration. We can see how the dotted line is less helpful because it has less time to help.

Figure 4.23 NICE vega profile

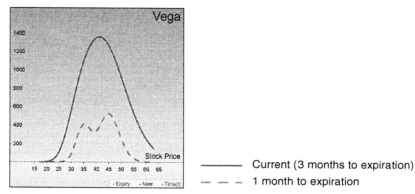

Current (3 months to expiration)

1 month to expiration

Now let's see how those two different strangles worked out. Figures 4.24 and 4.25 show the option chains for November 19.

Figure 4.24 NICE options chains for November 19

NICE SYSTEMS LTD

Symbol	Prev. Close	Current Close	High	Low	Volume
NICE	32.7	32.4	33.41	32.01	1166593

		Calls							Puts			
Symbol	Last	Bid	Ask	Vol	OpInt	Strike	Symbol	Last	Bid	Ask	Vol	OpInt
						2008-5 May						
2008EQJEF	5.3	5.2	5.5		45	30	2008EQJQF	0.7	2.15	2.55		1
2008EQJEG	3.3	2.85	3.2	17	47	35	2008EQJQG	1.95	4.8	5.3		123
2008EQJEH	1.45	1.5	1.7		276	40	2008EQJQH	6.9	8.4	8.9		212
2008EQJEI	0.85	0.65	0.9		153	45	2008EQJQI	6.8	12.6	13.3		66
						2008-2 Feb						
2008EQJBE	13.8	7.7	8.2		58	25	2008EQJNE	0.6	0.25	0.5		20
2008EQJBF	4	4	4.3	1	163	30	2008EQJNF	0.8	1.4	1.55		55
2008EQJBG	1.55	1.6	1.6	68	174	35	2008EQJNG	3.6	3.9	4.3	2	95
2008EQJBH	0.65	0.55	0.8	26	392	40	2008EQJNH	3.2	7.8	8.3		39
2008EQJBI	0.4	0.15	0.4		157	45	2008EQJNI	12.5	12.5	13.1		20

...and for December 10.

Figure 4.25 NICE options chains for December 10

NICE SYSTEMS LTD

Symbol	Prev. Close	Current Close	High	Low	Volume
NICE	31.47	31.24	31.86	31.14	1083593

Calls Symbol	Last	Bid	Ask	Vol	OpInt	Strike	Puts Symbol	Last	Bid	Ask	Vol	OpInt
						2006-5 May						
2008EQJEF	4.6	4.2	4.5	19	737	30	2008EQJQF	2.55	2.25	2.75	5	611
2008EQJEG	2.3	2.1	2.6	6	127	35	2008EQJQG	6.1	5.1	5.5		257
2008EQJEH	0.7	1.05	1.35		326	40	2008EQJQH	6.9	8.9	9.5		212
2006EQJEI	0.65	0.4	0.7		153	45	2008EQJQI	6.8	13.4	14.1		45
						2008-2 Feb						
2008EQJBE	5	6.6	7.2		64	25	2008EQJNE	0.4	0.25	0.45		31
2008EQJBF	3.6	2.9	3.3	5	174	30	2008EQJNF	1.35	1.4	1.65	1	74
2008EQJBG	1.05	0.9	1.1	44	263	35	2008EQJNG	4.3	4.3	4.7	13	249
2008EQJBH	0.2	0.3	0.45		575	40	2008EQJNH	10.1	8.6	9		44
2006EQJBI	0.4		0.2		157	45	2008EQJNI	12.5	13.4	14		

Table 4.13 NICE strangle comparison

		Trade exit date	
	Strangle entry	November 19	December 10
Value	23 Oct strangle (2.35)	(72% profit)	(83% profit)
		4.05	4.30
	2 Nov strangle (2.65)	(53% profit)	(62% profit)
Implied volatility	23 Oct strangle	Puts: % Calls:	Puts: 36.53% Calls: 34.61% (assuming in-between spread price of 0.10, actually no bid price given)
	2 Nov strangle		0%

Table 4.14 has a summary of the implied volatilities for the strangles.

Table 4.14 NICE strangle implied volatility comparisons

	October 23	November 2	November 19	December 10
Put implied volatility	34.99%	38.44%	39.22%	36.53%
Call implied volatility	32.87%	36.66%	39.19%	30.85% *

The October 23 and November 2 options have been calculated at the ask, and the November 19 and December 10 options have been calculated at the bid.

* The December 10 calls had no bid price as they are so far OTM that the implied volatility was calculated at an assumed price of 0.05.

As we can see, the only significant shift in implied volatility occurred between October 23 and November 2 as the earnings report loomed. Interestingly, even after the earnings report in early November, the implied volatility settled at the higher level as the stock continued its decline. It is unlikely that implied volatility would have sustained the higher level if the stock had started to climb as volatility is often accompanied by falling stock prices.

Other Factors to Note

We've largely finished our examination of straddles and strangles in this chapter. We return to these strategies later in the book as we create templates for our trading plans.

I want to mention a few other factors that you'll want to consider as you gain experience with these strategies.

Adjusting Trades and Gamma Trading

We've seen how implied volatility can rise before an earnings announcement. We know that implied volatility can fall immediately after an earnings announcement. And we also know the stock price can move dramatically after an earnings announcement.

When you enter into a straddle position, as the stock price and implied volatilities start to fluctuate, you can make adjustments to your trade in order to take advantage of these moves and take incremental profits even in advance of the earnings report and returning your position back to delta neutral. You achieve this by buying the stock when the price has declined and selling the stock when the price has increased.

A similar effect can be created by selling a portion of the profitable side of the trade when the stock price has moved. In other words, if the stock has made a move up, then the calls will be profitable, and the puts will be losers. In such cases, you would sell enough calls to bring the trade back to delta neutral. This strategy of adjustment works best if the stock is undulating back and forth and would involve incremental selling of both sides until the cost of the trade had been recouped leaving you in a free trade. If a trend takes hold, increment adjustments don't tend to work so well because you'd be continually selling your one profitable side (say the calls in an upward trend), not making the most of the entire move that's taken place. Such a strategy can even create losses if the incremental profits and final moves haven't been sufficient on the profitable side—the other side will be virtually worthless unless the stock rebounds the other way.

The same applies to gamma scalping using the underlying stock to make the adjustments.

An ATM straddle will have a delta very close to neutral. The idea is that we adjust our underlying stock position while holding onto the straddle.

Example

Let's say you have a stock at $100 and you buy 10 contracts of the ATM straddle. The historical volatility is 50%.

Stock	$100.00
Strike	100.00
Historical volatility	50%

Table 4.15 ATM straddle cost and delta

	Cost		Delta	
	Nominal	10 contracts	Nominal	10 contracts
Put	5.91	$5,910	-0.460	-460
Call	6.24	$6,240	0.539	+539
	12.15	$12,150	0.079*	79*

* rounded figures

Delta is roughly neutral here but not exactly (Table 4.15). Even though the stock is exactly ATM, calls and puts are valued slightly differently and also have slightly different deltas. The reason is because in theory it's easier for a stock to rise 20% than fall 20% because as it rises, each incremental increase becomes less significant in percentage terms. For example, when a $100 stock rises by $10, that's a 10% increase. However, when a $200 stock rises by $10, that's only a 5% increase. As a stock price falls, each incremental decrease becomes more significant. For example when a $200 stock falls by $10, that's a 5% decrease, but when a $100 stock falls by $10, that's a 10% decrease. Options prices reflect this distortion because they are based on the log of the change.

Back to our example: If the stock rises by $5.00, then the straddle position is now profitable on the call side and loss-making on the put side. The calls would be ITM and the puts OTM.

Table 4.16 Example with different stock and strike prices

Stock	**$105.00**
Strike	100.00
Historical volatility	50%

Table 4.17 Straddle value and delta after $5.00 move up

	Value		Delta	
	Nominal	**10 contracts**	**Nominal**	**10 contracts**
Put	3.92	$3,920	-0.338	-338
Call	9.24	$9,240	0.661	+661
	13.16	$13,160	0.323*	323*

* rounded figures

The call delta on the 10 contracts has increased from roughly 539 to 661. The put delta has inversely declined from roughly -461 to -338. The net position delta is now 323, a net increase of 245 from the starting point of 79.

To create a delta neutral position from here, we would have to sell short 323 shares at $105.

Let's say the stock now returns back to $100. The position delta of the original straddle plus the new addition of 323 short shares is now -246. To return to delta neutral we would buy back the shares.

Notice what we've achieved here. The stock fluctuated up then down. As the stock went up, the delta position became very positive as the calls became ITM and we therefore shorted 323 shares at $105 to return to delta neutral (though I should clarify that we didn't actually start at delta neutral). When the stock returned to $100, the delta position was negative by 245 deltas. If you wanted to continue adjusting the position, you would buy back 245 shares at $100, and those 245 shares would make a profit of $1,225, i.e., [245 x 5.00]. So the gamma scalping adjustment has made a profit while the straddle has probably lost some time value.

In this way you can make incremental profits leading up to an earnings season even as the stock price fluctuates around the original strike price of the straddle which may not yet be making profits. If you decided to buy back the entire 323 shares shorted at $105, your profit would be $1,615, over 10% of the straddle cost recouped even though the stock price has returned back to the strike price.

If the stock then declined by a few dollars, you would return to delta neutral by buying shares at the lower stock price and selling them as the stock bounced back to nearer the strike price, thereby allowing you to pocket further profits.

Gamma scalping is very useful if the implied volatility of the straddle declines. It's also useful to recoup some time decay as well as the difference in the bid-ask spreads of the options. However, gamma scalping can be problematic if the stock price moves in one direction and then keeps going in that same direction. Say the stock price rises to $105 and you therefore short shares at $105 to get your position back to delta neutral. If the stock makes another jump up, now to $110, your short stock position is down by five points, or $1,615, thereby negating much of your straddle profits.

Inside Information

One of the ways insiders try to camouflage their trades is via the derivatives markets. A key time for insider activity is before news events such as earnings announcements, economic data reports, and corporate takeover scenarios. Cheating opportunists know that options offer significant leverage particularly OTM. So look out for unusual spikes in the option volumes. Unusual activities in underlying stocks and their option chains are rife in advance of major news "surprises." Look out for unusual volume fluctuations and exaggerated implied volatility spikes in the front month expiration options in advance of the news event. Such spikes can occur OTM and ATM.

Strike Pinning

A phenomenon of trading liquid stocks is that of the prices "pinning" to a strike price. Jeff Augen's book, *The Volatility Edge in Options Trading*, documents this phenomenon. I first appreciated it in my own trading when GOOG was right in between two strikes that were $10 apart. In the last 30 minutes of the trading day, which was the last day of expiration and after an unusually quiet day, Jeff suggested that the stock could rise to $530 before the close. Bearing in mind how little the stock had moved that day, I made a mental note while not holding my breath—it just didn't seem possible, particularly when the clock had struck 3:45 p.m. Eastern Time, just 15 minutes before the close.

Suddenly within three 5-minute bars, the stock surged $5 out of the blue, sucked right onto the strike price at $530. This is just one example of pinning that can occur. For more information on this, *The Volatility Edge in Options Trading* by Jeff Augen is required reading.

Expiration Day Trading

So it's possible to trade volatility during the expiration day. This is highly specialized and therefore to be handled with great care.

Most traders would only consider *selling* straddles and strangles on the last day in order to take advantage of rapid time decay. So they might sell the remaining premiums, hope the stock remains flat for the day, and see the options diminish in value ever more rapidly as the hours go by. One strategy is to sell the straddle or strangle (if prices are high enough) the night before, hoping that no news materializes before the final day opening, in which case the options will have fallen in value owing to the 17 hours of overnight time decay. The options can be then bought back for less than they were sold for, but during the overnight period the position has unlimited risk, so this is a risky strategy.

Similarly, the final day can be subject to big moves in the stock price that can make shorting options highly dangerous.

Learning Points

In this chapter you've learned the criteria that make up a great straddle and also those factors you need to be wary of. Let's review them again now:

Straddle Checklist

- Volatility—implied and historical
- News events such as earnings reports
- Time decay
- Straddle cost
- Strike price positioning
- Stock chart patterns
- Breakeven points

The straddle and strangle are wonderful strategies when you get them right. The checklist here is part of your due diligence, which you must undertake without bias in order to ensure the quality of your analysis is as good as it can be.

chapter 5

Ratio Backspreads

In the last chapter you learned about how to trade when you're anticipating an increase in volatility but where you have no bias as to the direction the stock may go in. But what if you do have a bias? What if you feel sure of volatility and you're biased in one particular direction—is there a way we can take advantage of that?

The answer is yes, and it comes in the form of *ratio backspreads*.

If you believe volatility is about to rise and your bias is bullish, you would trade a *call ratio backspread*, and if your bias is bearish, you would trade a *put ratio backspread*. The idea is that when you get it right, you are rewarded by faster increases in profit. When you get it very wrong, you're not punished because at least you anticipated volatility, if not the right direction. Where you do get punished is if there is no volatility and if the stock price doesn't move. Even so, if you get in and out quickly enough, you won't suffer too badly. We'll see this in due course.

Call Ratio Backspreads

The call ratio backspread enables you to make accelerated profits provided the stock moves sharply upward. Increasing volatility is very helpful because you're net long in calls. The worst thing that can happen is that the stock price doesn't move at all, and even a sharp move down can be profitable or at the very least preferable to no movement at all.

The call ratio backspread involves buying and selling different numbers of the same expiration calls. You buy more calls than you sell, so you are always a net buyer. This gives you the uncapped profit potential. It also reduces the net cost of making the trade such that you can even create a net credit. Furthermore, your risk is capped, though you need to investigate the strategy further in order to understand it properly.

The call ratio backspread has two steps:

Step 1: Sell lower strike calls

Step 2: Buy a greater number of higher strike calls

The idea behind the ratio part of the strategy is (a) to reduce the cost of the trade, sometimes to nil, and (b) to protect the downside of the side you're not biased about. We'll come to that a bit later. Remember also that you're selling nearer the money (NTM) calls, which will have higher deltas than the higher strike calls, so to balance your deltas you need to buy more out of the money (OTM) calls than the NTM calls that you're selling. It's also worth noting that the NTM calls are worth more than the OTM calls.

Note that in Figure 5.1 I've specified the ratios of 2:1 and 3:2. In reality the ratios don't have to be fixed to those proportions, but I'll use them for illustration purposes in the coming examples.

Figure 5.1   Call ratio backspread components

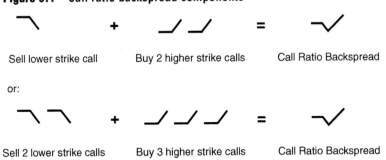

Sell lower strike call   Buy 2 higher strike calls   Call Ratio Backspread

or:

Sell 2 lower strike calls   Buy 3 higher strike calls   Call Ratio Backspread

The risk profile of the call ratio backspread is as shown in Table 5.1.

Table 5.1 Call ratio backspread risk profile

Maximum risk	[difference in strike prices] - [net credit received] or + [net debit paid]
Maximum reward	Unlimited to the upside Limited to the [lower strike price + net credit] downside
Breakeven on the downside (at expiration)	[lower strike + net credit]
Breakeven on the upside (at expiration)	[higher strike price + (difference in strike prices x number of short calls) / (number of long calls - number of short calls) - [net credit received] or + [net debit paid]]

The ratio backspread is peculiar in that sometimes it has two breakevens, and sometimes it doesn't.

Let's take an example and illustrate how the call ratio backspread risk profile is affected by the following:

- The ratio itself
- The strike prices
- The expiration dates

Example

ACME is trading at $100.00 on February 18. Historical volatility of the stock is at 50%, and both options' implied volatilities are around the same level.

- Sell one July 100 strike call at 13.45
- Buy two July 110 strike calls at 9.55

Table 5.2 Call ratio backspread example results

Net debit	premium bought – premium sold **19.10 – 13.45 = 5.65**
Maximum risk	difference in strikes + net debit **10.00 + 5.65 = 15.65**
Interim risk *	same as net debit * **5.65**
Maximum reward	uncapped

Table 5.2   Call ratio backspread example results (continued)

Interim reward *	n/a because the trade is a net debit in this case *
Lower breakeven	lower strike + net credit **n/a because we have a net debit here**
Higher breakeven	higher strike + (difference in strikes × # short calls) / (long calls - short calls) + net debit (or - net credit) **110.00 + (10.00 / 1) + 5.65 = 125.65**

* The interim risk is the horizontal section of the risk profile at expiration line shown in Figure 5.2. It signifies the risk at expiration if the stock price falls below the lower strike price. If the horizontal line is above the breakeven line then it would be called the interim reward. We only get an "interim reward" if the ratio backspread trade is executed at a net credit.

Notice in Figure 5.2 how the risk curve migrates to the expiration line. See how the thinner solid curve today has a breakeven near the current stock price of $100? This tells us that if volatility remains constant at 50% but the stock rises, we're going to be in profit. However, if we allow the trade to linger for a few months, we migrate to the dashed line. This dashed line is our risk profile with one month left until expiration; in other words, we've kept hold of the trade for four months. See how the breakeven has moved out to around $120? That's quite a shift. And at expiration the breakeven moves all the way out to $125.65.

Figure 5.2   February 18 call ratio backspread risk profile with implied volatility at 50%

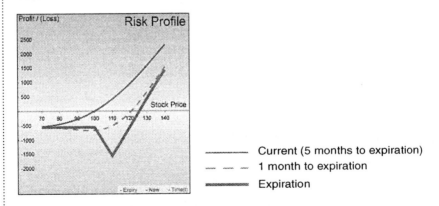

The moral of that particular story is don't hang onto a ratio backspread. Place it before your earnings date and close it once the news is out. Be careful not to buy high implied volatilities as you're net long options.

Let's see what happens if we change one component at a time. First is how an increase in volatility changes the risk profile (see Figure 5.3).

If the option volatility were to rise from 50% to 60%, our trade would immediately be in profit, and the breakeven would go down to just over $90. The breakeven with one month until expiration would be under $120 now, and our breakeven at expiration would remain unchanged.

What if we suffered a volatility crunch in the aftermath of a dull earnings announcement and the options implied volatilities shrunk to 40%?

Figure 5.3 February 18 call ratio backspread risk profile with implied volatility increased to 60%

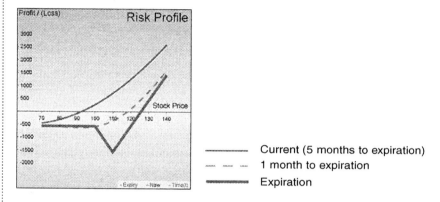

This time the immediate breakeven would be almost $110 (see Figure 5.4), and the breakeven with one month until expiration would shift out to over $120.

Figure 5.4 February 18 call ratio backspread risk profile with implied volatility decreased to 40%

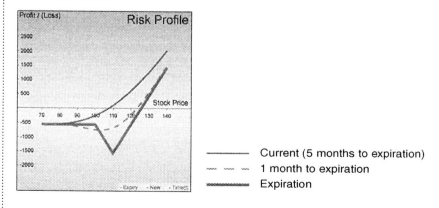

So we can see how important it is that implied volatilities rise (or at least don't fall) once we're in this trade.

In the next diagram, Figure 5.5, I'm changing our dotted line to show us our risk profile when we're three months from expiration, i.e., two months into the trade, assuming the option volatilities have remained constant at the original 50%.

Figure 5.5   February 18 call ratio backspread risk profile with dotted line 3 months from expiration

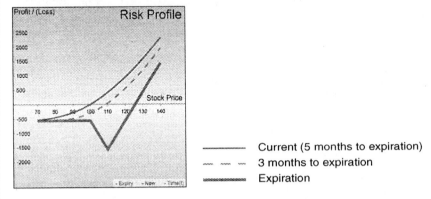

The 3-months to expiration dotted line breaks even at around $110 (see Figure 5.5). Remember we entered the trade on February 18, which is five months before the July expiration. Just two months into the trade, our breakeven moves from around $100 to $110. In another two months, in June, the breakeven would be around $120. Time decay is hurting our position, and one of the effects of it is to push out our breakeven further away from the current stock price of $100.

What happens if we change the ratio from 2:1 to 3:2? Well, we're buying proportionately less calls, so the position will take longer to get into profit but will cost less. Let's compare by looking at Table 5.3.

Table 5.3   Call ratio backspread ratio comparisons

	2 : 1 CRB	3 : 2 CRB
Net debit	5.65	1.75
Maximum risk	15.65	21.75
Interim risk	5.65	1.75
Maximum reward	uncapped	uncapped
Interim reward	n/a	n/a
Lower breakeven	n/a	n/a
Higher breakeven	125.65	131.75

The 3:2 trade costs only 1.75 compared with 5.65. This is no surprise as the ratio is 3:2 as opposed to 2:1. The expiration breakeven is further away at $131.75. This is because the maximum loss is greater for the 3:2 than with the 2:1 ratio backspread, so the 3:2 climbs into profit slightly later than the 2:1.

So which is better? Well, if the stock moves sharply up, the 2:1 is better as we're in profit much faster. If the stock doesn't move at all, the 2:1 is better because the maximum risk is lower. But if the stock moves sharply down, the 3:2 is better (see Figure 5.6) because the interim risk is lower.

Figure 5.6   3:2 ratio backspread

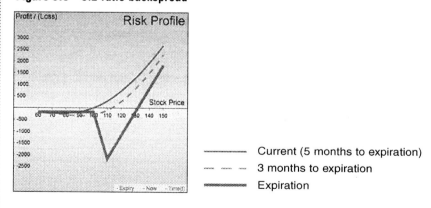

——————— Current (5 months to expiration)

—— —— —— 3 months to expiration

▬▬▬▬▬ Expiration

Is it possible to do one of these trades at a net credit? Yes. All we need is a volatility skew such that the OTM calls have lower implied volatility than the NTM options, and the possibility will exist.

Let's take the original example again and adjust some of the inputs.

ACME is trading at $100.00 on February 18. Historical volatility of the stock is at 50%.

● Sell two July 100 strike calls at 13.50 (implied volatility = 50.16%)

● Buy three July 110 strike calls at 9.00 (implied volatility = 47.80%)

Bearing in mind we always have the bid-ask spread to consider, we've found a situation here where we're buying lower implied volatility than what we're selling. Let's look at the analysis of the trade in Table 5.4.

Table 5.4   3:2 call ratio backspread trade summary

Net debit	premium bought - premium sold **27.00 - 27.00 = 0.00**
Maximum risk	[number of short calls x difference in strikes] + net debit **[2 x 10.00] + 0 = 20.00**
Interim risk	same as net debit **0.00**
Maximum reward	uncapped
Interim reward	**0.00**
Lower breakeven	lower strike + [net credit / number of short calls] **100 + 0 = 100**
Higher breakeven	higher strike + (difference in strikes x number of short calls) / (long calls - short calls) + net debit (or - net credit) **110.00 + (10.00 x 2 / 1) + 0 = 130.00**

So here we have a scenario where we have two breakevens because we recouped from selling options at least as much as we spent on the long side.

Notice in Figure 5.7 how the expiration line breaks even to the downside at $100 and then moves horizontal along the breakeven line from right to left.

If the implied volatility is skewed any further to make the OTM calls less valuable, then we'd have a net credit trade here. Let's modify the example some more.

ACME is trading at $100.00 on February 18. Historical volatility of the stock is at 50%.

- Sell two July 100 strike calls at 13.50 (implied volatility = 50.16%)

- Buy three July 110 strike calls at 8.50 (implied volatility = 45.85%)

Figure 5.7   3:2 call ratio backspread risk profile

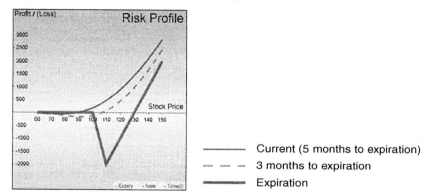

Current (5 months to expiration)
3 months to expiration
Expiration

Notice in Figure 5.8 how the expiration line breaks even to the downside at $100.75, continues up for a bit, then moves horizontally above the breakeven line from right to left. So even by getting the direction wrong, we still make a small profit if we play the volatility skew where the OTMs are relatively undervalued compared with the NTMs.

Figure 5.8   3:2 call ratio backspread risk profile with lower implied volatility for the long OTM calls

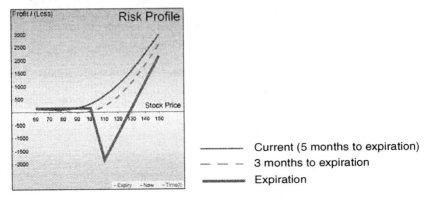

─────────── Current (5 months to expiration)
─ ─── ─── 3 months to expiration
━━━━━━━━━ Expiration

Strike Price Impact

What if we alter the distance between the strike prices? If we push out the higher strike price, we're going to pay less for the OTM calls because they're further OTM than before. Also the distance to the higher breakeven is going to be wider than before. Again, let's go back to our original 2:1 call ratio backspread and compare.

ACME is trading at $100.00 on February 18. Historical volatility of the stock is at 50% and both options' implied volatilities are around the same level.

- Sell one July 100 strike call at 13.45
- ~~Buy two July 110 strike calls at 9.55~~
- Buy two July 120 strike calls at 6.70

Table 5.5   100-110 and 100-120 call ratio backspread comparison

	100–110 CRB	100–120 CRB
Net debit	5.65	n/a
Net credit	n/a	0.05
Maximum risk	15.65	19.95
Interim risk	5.65	n/a
Maximum reward	uncapped	uncapped
Interim reward	n/a	0.05
Lower breakeven	n/a	100.05
Higher breakeven	125.65	139.95

Notice in Figure 5.9 how the wider backspread is at a net credit, thereby giving us protection if the stock price goes down. This is because we're buying much cheaper options as they're further OTM. The risk is higher, however, and the higher breakeven is pushed further out. Remember though, we would never hold one of these to expiration.

Figure 5.9   100–120 call ratio backspread risk profile

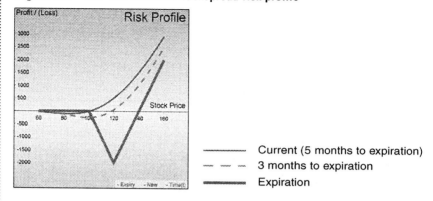

The higher breakeven is a long way off. What happens if we shift both strike prices down $10 in relation to the original trade? In the original trade we sold one July 100 strike call and bought two July 110 strike calls.

● Sell one July 90 strike call at 18.55

● Buy two July 100 strike calls at 13.45

Table 5.6   100-110 and 90-100 call ratio backspread comparison

	100–110 CRB	90–100 CRB
Net debit	5.65	8.35
Net credit	n/a	n/a
Maximum risk	15.65	18.35
Interim risk	5.65	8.35
Maximum reward	uncapped	uncapped
Interim reward	n/a	n/a
Lower breakeven	n/a	n/a
Higher breakeven	125.65	118.35

As you can see in Table 5.6, by shifting the strikes down we've brought the higher breakeven down, which is good, but we're paying more and absorbing more risk for that particular privilege. With the stock at $100 if the stock price moves immediately, we're making money very quickly as the current risk profile (the thinner solid line below) breaks even at around $100, provided the implied volatility of the options remains the same. Anything above $100 represents ITM, so the position quickly moves to its maximum speed (or delta) as soon as we're in profit.

Figure 5.10   90-100 call ratio backspread risk profile with implied volatility at 50%

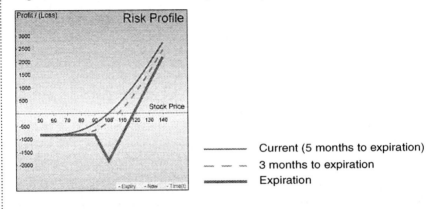

Is this better than the original call ratio backspread? Well, if the stock price explodes by $20 overnight, perhaps. If it goes down by $20 overnight, probably not.

Let's see what a change in volatility does to the new ITM ratio backspread trade.

If the implied volatilities go down to 40%, the current breakeven pushes out to around $105 (see Figure 5.11).

Figure 5.11   90-100 call ratio backspread risk profile with implied volatility decreased to 40%

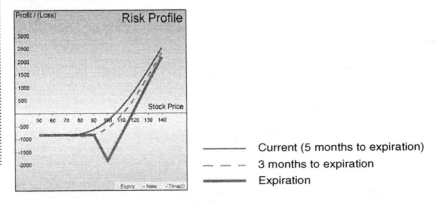

If the implied volatilities rise to 60%, the current breakeven will come in to around $92.

Figure 5.12 90-100 call ratio backspread risk profile with implied volatility increased to 60%

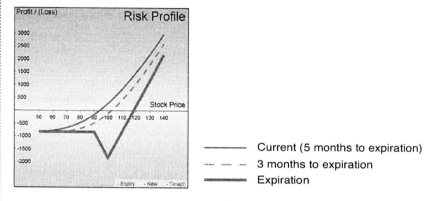

Current (5 months to expiration)
3 months to expiration
Expiration

Therefore if you place this trade nine days or so before earnings after which implied volatilities rise right up to the earnings date where you sell (say just before the adjustment), a 10% increase in implied volatility could translate to much greater profit and a much easier breakeven target.

So now we've examined adjusting the ratio itself and the strikes, let's see what the impact is if we adjust the expiration dates.

So far we've looked at these trades with expiration about five months away. Let's now try one month to expiration with all the other variables the same. The trade is now as follows:

● Sell one March* 100 strike call at 6.15

● Buy two March* 110 strike calls at 2.60

As shown in Figure 5.13, expiration breakeven is $120, but amazingly even using the same volatilities of 50%, with the shorter term trade, we now have a net credit and therefore an interim profit even if this stock falls below $100.95.

---

* March is one month from expiration.

Figure 5.13   100-110 call ratio backspread risk profile with implied volatility at 50%

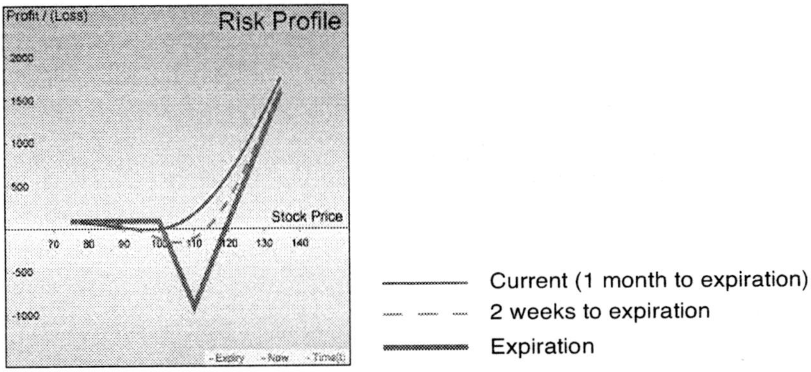

—————— Current (1 month to expiration)

— — — 2 weeks to expiration

▬▬▬▬▬ Expiration

Let's take a look at Table 5.7 and compare the two trades.

Table 5.7   100-110 call ratio backspread comparisons for July and March expirations

	100–110 July CRB	100–110 March CRB
Net debit	5.65	n/a
Net credit	n/a	0.95
Maximum risk	15.65	9.05
Interim risk	5.65	n/a
Maximum reward	uncapped	uncapped
Interim reward	n/a	0.95
Lower breakeven	n/a	100.95
Higher breakeven	125.65	119.05

We can immediately see that the March expiration trade is much more responsive. It has less risk and has a net credit, not a net debit.

Now look at the two-week line to expiration (the dotted line). See how with only two weeks left to expiration the risk profile moves below the breakeven line before climbing back up again, breaking even at around $114. Provided the option volatilities don't take a significant downturn, the trade has very limited risk for the first two weeks—notice how the dotted line barely moves below the breakeven line.

The issue with the March (one-month) expiration is that time decay will be kicking in much sooner than with the longer terms to expiration. After three weeks in the trade and with only one week left, we can see the difference in that dotted line in Figure 5.14.

Figure 5.14 100-110 call ratio backspread risk profile with 1 week left to expiration

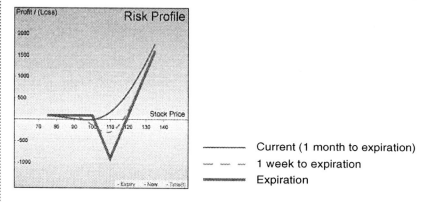

——————— Current (1 month to expiration)

—— —— —— 1 week to expiration

▓▓▓▓▓▓▓▓▓ Expiration

Now let's imagine that the implied volatilities are crunched from 50% to 40%...

We can see in Figure 5.15 that dotted line migrates downward toward the expiration risk profile.

Figure 5.15 100-110 call ratio backspread risk profile with 1 week left to expiration and implied volatility decreased to 40%

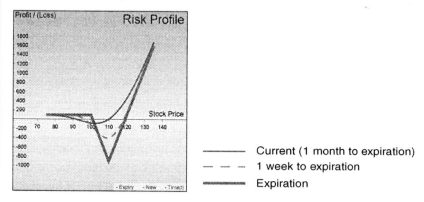

——————— Current (1 month to expiration)

—— —— —— 1 week to expiration

▓▓▓▓▓▓▓▓▓ Expiration

So we've observed that ratio backspreads are affected by

● The ratios of bought-to-sold calls

● The position of and distance between the strike prices

● The time to expiration

An aggressive trade would combine a high ratio of bought-to-sold calls with a short distance between strikes and a short time to expiration. In such a case you'd want the stock to make a very fast move and identify a way of exiting the trade very quickly.

In many ways the call ratio backspread offers a better solution than the straddle. Because you're both long and short calls, you're afforded some protection against both time decay and a decline in volatility, both of which impact a straddle much more severely. As we saw in Figure 5.15, the dotted line moved down into further risk territory relatively slowly until we imposed both increasing time decay and decreasing volatility into the equation.

In terms of trade management, the risk profile diagrams just provided serve to emphasize that you must select your expiration dates with plenty of time to spare and ensure you exit the trade in a timely fashion, whatever happens with the stock.

Context

It's clear that we're anticipating higher volatility together with an upward directional bias in the stock price. Depending on the options premiums and the ratios, we can execute this strategy with a negligible cash outlay. However, we'll be required to have sufficient funds in the account to cover the potential risk of the trade.

Greeks

Going back to the ACME example on February 18, the stock was $100, historical volatility was 50%, and we were selling one July 100 call at 13.45 and buying two July 110 calls at 9.55 each.

As the stock rises above the second strike price, the position moves in line with the stock, and delta reaches its peak when the position is deep ITM. As the stock price falls, the position moves into negative territory, and delta slows down (see Figure 5.16).

Figure 5.16   Call ratio backspread delta profile

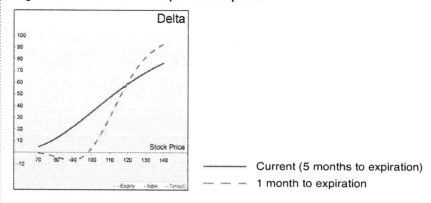

——————— Current (5 months to expiration)

— — — 1 month to expiration

Gamma peaks around the higher strike price, as shown in Figure 5.17, illustrating the position's pivotal strike price level. This is where the position's rate of change is at its fastest.

Figure 5.17   Call ratio backspread gamma profile

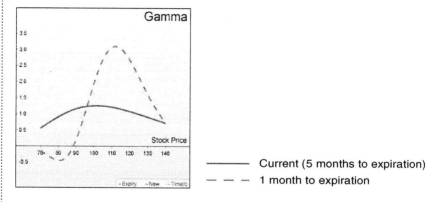

——————— Current (5 months to expiration)

— — — 1 month to expiration

Time decay is harmful to the position unless the stock falls dramatically. Notice in Figure 5.18 how with the dotted line, which has only one month to expiration, theta decay is far more destructive, as depicted by the dotted line being lower than the solid line, which has five months to expiration.

Figure 5.18   Call ratio backspread theta profile

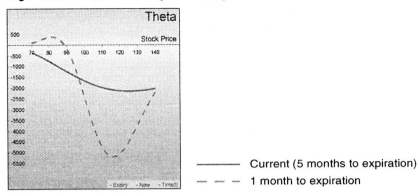

——————— Current (5 months to expiration)
—— —— —— 1 month to expiration

Not surprisingly vega is positive here, as shown in Figure 5.19, illustrating how volatility is helpful to the position. Notice how the solid line is higher than the dotted line. This is because with five months to expiration volatility has more time to help the position. Vega peaks around the higher strike price. This is because the higher strike price represents the lowest point of the risk profile curve, so any increase in volatility at this point will be helpful to the position as it will push the risk curve away from the maximum loss area. Remember also, we are net long options, meaning that increases in volatility will generally help the position.

Figure 5.19   Call ratio backspread vega profile

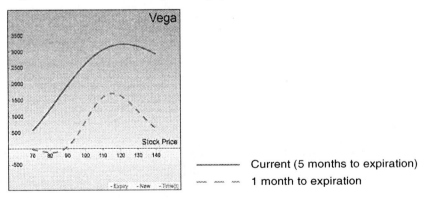

——————— Current (5 months to expiration)
—— —— —— 1 month to expiration

In a low interest rate environment, you don't worry too much about rho, but you may note that higher interest rates are generally helpful to the position. Notice in Figure 5.20 how the solid line is above the dotted line. This shows that the more time the position has to expiration, the more interest rates can help the position. This is, of course, common sense.

Figure 5.20   Call ratio backspread rho profile

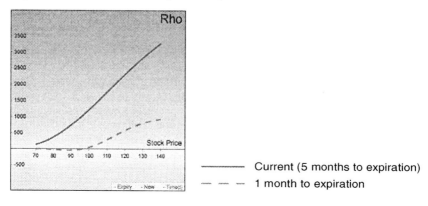

——————— Current (5 months to expiration)

~~~~ ~~~~ ~~~~ 1 month to expiration

Put Ratio Backspreads

The put ratio backspread is the opposite of the call ratio backspread. It is bearish while the call ratio backspread is bullish and is based on the use of puts rather than calls.

The put ratio backspread enables you to make accelerated profits, provided the stock moves sharply downward. Increasing volatility is very helpful to the position because you're net long (in options). The worst thing that can happen is that the stock doesn't move at all, and even a sharp move up can be profitable or at the very least preferable to no movement at all.

As you'd expect, the put ratio backspread involves buying and selling different numbers of the same expiration puts. You buy more puts than you sell, so you are always a net buyer. This gives you the ongoing profit potential until the stock reaches zero. It also reduces the net cost of making the trade so that you can even create a net credit. Furthermore, your risk is capped. In the coming sections we investigate the strategy further to help you understand it better.

The put ratio backspread involves two steps:

Step 1: Sell higher strike puts

Step 2: Buy a greater number of lower strike puts

We know that the ratio enables you to reduce the cost of the trade and protect the downside of the "wrong side." The put ratio backspread is a bearish strategy, so the wrong side comes into play if the stock rises, in which case the strategy protects you from such a scenario. Again, this is a classic example of the Rule of the Opposites (from Chapter 1, "Introduction to Options"). The put ratio backspread is the precise opposite of the call ratio backspread.

Remember also that you're selling the NTM puts, which will have higher (negative) deltas than the lower strike puts, so to balance your deltas, you need to buy more OTM puts than the NTM puts that you're selling. It's also worth noting that the NTM puts are worth more than the OTM puts.

Figure 5.21 Put ratio backspread components

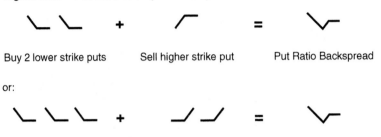

Remember, the ratios don't have to be fixed to the 2:1 and 3:2 proportions, but as with the call ratio backspreads, we'll use them for illustration purposes in our examples.

The risk profile of the put ratio backspread is as follows:

Table 5.8 Put ratio backspread risk profile

Maximum risk	[difference in strike prices] - [net credit received] or + [net debit paid]
Maximum reward	[breakeven on the downside x difference between number of bought and sold options]
Breakeven on the downside (at expiration)	[lower strike price - (((difference in strike prices × # short puts) + net debit or - net credit) / (number of long puts - number of short puts))]
Breakeven on the upside (at expiration)	[higher strike - (net credit / # short puts)]

As we know from the call ratio backspread, the ratio backspread is a peculiar strategy in that sometimes it has two breakevens, and sometimes it doesn't.

Let's now take our examples from before and apply them to the put ratio backspread. The strategy is still affected by

● The ratio itself

● The strike prices

● The expiration dates

Example

ACME is trading at $100.00 on February 18. Historical volatility of the stock is at 50%, and both options' implied volatilities are around the same level.

● Sell one July 100 strike put at 12.00

● Buy two July 90 strike puts at 7.25

Table 5.9 Put ratio backspread example

Net debit	premium bought - premium sold **14.50 - 12.00 = 2.50**
Maximum risk	difference in strikes + net debit **10.00 + 2.50 = 12.50**
Interim risk *	same as net debit * **2.50**
Maximum reward	Lower breakeven × # (bought - sold options) **77.50**
Interim reward *	n/a because the trade is a net debit in this case *
Lower breakeven	[lower strike price - (((difference in strike prices × # short puts) + net debit or - net credit) / (number of long puts - number of short puts))] **77.50**
Higher breakeven	[higher strike - (net credit / # short puts)] **n/a because the trade is a net debit in this case**

*The interim risk is the horizontal section of the risk profile at expiration line shown in Figure 5.22. It signifies the risk at expiration if the stock rises above the higher strike price. If the horizontal line is above the breakeven line, then it would be called the interim reward. You only get an "interim reward" if the ratio backspread trade is executed at a net credit.

Note that with the put ratio backspread, the higher your breakeven the better as the risk curve goes from bottom right to top left (i.e., the opposite of the call ratio backspread). See the risk profiles in Figure 5.22.

Figure 5.22   February 18 put ratio backspread risk profile with implied volatility at 50%

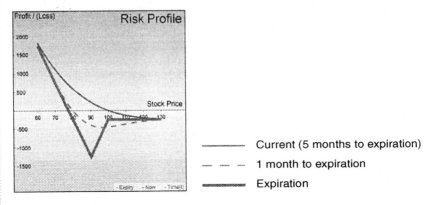

As we saw earlier with the call ratio backspread risk profiles, the risk curve migrates to the expiration line. See how the thinner solid curve on this day has a breakeven near the current stock price of $100. This tells us that if volatility remains constant at 50% but the stock rises, we're going to be in profit. However, if we allow the trade to linger for a few months we migrate to the dotted line. This dotted line is our risk profile with one month left to expiration; in other, words we've kept hold of the trade for four months. Note how the breakeven has moved out to around $80. At expiration the breakeven moves all the way out to $77.50.

As before, you don't hang onto a ratio backspread. Open the trade before the earnings date and close it once the news is out. You also need to be careful not to buy high implied volatilities as you're net long options.

Taking one variable at a time, let's see how an increase in volatility would change the picture, as shown in Figure 5.23:

Figure 5.23   February 18 put ratio backspread risk profile with implied volatility increased to 60%

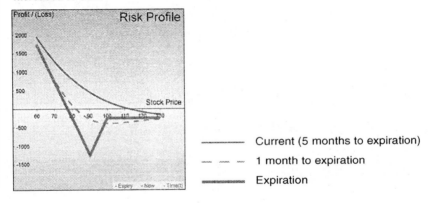

If the option volatility were to rise from 50% to 60%, our trade would immediately be in profit, and the breakeven would go up to around $110. The breakeven with one month to expiration would be over $80 now, and the breakeven at expiration would remain unchanged.

What if we suffered a volatility crunch in the aftermath of a moribund earnings announcement and the options implied volatilities shrunk to 40%?

This time the immediate breakeven would be around $90, and the breakeven with one month to expiration would shift out to under $80 (see Figure 5.24).

Figure 5.24   February 18 put ratio backspread risk profile with implied volatility decreased to 40%

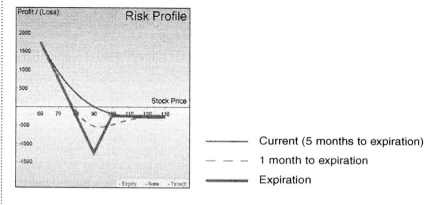

Again, we can see how important it is that implied volatilities rise (or at least don't fall) once we're in this trade.

In Figure 5.25, I'm adjusting the dotted line to show us the risk profile when we're three months from expiration, i.e., two months into the trade, assuming the option volatilities have remained constant at the original 50%.

Figure 5.25   February 18 put ratio backspread risk profile with dotted line 3 months to expiration

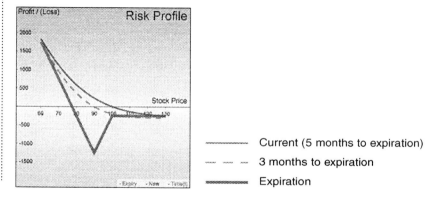

The three months to expiration dotted line breaks even at around $90. Remember we entered the trade on February 18, which is five months before the July expiration. Just two months into the trade, our breakeven moves from around $100 to $90. In another two months, in June, the breakeven would be around $80. Time decay is hurting our position, and one of the effects of it is to push out our breakeven further away from the current stock price of $100.

What happens if we change the ratio from 2:1 to 3:2? Well, we're buying proportionately fewer puts, so the position will take longer to get into profit but will cost less. Let's compare in Table 5.10.

Table 5.10   2:1 and 3:2 put ratio backspread comparison

	2:1 PRB	3:2 PRB
Net debit	2.50	n/a
Net credit	n/a	2.25
Maximum risk	12.50	17.75
Interim risk	2.50	n/a
Maximum reward	77.50	72.25
Interim reward	n/a	2.25
Lower breakeven	77.50	72.25
Higher breakeven	n/a	98.875

Can you see here that the 3:2 trade is actually a net credit, not a net debit? The 3:2 trade pulls in 2.25 net credit compared with the 2:1 trade net debit of 2.50. This is because the bought/sold ratio is 3:2 as opposed to 2:1. The other by-product of having a net credit is that the 3:2 trade has two breakevens. It has an upper breakeven of 98.88, which the 2:1 does not have. The lower breakeven of the 3:2 is further away at 72.25 compared with 77.50 (remember the stock price is $100). This is because the 3:2 trade has a lower maximum loss, meaning it has further to travel in order to get into profit.

So which is better? Well, if the stock moves sharply up, then the 2:1 is better as you're in profit much faster. If the stock doesn't move at all, the 2:1 is better because the maximum risk is lower. But if the stock moves sharply down, the 3:2 is better because the interim risk is in fact positive because the trade is a net credit.

Figure 5.26 3:2 ratio backspread

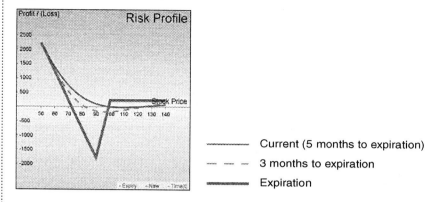

------- Current (5 months to expiration)

----- 3 months to expiration

■■■■■■ Expiration

So even without a volatility skew, by changing the ratios we've created a net credit trade.

Strike Price Impact

As before, let's see what happens if we change the strike prices. If we push out the lower strike price, we're going to pay less for our OTM puts because they're even further OTM than before. Also the distance to the lower breakeven is going to be wider than before. Again, let's go back to our original 2:1 put ratio backspread and compare.

ACME is trading at $100.00 on February 18. Historical volatility of the stock is at 50%, and both options' implied volatilities are around the same level.

● Sell one July 100 strike put at 12.00

● ~~Buy two July 90 strike puts at 7.25~~

● Buy two July 80 strike puts at 3.80

Table 5.11 90-100 versus 80-100 put ratio backspread comparison

	90–100 PRB	80–100 PRB
Net debit	2.50	n/a
Net credit	n/a	4.40
Maximum risk	12.50	15.60

Table 5.11   90-100 versus 80-100 put ratio backspread comparison

	90–100 PRB	80–100 PRB
Interim risk	2.50	n/a
Maximum reward	77.50	64.40
Interim reward	n/a	4.40
Lower breakeven	77.50	64.40
Higher breakeven	n/a	95.60

Notice how the wider backspread is at a net credit, thereby giving us protection if this trade goes the other way (up). This is because we're buying much cheaper options as they're further OTM. The risk is higher, however, and the lower breakeven is pushed further away downward. Remember though, we would never hold one of these to expiration.

The lower breakeven is a long way off (see Figure 5.27). What happens if we shift both strike prices up by $10 in relation to the original trade? In the original trade we sold a one July 100 strike put and bought two July 90 strike puts.

● Sell one July 110 strike put at 18.00

● Buy two July 100 strike puts at 12.00

Figure 5.27   80-100 put ratio backspread risk profile

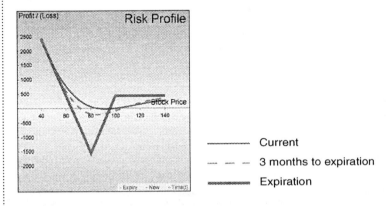

_____ Current

___ ___ ___ 3 months to expiration

▬▬▬▬▬ Expiration

Table 5.12   90-100 versus 100-110 put ratio backspread comparison

	90–100 PRB	100–110 PRB
Net debit	2.50	6.00
Net credit	n/a	n/a
Maximum risk	12.50	16.00
Interim risk	2.50	6.00
Maximum reward	77.50	84.00
Interim reward	n/a	n/a
Lower breakeven	77.50	84.00
Higher breakeven	n/a	n/a

By shifting the strikes up we've brought our lower breakeven up, which is good, but we're paying more and absorbing more risk for that privilege. With the stock at $100, if the stock moves down immediately, then we're making money very quickly as today's risk profile (the thinner solid line in Figure 5.28) breaks even at around $100—provided the implied volatility of the options remains the same. Because anything below $100 represents ITM, the position quickly moves to its maximum speed (or delta) as soon as we're in profit.

Figure 5.28   100-110 put ratio backspread with implied volatility at 50%

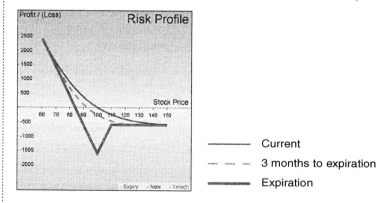

Current
3 months to expiration
Expiration

Is this better than the original call ratio backspread? Well, if the stock price explodes downward by $20 overnight, perhaps. If it goes up by $20 overnight, then probably not.

Let's see how a change in volatility affects the new ITM put ratio backspread trade.

If the implied volatilities go down to 40%, the current breakeven pushes out to around $92 (see Figure 5.29), which is further away.

Figure 5.29   100-110 put ratio backspread with implied volatility decreased to 40%

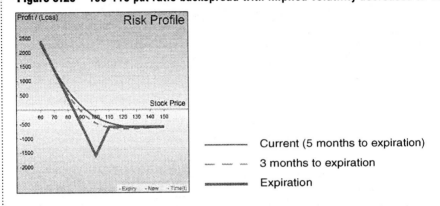

Current (5 months to expiration)

3 months to expiration

Expiration

If the implied volatilities rise to 60%, the current breakeven will come in to around $110, which would mean an immediate profit (see Figure 5.30).

Figure 5.30   100-110 put ratio backspread with implied volatility increased to 60%

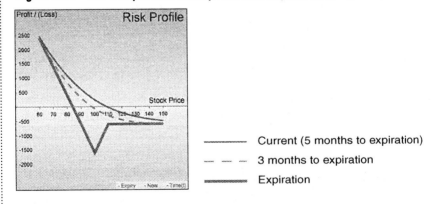

Current (5 months to expiration)

3 months to expiration

Expiration

Therefore if we place this trade, say, nine days before earnings, after which implied volatilities rise right up to the earnings date, whereupon we sell, then a 10% increase in implied volatility could translate into much greater profit and a much nearer breakeven target.

So now that we've examined adjusting the ratio itself and the strikes, let's examine the impact of adjusting the expiration dates. So far we've looked at these trades with expiration about five months away. Let's now try an example with one month to expiration with all the other variables the same. The trade is now as follows:

- Sell one March* 100 strike put at 5.80
- Buy two March* 90 strike puts at 2.00

The lower expiration breakeven is $81.80, but now, even using the same volatilities of 50% with the shorter term trade, we have a net credit and therefore an interim profit even if this stock rises above $98.20 (see Figure 5.31).

Figure 5.31   90-100 put ratio backspread with one month to expiration

Current (1 month to expiration)
2 weeks to expiration
Expiration

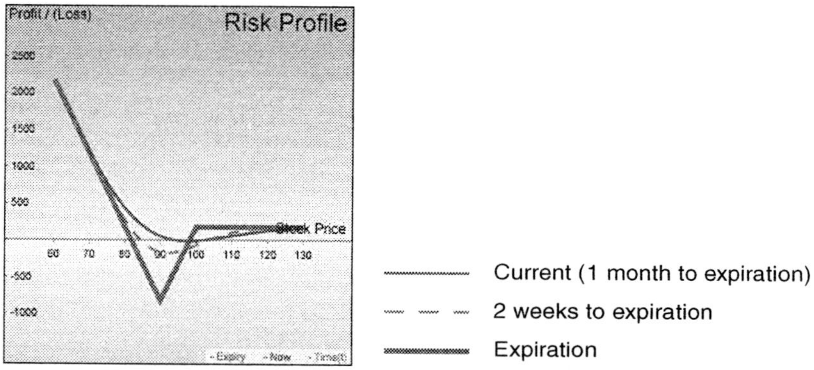

Let's look at Table 5.13 and compare the two trades.

---

* March is one month from expiration.

Table 5.13   90-100 March versus July put ratio backspread

	90–100 July PRB	90–100 March PRB
Net debit	2.50	n/a
Net credit	n/a	1.80
Maximum risk	12.50	8.20
Interim risk	2.50	n/a
Maximum reward	77.50	81.80
Interim reward	n/a	1.80
Lower breakeven	77.50	81.80
Higher breakeven	n/a	98.20

We can immediately see that the March expiration trade is much more responsive. It has less risk and has a net credit, not a net debit.

Now look at the two-week line to expiration (the dotted line in Figure 5.31). See how with only two weeks left to expiration (which happens to be in two weeks' time), the risk profile moves below the breakeven line before climbing back up again, breaking even at around $84. Provided the options' volatilities don't take a significant downturn, the trade has very limited risk for the first two weeks, as you can see by how the dotted line only goes a little below the breakeven line.

The issue with the March (one-month) expiration is that time decay will kick in much faster than with the longer terms to expiration. After three weeks in the trade and with only one week left, we can see the difference in that dotted line (Figure 5.32).

Figure 5.32   90-100 March put ratio backspread with dotted line one week to expiration and implied volatility at 50%

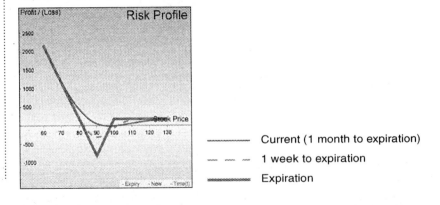

——————— Current (1 month to expiration)

— —— — 1 week to expiration

▬▬▬▬▬ Expiration

Now let's see what happens when the implied volatilities are squeezed from 50% to 40%...

Figure 5.33   90-100 March put ratio backspread with dotted line one week to expiration and implied volatility decreased to 40%

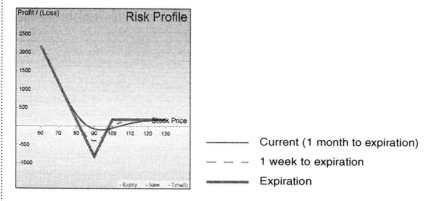

———————— Current (1 month to expiration)

— —— —— 1 week to expiration

▬▬▬▬▬▬ Expiration

We can see in Figure 5.33 the dotted line migrating ever downward toward the expiration risk profile.

So we've learned that put ratio backspreads are affected by

● The ratios of bought-to-sold puts

● The position of and distance between the strike prices

● The time to expiration

An aggressive trade would be a high ratio of bought-to-sold puts, with a short distance between strikes and a short time to expiration. In such a case you'd want the stock to make a very fast move (preferably downward), and you'd want to exit the trade very quickly.

If you're bearish the put ratio backspread offers a potentially better solution than the straddle. Because you're both long and short puts, you're afforded some protection against both time decay and a decline in volatility, both of which impact a straddle much more severely. As we observed in Figure 5.33, the dotted line moved down into further risk territory relatively slowly until we imposed the double whammy of increasing time decay and decreasing volatility into the equation.

In terms of trade management, the risk profile diagrams provided here serve to emphasize that you must select your expiration dates with plenty of time to spare and ensure that you exit the trade in a timely fashion, whatever happens with the stock.

Context

With put ratio backspreads, it's clear that you're anticipating higher volatility together with a downward directional bias in the stock price. Depending on the options premiums and the ratios, you can execute this strategy with a negligible cash outlay. However, you'll be required to have sufficient funds in the account to cover the potential risk of the trade.

Greeks

Going back to the ACME example on February 18 the stock was $100, historical volatility was 50%, and we were selling one July 100 put at 12.00 and buying two July 90 calls at 7.25 each.

As the stock falls below the second strike price, the position moves in line with the stock, and delta inversely reaches its peak (negative here) when the position is deep ITM. As the stock price rises the position moves into negative territory and delta slows down (note how the curve flattens in Figure 5.34).

Figure 5.34   Put ratio backspread delta profile

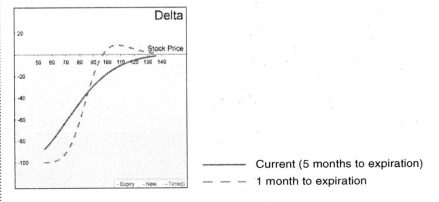

Gamma peaks around the lower strike price, illustrating the position's pivotal strike price (see Figure 5.35). This is where the position's rate of change is at its fastest.

Figure 5.35   Put ratio backspread gamma profile

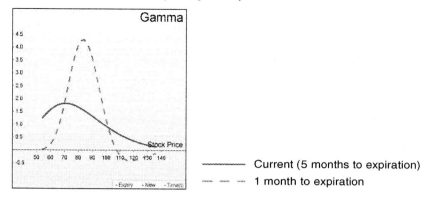

────────── Current (5 months to expiration)
─ ─ ─ ─ 1 month to expiration

Time decay is harmful to the position unless the stock falls dramatically. Notice how with the dotted line having only one month to expiration, theta decay is far more destructive, as depicted by the dotted line moving lower than the solid line which has five months to expiration (see Figure 5.36).

Figure 5.36   Put ratio backspread theta profile

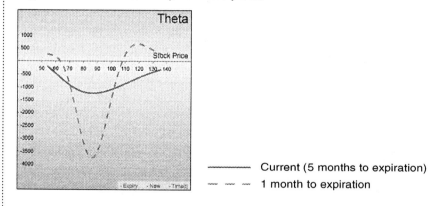

────────── Current (5 months to expiration)
─ ─ ─ ─ 1 month to expiration

Not surprisingly, vega is positive here in Figure 5.37, illustrating how volatility helps our position. Notice how the solid line is higher than the dotted line. This is because with five months to expiration, volatility has more time to help the position. Vega peaks around the lower strike price. This is because the lower strike price represents the lowest point of the risk profile curve, so any increase in volatility at this point will be helpful to the position as it will push the risk curve away from the maximum loss area. Remember also, we are net long options, meaning that increases in volatility will generally help our position.

Figure 5.37   Put ratio backspread vega profile

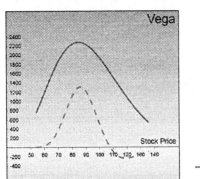

——————— Current (5 months to expiration)
‒ ‒ ‒ ‒ 1 month to expiration

As mentioned earlier, in a low interest rate environment you don't worry too much about rho, but you may observe that higher interest rates are generally unhelpful to the put ratio backspread position (remember higher interest rates were actually helpful to the call ratio backspread). Notice how the solid line is below the dotted line. This is demonstrating that the more time the position has to expiration, the more interest rates can harm the position (Figure 5.38).

Figure 5.38   Put ratio backspread rho profile

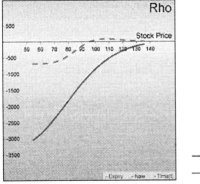

——————— Current (5 months to expiration)
‒ ‒ ‒ ‒ 1 month to expiration

Learning Points

In this chapter you've learned how you can create volatility trades that match a directional bias you may have for a stock while simultaneously reducing the cost of the trade—and in some cases even executing the trade for a net credit.

We know that both call and put ratio backspreads are going to be affected by

● Volatility

● Strike price positions

● Expiration date

● The ratios themselves

Before proceeding to the next chapter, let's take one more example of each of these ratio backspreads and compare the 2:1 ratio with a more aggressive 3:1.

Here's our stock again: ACME is trading at $100.00 on February 18. Historical volatility of the stock is at 50%, and both options' implied volatilities are around the same level (see Table 5.14).

Starting with the call ratio backspread:

● Sell one July 100 strike call at 13.45

● Buy two July 110 strike calls at 9.55

Table 5.14   2:1, 100-110 strike call ratio backspread example

Net debit	premium bought – premium sold **19.10 – 13.45 = 5.65**
Maximum risk	difference in strikes + net debit **10.00 + 5.65 = 15.65**
Interim risk *	same as net debit * **5.65**
Maximum reward	uncapped
Interim reward *	n/a because the trade is a net debit in this case *
Lower breakeven	lower strike + net credit **n/a because we have a net debit here**
Higher breakeven	higher strike + (difference in strikes × # short calls) / (long calls - short calls) + net debit (or - net credit) **110.00 + (10.00 / 1) + 5.65 = 125.65**

* The interim risk is the horizontal section of the risk profile at the expiration line. It signifies the risk at expiration if the stock rises above the higher strike price. If the horizontal line is above the breakeven line, then it would be called the interim reward. You only get an "interim reward" if the ratio backspread trade is executed at a net credit.

Now let's compare this with the 3:1 call ratio backspread (Table 5.15):

Table 5.15   2:1 versus 3:1 call ratio backspread comparison

	2:1 CRB	3:1 CRB
Net debit	5.65	15.20
Maximum risk	15.65	25.20
Interim risk	5.65	15.20
Maximum reward	uncapped	uncapped
Interim reward	n/a	n/a
Lower breakeven	n/a	n/a
Higher breakeven	125.65	122.60

As we'd expect, the 3:1 trade costs more and has more risk. However, the breakeven is slightly lower even despite the greater risk of the trade. This is because once the trade is ITM, it is moving at a delta twice the speed of the stock price's movement. Remember we're buying three calls and selling one. The net difference is 2. So delta eventually levels out at a speed of 2. It doesn't make itself obvious on the risk profile chart (Figure 5.39) because of the way the chart is scaled, but the diagonal lines from bottom left to top right are moving at twice the rate of the stock, so when the trade is ITM, for every dollar the stock is moving up, the 3:1 call ratio backspread is moving up $2. In other words the 3:1 is a far more aggressive trade. If the stock moves sharply up, you'll be making accelerated profits almost immediately. The same applies in the case of an upturn in volatility.

Figure 5.39   3:1, 100-110 strike call ratio backspread risk profile

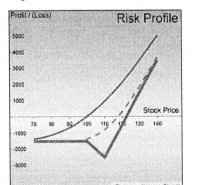

——————— Current (5 months to expiration)
— — — — — 1 month to expiration
▬▬▬▬▬▬ Expiration

As we can see in Figure 5.40, delta reaches 200 (i.e., referring to 200 shares). For 200, read "two" contracts.

Now let's do the same with the put ratio backspread. Remember the original 2:1 trade from February 18:

● Sell one July 100 strike put at 12.00

● Buy two July 90 strike puts at 7.25

Figure 5.40   3:1 call ratio backspread delta profile

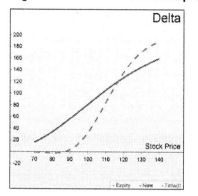

—————————— Current (5 months to expiration)

—— —— —— 1 month to expiration

Table 5.16   2:1 put ratio backspread example summary

Net debit	premium bought – premium sold **14.50 – 12.00 = 2.50**
Maximum risk	difference in strikes + net debit **10.00 + 2.50 = 12.50**
Interim risk *	same as net debit * **2.50**
Maximum reward	Lower breakeven × #(bought - sold options) **77.50**
Interim reward *	n/a because the trade is a net debit in this case *
Lower breakeven	[lower strike price - (((difference in strike prices × # short puts) + net debit or - net credit) / (number of long puts - number of short puts))] **77.50**
Higher breakeven	[higher strike – (net credit / # short puts)] **n/a because the trade is a net debit in this case**

* The interim risk is the horizontal section of the risk profile at the expiration line. It signifies the risk at expiration if the stock rises above the higher strike price. If the horizontal line is above the breakeven line, then it would be called the interim reward. You only get an "interim reward" if the ratio backspread trade is executed at a net credit.

Let's compare that with the 3:1 put ratio backspread (Table 5.17):

Table 5.17   2:1 versus 3:1 put ratio backspread

	2:1 PRB	3:1 PRB
Net debit	2.50	9.75
Net credit	n/a	n/a
Maximum risk	12.50	19.75
Interim risk	2.50	9.75
Maximum reward	77.50	160.25
Interim reward	n/a	n/a
Lower breakeven	77.50	80.125
Higher breakeven	n/a	n/a

Look at the difference between the maximum reward figures. The 3:1 trade is moving at two deltas (inversely) once the stock is below the lower strike price. This means for every dollar the stock falls, the 3:1 put ratio backspread is gaining two. As such, when the stock reaches zero, the 3:1 put ratio backspread is at 160.25. The steepness of the diagonal line isn't apparent because of the chart scaling, but do be aware of what's happening. With this strategy and this trade in particular, if the stock does gap down or crash, it's great news.

So just like before, the 3:1 trade costs more and has more risk. The breakeven is slightly higher despite the greater risk of the trade. Once the trade is ITM, it is moving at an inverse delta twice the speed of the stock. As the stock price goes down, our put ratio backspread becomes more valuable, explaining delta's inverse (or negative) value. Remember we're buying three puts and selling one. The net difference is two. So delta eventually levels out at a speed of -2. The 3:1 is a far more aggressive trade than the 2:1 (see Figure 5.41). If the stock moves sharply down, we'll be making accelerated profits almost immediately. The same applies if there is an upturn in volatility.

Figure 5.41   3:1, 90-100 strike put ratio backspread risk profile

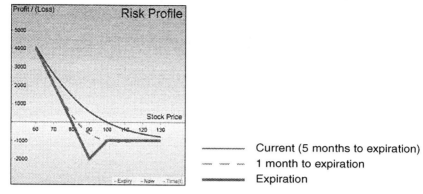

Current (5 months to expiration)
1 month to expiration
Expiration

As we can see in Figure 5.42, delta reaches -200 (i.e., referring to 200 shares). For -200, read "minus two" contracts.

Figure 5.42   3:1, 90-100 strike put ratio backspread delta profile

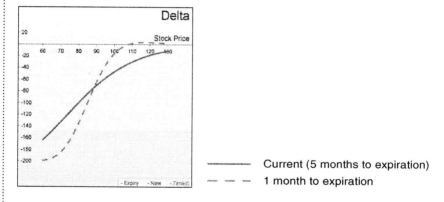

Current (5 months to expiration)
1 month to expiration

That concludes this exciting chapter. Ratio backspreads are ideal when you play them conservatively. The key is to ensure that if you get it wrong you're not too badly punished. That means picking the appropriate strike price, expiration, and ratio combinations.

The next chapter introduces an income strategy, which is also in fact a volatility strategy.

Diagonal Spreads

The *diagonal spread* is an income generating strategy that requires the right tools to trade it properly. In order to emphasize how powerful it is when in the right hands and how critical it is to analyze it correctly, I teach you how to do it wrong before we get to do it right! The reason I do this is because the diagonal spread is one of the most mistaught strategies out there. Without the right tools, people will do it wrong and teach it wrong. With the right tools, it will become one of your favorite strategies.

The diagonal is not often spoken about as a volatility strategy but more of an income strategy. However, in this chapter I demonstrate to you that it is, in fact, both.

The Basic Covered Call

Let's start from the premise that you want to enhance your monthly income from your trading portfolio. Many people default into writing covered calls. Covered calls are easy. With a *covered call* you buy (or already own) the stock and then sell OTM (or sometimes ATM) calls against that long stock position. If the stock is bought simultaneously with writing the call contract, the strategy is commonly referred to as a "buy-write."

1. Buy (or own) the stock
2. Sell calls either ATM or more commonly one or two strike prices OTM (i.e., calls with strike prices one or two strikes price higher than the stock)

Figure 6.1   Covered call components

Buy stock   Sell OTM call   Covered Call

Typically the strategy involves selling the calls on a monthly basis. In this way you capture more in premium over several months, provided you are not exercised in the meantime. Selling premium each month will cumulatively net you more over a period of time than selling one single premium with a long way to expiration. Remember, whenever you sell options premium, time decay works in your favor. Time decay is at its fastest rate in the last 20 trading days (i.e., the last month), so when you sell option premiums, it is best to sell with a month left to expiration and repeat the process the following month.

If you're selling OTM options, there's a better chance the option will expire worthless. In theory, having sold the call option short, you have to buy it back in order to close the trade. In reality you don't have to buy it back if it expires worthless, which it will if it expires either OTM or ATM.

If trading U.S. stocks and options, you will be required to buy or be long in 100 shares for every option contract that you sell in order for the position to be completely covered.

If the stock rises beyond the strike price, then the call buyer will exercise the right to buy the stock from you at the strike price. Because you already own the stock, you are covered no matter how far up the stock travels. A buyer may exercise an ITM call, or if no buyer does so at expiration, the Options Clearing Corporation (OCC) will execute an automatic exercise.

The idea is that by selling the right to buy your shares from you every month, you collect a "rent" on those shares. That rent can be anything from less than one percent to several percentage points every month.

Remember that your maximum gain is capped when the stock reaches the level of the call's strike price. No matter how high the stock goes beyond that, you still cannot make any more. However, the actual profit from a covered call has three components. First, you keep the premium from selling the call. Second, you earn dividends. Third, you get a capital gain as long as the strike is higher than your original cost for the stock.

- If the stock price rises above the strike price, you'll be exercised; that is, you'll be obligated to sell the shares at the strike price level even if the stock has traveled well above that price. Your profit will be [strike price - stock price paid + dividends earned + premium received].

- If the stock price falls your maximum loss is [stock price paid + dividends earned - premium received].

- The breakeven of the covered call, exclusive of dividends, is [stock price - premium received].

Table 6.1   Covered call risk profile components

Profile	Description	Risk	Reward	Breakeven
/	Buy stock	Purchase price	Unlimited as the stock rises	**Purchase price**
\	Sell call	Unlimited as the stock rises	Limited to the call premium received	**Strike price + call premium**
/‾	**Covered Call**	Cost of stock less call premium received	Limited to the call strike price less the stock price paid plus the call premium received	**Stock price paid less the call premium received**

With a covered call your outlook is neutral to bullish. You're expecting a steady rise in the stock price, certainly nothing too ambitious. Remember, the covered call is not a "volatility strategy." It's an income strategy that you can improve by converting it into a combined volatility and income strategy. Let's take a look at a trade.

Example

AAPL is trading at 148.28 on September 24, 2007. The stock has just broken through a resistance area and made its highest close in almost two months.

We like the look of the chart in Figure 6.2 and want to place a trade where we make profit if the stock rises. We also want to collect some bonus income, just in case the stock moves sideways for a while. A covered call seems appropriate for our bullish outlook.

Figure 6.2   AAPL breakout chart

TC2000®.com. Courtesy of Worden Brothers Inc.

● Buy stock at 148.28

● Sell November 155 calls at 7.30

There's about six weeks left to expiration, and the yield here is a phenomenal 4.9%. Note that AAPL rose from $110 in August to $140 in just over one month, which explains why slightly ITM call options are so pricey—the calls are in great demand.

Remember, for every call you sell you have to buy 100 shares of AAPL in order for each short call to be covered.

Now, there's nothing wrong with this trade (see Table 6.2). A covered call is a perfectly legitimate strategy for generating monthly income. We know it's not a volatility strategy like the straddle or ratio backspread, but of course, if the calls have high implied volatility, then the premium and income return will be high. But typically if you're anticipating higher volatility, you wouldn't choose the covered call because the potential profit is capped (see Figure 6.3).

Table 6.2 AAPL trade summary

	November 155 covered call
You pay (net debit)	Stock - premium 148.28 - 7.30 = 140.98
Maximum risk	140.98
Maximum reward	Strike - stock + premium 155 - 148.28 + 7.30 = 14.02
Initial yield	7.30 / 148.28 = 4.92%
Maximum yield if exercised	14.02 / 148.28 = 9.46%
Breakeven at expiration	$140.98
Call implied volatility	43.07%

Figure 6.3 Covered call risk profile

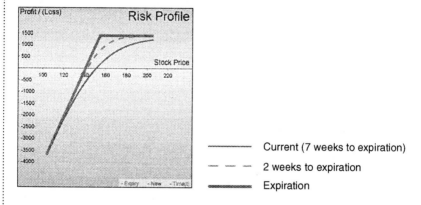

Current (7 weeks to expiration)

2 weeks to expiration

Expiration

Figure 6.4 shows the full profile for this trade.

Figure 6.4   Covered call risk profile and Greeks

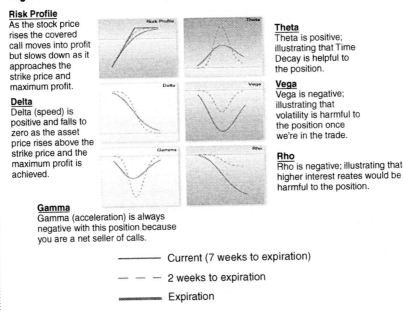

Risk Profile
As the stock price rises the covered call moves into profit but slows down as it approaches the strike price and maximum profit.

Delta
Delta (speed) is positive and falls to zero as the asset price rises above the strike price and the maximum profit is achieved.

Gamma
Gamma (acceleration) is always negative with this position because you are a net seller of calls.

Theta
Theta is positive; illustrating that Time Decay is helpful to the position.

Vega
Vega is negative; illustrating that volatility is harmful to the position once we're in the trade.

Rho
Rho is negative; illustrating that higher interest reates would be harmful to the position.

——————— Current (7 weeks to expiration)

— — —   2 weeks to expiration

▬▬▬▬▬▬ Expiration

Notice the vega chart. It shows that volatility is harmful to the covered call once we're actually in the trade. When we're placing the trade, high implied volatility will be reflected in the option premium, which of course is good for us. Once we're in the trade, as a net options seller, we now want volatility to fall. In such a case, if we had to buy the option back to close, we'd be able to do so at a lower price. As a rule of thumb, when we buy options, we want implied volatility to rise; when we sell options, we want implied volatility to fall.

In this example our profit potential is capped at 14.02 for seven weeks. That's pretty good. In real terms, if buying the minimum amount of 100 shares and selling one call, that's a profit of $1,402, or 9.46%. Even if you were super-bullish on AAPL at this time, would we be happy with such a yield? Possibly...a profit is a profit, and if you annualize that 9.46%, it would end up at around 85.55% for the year (compounding 9.46% every 7.6 weeks).

If you like this type of strategy, is there a way that you could extract a greater return from it?

The answer is...yes.

The next question is...how?

There are three flawed ways to improve the yield from a covered call. After looking at those, I show you a better way, which is a diagonal spread using calls.

So, how can we squeeze some extra yield out of the covered call? Well, a yield depends on two components:

a. The principle that you invest

b. The income that you receive

Let's look at (b) first and see how we can improve upon the income we receive. The first thing we could do is to sell a lower strike price call as that would bring in a higher premium.

Originally you sold the 155 strike price for a premium of 7.30 at the bid. If you sell the 150 strike call, you can get 9.50, as shown in Figure 6.5. Let's see how the trade is affected by looking over Table 6.3.

Figure 6.5 AAPL options chain

Apple Computer Inc

Symbol	Prev. Close	Current Close	High	Low	Volume
AAPL	146.73	148.28	149.85	146.65	37369000

Calls							Puts					
Symbol	Last	Bid	Ask	Vol	OpInt	Strike	Symbol	Last	Bid	Ask	Vol	OpInt
2007-11 Nov												
2007QAAKR	59	59.1	59.3	40		90	2007QAAWR	0.15	0.05	0.1	1	
2007QAAKS	54.7	54.2	54.4	40		95	2007QAAWS	0.15	0.1	0.15	23	
2007QAAKT	48.4	49.3	49.5	40		100	2007QAAWT	0.25	0.2	0.25	33	
2007QAAKA	43.7	44.5	44.7	20		105	2007QAAWA	0.37	0.3	0.35	69	
2007QAAKB	40.14	39.7	39.9	40		110	2007QAAWB	0.45	0.45	0.55	237	
2007QAAKC	34.3	35	35.2	3		115	2007QAAWC	0.8	0.75	0.8	183	
2007QAAKD	30.6	30.5	30.7	56		120	2007QAAWD	1.2	1.15	1.25	2661	
2007APVKE	26	26.1	26.4	35		125	2007APVWE	1.9	1.8	1.9	7259	
2007APVKF	21.82	22	22.3	366		130	2007APVWF	2.85	2.65	2.75	6688	
2007APVKG	18	18.3	18.5	523		135	2007APVWG	3.9	3.8	4	4027	
2007APVKH	14.72	14.9	15.1	1086		140	2007APVWH	5.6	5.4	5.6	5179	
2007APVKI	11.9	12	12.2	2171		145	2007APVWI	7.7	7.5	7.6	3390	
2007APVKJ	9.59	9.5	9.6	4432		150	2007APVWJ	10	9.9	10.1	1880	
2007APVKK	7.5	7.3	7.5	5746		155	2007APVWK	13.6	12.8	13	302	
2007APVKL	5.6	5.6	5.8	2273		160	2007APVWL	16.4	16.1	16.3	278	
2007APVKM	4.3	4.3	4.4	2507		165	2007APVWM	20.8	19.8	20	145	

Table 6.3 150 versus 155 strike covered call comparison

	November 155 covered call	November 150 covered call
You pay (net debit)	Stock - premium 148.28 - 7.30 = **140.98**	Stock - premium 148.28 - 9.50 = **138.78**
Maximum risk	**140.98**	**138.78**
Maximum reward	Strike - stock + premium 155 - 148.28 + 7.30 = **14.02**	Strike - stock + premium 150 - 148.28 + 9.50 = **11.22**
Initial yield	7.30 / 148.28 = **4.92%**	9.50 / 148.28 = **6.41%**
Maximum yield if exercised	14.02 / 148.28 = **9.46%**	11.22 / 148.28 = **7.57%**
Breakeven at expiration	**$140.98**	**$138.78**
Call implied volatility	**43.07%**	**43.71%**

By selling a lower strike price, you pull in more initial income (9.50 versus 7.30), but your maximum yield drops to 7.57% from 9.46%. This is because you would be exercised at the lower strike price, which is always where you achieve your maximum yield. Remember your maximum profit is derived from the amount of premium we receive plus the difference between the strike price and the stock price paid. The lower the strike price, the bigger the premium will be but the less the maximum potential return will be.

To compensate for this, our lower strike (150) covered call has a lower breakeven target and therefore has a greater probability of becoming profitable. However, if AAPL rises sharply, you're not going to benefit from that beyond the $150 mark where you hit your maximum profit.

Some fund managers will write ATM or even slightly ITM covered calls in order to make a high probability yield with a large "buffer," i.e., where the breakeven is lower. The high initial yield is offset by the inferior maximum yield, but the fund manager is happy if he's making around 2+% per month for the client with supposedly lower risk than if they simply owned the stock. This is fine while stocks are going sideways or rising moderately. The problem is that such a strategy never takes advantage of a big upside. Complex statistical algorithms would illustrate that for volatile stocks, the covered call, comparatively speaking, wouldn't be the optimum strategy because your profits are always capped.

So although you can enhance your initial income and yield by lowering the strike price, it's not a satisfactory solution if you're anticipating some volatility in the near future. How else, then, can you improve your income yield?

Sell more option premium?

There are three ways to consider this...and you don't want to do any of them! But let's go through the exercise anyway because with options trading, you need to understand what's right in the context of what's wrong.

Synthetic Short Straddle (Do Not Trade This Strategy!)

The first way of bringing in more premium is to sell another call. So instead of selling one call contract per 100 shares bought, you sell two calls per 100 shares owned. This creates a *synthetic short straddle*.

Notice how in Figure 6.6 the covered call has changed shape and has become an upside-down straddle. What was a horizontal line with the covered call is now a downward diagonal line that crosses the breakeven line at 176.32. So in this case, provided AAPL remains between 133.68 and 176.32 for the next seven weeks, then you make a profit. Bearing in mind that AAPL has moved almost $50 in the last two months, that's not a bet you'd want to take, particularly when you have an uncapped risk profile with the synthetic short straddle.

Figure 6.6 AAPL November 155 synthetic short straddle

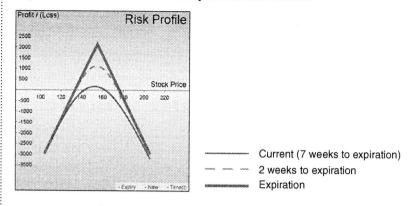

The lower breakeven of 133.68 is lower than the covered call's equivalent of 140.98 (see Table 6.4).

Table 6.4 155 strike covered call versus 155 strike synthetic short straddle comparison

	November 155 covered call	November 155 synthetic short straddle
You pay (net debit)	Stock - premium 148.28 - 7.30 = 140.98	Stock - premiums 148.28 - 14.60 = 133.68
Maximum risk	**140.98**	**133.68 if the stock falls** **Unlimited if the stock rises**
Maximum reward	Strike - stock + premium 155 - 148.28 + 7.30 = **14.02**	Strike - stock + premiums 150 - 148.28 + 14.60 = **21.32**
Initial yield	7.30 / 148.28 = **4.92%**	14.60 / 148.28 = **9.84%**
Maximum yield if exercised	14.02 / 148.28 = **9.46%**	**9.84%** only if the stock price is equal to the strike price at expiration
Breakeven at expiration	**$140.98**	**$133.68 and $176.32**

If the idea is to profit from increasing volatility, then the synthetic short straddle fails spectacularly. If the idea is to profit from falling volatility, then this would be worth considering. However for the purposes in this book, I am only considering long volatility strategies, so the synthetic short straddle is not appropriate.

So you're not going to sell an extra call in order to increase your income yield. But how about selling a put instead of the extra call? In other words, you're long the stock, and so now you're going to sell the 155 strike call *and* the 155 strike put. (Remember, this is purely for illustrative purposes so you know what NOT to do!)

Covered Short Straddle (Do Not Trade This Strategy!)

As the strategy name implies, the *covered short straddle* involves shorting a straddle while being covered by way of owning the stock.

- Buy stock at 148.28
- Sell November 155 calls at 7.30
- Sell November 155 puts at 12.80

Because the call and put share the same strike price, one of them will inevitably be OTM, and the other must be ITM. Here, the call is OTM, and the put is ITM. Remember, you're short both options, so unless the stock is at $155.00 on expiration date, one of these options will be exercised, and you may not like that.

If the stock finishes above $155 at expiration, the call will be ITM and will be exercised. This means the stock will be "called away" from you at the strike price, bringing you a tidy profit by way of

a. The stock rising from $148.28 to $155.00 (you won't get any more than that even if the stock keeps rising).

b. The call premium of 7.30 you collected.

c. The put premium of 12.80 you collected. Remember the put has expired OTM, so you simply keep the premium with no other consequences in this instance.

d. Dividends earned during the time you owned the stock

If the stock is trading below $155 at expiration, the put will be ITM and will be exercised. This means you will be contractually obligated to buy an additional 100 shares per contract at $155.00 no matter where the stock has fallen to. Because you're never going to trade this strategy, I'm not going to go into huge detail here, but consider the impact of AAPL falling if you're trading a covered short straddle.

Let's look closely at the risk profile and see if there's anything we don't like about it (refer to Table 6.5 and Figure 6.7).

Table 6.5   Covered short straddle risk profile

Maximum risk	[stock price paid + strike price - put premium - call premium]
Maximum reward	[call and put premiums received + strike price] - [stock price paid]
Breakeven	[strike price - [half of the options premiums received] + [half of the difference between the stock price and the strike price]]

Figure 6.7   AAPL November 155 covered short straddle

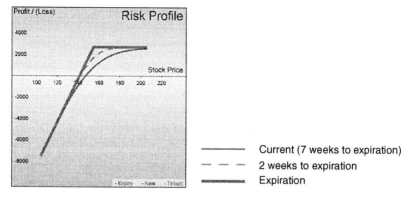

------------- Current (7 weeks to expiration)
------- 2 weeks to expiration
------------- Expiration

Notice the maximum risk here:

[Stock price + strike price - both premiums]
[148.28 + 155.00 - 7.30 - 12.80] = **283.18**

The risk on this trade if it went seriously wrong is $283.18, or $28,318 with just one contract sold on each side! Ouch! How can this be? Well, it's simple. The covered call had a maximum risk of 140.98. By selling a put you now gain $12.80 less risk for the put premium you receive, but you risk the strike price of the sold put, which adds a further $155.00 to your risk.

Now, of course it's unlikely that AAPL will drop to zero, thereby triggering your maximum risk nightmare scenario; however, what you may have noticed is that as the stock falls below the strike price of 155, the position is losing money at *double* speed (i.e., 2 deltas) because you've added a short put (+1 delta) to the long stock (+1 delta) you already own.

Let's compare the original covered call with this covered short straddle and then consign both to the trash can before we investigate how else we can increase our yields and profit from volatility at the same time (see Table 6.6).

Table 6.6   155 strike covered call versus 155 strike covered short straddle comparison

	November 155 covered call	November 155 covered short straddle
You pay (net debit)	Stock - premium 148.28 - 7.30 = 140.98	Stock - premiums 148.28 - 20.10 = 128.18
Maximum risk	**140.98**	**283.18**
Maximum reward	Strike - stock + premium 155 - 148.28 + 7.30 = **14.02**	Premiums + strike - stock 20.10 + 155 - 148.28 = **26.82**
Initial yield	7.30 / 148.28 = **4.92%**	20.10 / 148.28 = **13.56%**
Maximum yield if exercised	14.02 / 148.28 = **9.46%**	(20.10 + 6.72) / 148.28 = **18.1%** if the call is exercised
Maximum yield on risk	14.02 / 140.98 = **9.94%**	26.82 / 283.18 = **9.47%**
Breakeven at expiration	**$140.98**	**$141.59**

As we can see, the covered short straddle has more than double the risk of the covered call, while the yield on *risk* is roughly the same. Of course the initial yield and maximum yield if exercised are higher with the covered short straddle because we're measuring the extra income against the cost of buying the stock. But the cost of buying the stock is only a fraction of the risk you take on with the covered short straddle. This is because of the sold put component.

All in all, the covered short straddle is an entirely unsatisfactory strategy for our purposes here, so we move on. You're hit by the double whammy of a huge downside risk if the stock falls dramatically, plus the almost certain scenario that one of your options is going to be exercised as they both share the same strike price.

Is there anything you could do to it in order to at least mitigate one of those issues?

Well, you can mitigate the problem of almost certain assignment (exercise) by lowering the strike price of the put. Now, don't get too excited, we're still not quite there with a satisfactory solution to our challenge, but let's at least take a look at this new strategy, the covered short strangle.

Covered Short Strangle (Do Not Trade This Strategy!)

This is an interesting strategy to examine briefly. A while ago I was invited into one of the private client trading desks of one of the major investment banks in New York. One of the senior traders called me over to discuss a trade he'd placed for his own account. He'd bought the stock, written OTM calls and

OTM puts, and was very pleased because he was getting a better yield than he'd have gotten with a plain vanilla covered call.

His smile turned to a frown when I showed him that if the stock had a bad earnings report in a few days, his losses would accelerate at twice the speed if the stock fell below the put strike price—he'd be long the stock ($+1$ delta) and short the put ($+1$ delta), so if the stock fell severely his position would lose money at the speed of 2 deltas, i.e., double the speed of the stock price decline below the put strike price.

Here was a classic case of someone who did not understand an options trade that they had placed. He had no idea of his risk profile and the dangers of a potential gap down in the stock. But the real shocker was that this trader was within the premier investment bank on Wall Street and trading like this on behalf of his private clients! So you should appreciate the need to understand these things yourself, which is why I'm showing you how *not* to do things as well as how *to* do things correctly!

So back to the strategy itself. As its name implies, the covered short strangle involves shorting a strangle while being covered by owning the stock.

- Buy stock at 148.28
- Sell November 155 calls at 7.30
- Sell November 145 puts at 7.50

In contrast to the covered short straddle, you're now selling OTM puts as well as OTM calls (no difference with the calls).

As a result, provided the stock price remains between the strikes of $145 and $155, then you won't be exercised either way.

If the stock finishes above $155 at expiration, the call will be ITM and exercised in the same way as before. This means you'll make a profit composed of

a. The stock rising from $148.28 to $155.00 (you won't get any more than that even if the stock keeps rising).

b. The call premium of 7.30 you collected.

c. The put premium of 7.50 you collected. The put has expired OTM so you simply keep the premium with no other consequences in this instance.

d. Dividends paid to you while you owned the stock.

If the stock is trading between $145 and $155 at expiration, then both options are OTM, and neither will be exercised. Therefore you keep both premiums in their entirety and any increase or decrease that the stock price may have made.

If the stock has fallen from $148.28, you'll make a loss on that portion, and if it's risen from $148.28, then you'll make a profit on that portion too.

If the stock finishes below $145 at expiration the put will be ITM and will be exercised. This means you will be obligated to buy 100 more shares per contract at $145.00 no matter where the stock has fallen to. This is a problem similar to that of the covered short straddle. Again I'm not going into huge detail with a strategy you shouldn't trade, but you should be getting a feel for this now and why we wouldn't be interested in this strategy.

Let's look at the risk profile in Table 6.7 and in Figure 6.8 and see exactly what we don't like about it.

Table 6.7   Covered short strangle risk profile

Maximum risk	[stock price paid + put strike - put premium - call premium]
Maximum reward	[call and put premiums received + call strike - stock price paid]
Breakeven	Varies depending on the relationship between the stock price, the premiums received, and the strike prices.

Figure 6.8   AAPL November 155 covered short strangle

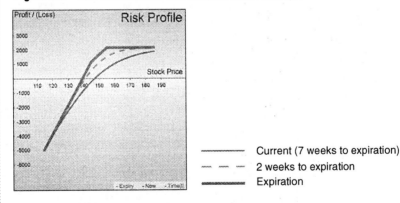

Notice the maximum risk here:

[Stock price + put strike price - both premiums]
[148.28 + 145.00 - 7.30 - 7.50] = **278.48**

The risk on this trade if it went seriously wrong is $278.48, or $27,848 with just one contract sold on each side. That's another ouch! Remember, the covered call had a maximum risk of 140.98. By selling the 145 strike put, you now gain $7.50 less risk for the put premium you receive, but you risk the strike price of the sold put, which adds a further $145.00 to the risk.

If the stock falls below the put strike of 145, the position will lose money at *double* speed (i.e., 2 deltas) because you've added a short put (+1 delta) to the long stock (+1 delta) you already own.

Let's compare the original covered call with this covered short strangle in Table 6.8 and again consign both to the trash can before we investigate how else we can increase our yields and profit from volatility at the same time.

Table 6.8   155 strike covered call versus 155 strike covered short strangle comparison

	November 155 covered call	November 155 covered short strangle
You pay (net debit)	Stock - premium 148.28 - 7.30 = 140.98	Stock - premiums 148.28 - 14.80 = 133.48
Maximum risk	**140.98**	**278.48**
Maximum reward	Strike - stock + premium 155 - 148.28 + 7.30 = **14.02**	Premiums + call strike - stock 14.80 + 155 - 148.28 = **21.52**
Initial yield	7.30 / 148.28 = **4.92%**	14.80 / 148.28 = 10%
Maximum yield if exercised	14.02 / 148.28 = **9.46%**	(14.80 + 6.72) / 148.28 = **14.5%** if the call is exercised
Maximum yield on risk	14.02 / 140.98 = **9.94%**	21.52 / 278.48 = **7.73%**
Breakeven at expiration	**$140.98**	**$139.24**

The covered short strangle has almost double the risk of the covered call, while the yield on *risk* is actually lower. The initial yield and maximum yield if exercised are higher for the covered short strangle because we're measuring the extra income against the cost of buying the stock. But the cost of buying the stock is only a fraction of the risk you take on with the covered short strangle. This is because of the sold put component of the strategy.

All in all, the covered short strangle is marginally better than the covered short straddle in terms of risk, but it's still unsatisfactory for our purposes here, so again we move on.

Increasing Your Yield by Spending Less on the Trade

We have now extinguished all methods of increasing the covered call yield by increasing the income we bring in by selling options. The only other method by which we can increase the yield is to *spend less* on the trade. So instead of buying the stock, why not buy a call option?

The next question is...which call option do we buy? And that's the critical question. I take you through just one more example of what *not* to do before we arrive at the diagonal call spread, so please bear with me. It's crucial that you understand what not to do and why before we study how to do it the right way. The idea is that you gain the experience of getting it wrong without actually losing any money.

The issue of which call to buy is complex and controversial. I'm typically cautious and rarely affected by nasty surprises. A super-aggressive trader will want to minimize their outgoings on the trade and will seek to buy a cheap longer term call against which they will sell the OTM call leg (as per the covered call). A cheap call would be OTM.

Calendar Call Spread

The *calendar call* involves buying and selling equal numbers of calls with the same strike price but with different expiration dates. You buy the longer term expiration date and sell the shorter term expiration date. In buying the call (instead of the stock) you radically reduce your trade cost; however, you also radically alter your risk profile.

Continuing with the AAPL example, there weren't any 155 strike calls for the longer term expiration options, so we're going to use the 150 strikes. Typically, calendar traders will use the ATM calls or one strike above ATM so we're using normal parameters here.

- Buy January 150 calls at 14.40
- Sell November 150 calls at 9.50

Let's look at the risk profile in Table 6.9 and Figure 6.9.

Table 6.9   Calendar call risk profile

Maximum risk	Net debit paid (4.90 here)
Maximum reward	[Long call value at the time of the short call expiration when the stock price is at the strike price - net debit]
Lower breakeven	Depends on the value of the long call at the time of the short call expiration
Higher breakeven	Depends on the value of the long call at the time of the short call expiration

As we can see, the success of this trade largely depends on the value of the long call at the time of the short call's expiration. The maximum reward occurs when the stock price is equal to the strike price at the time of the short call's expiration.

Figure 6.9   AAPL 150 November-January calendar call spread

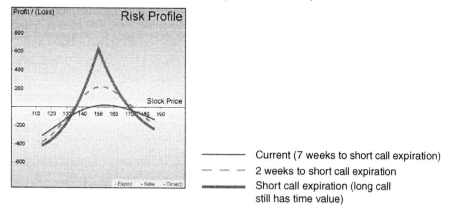

- .... Current (7 weeks to short call expiration)
- ---- ------- ----- 2 weeks to short call expiration
- ▬▬▬▬▬ Short call expiration (long call still has time value)

The risk on this trade if it were to go seriously wrong is only $4.90, or in real terms with one contract, $490. Now compare that with the covered short straddle and covered short strangle we looked at earlier. This is much more acceptable, although we have to acknowledge that it's virtually impossible that AAPL would drop to zero during the time of our investment.

Now, remember we're talking about how to profit from volatility here. Looking at the risk profile chart in Figure 6.9, there's something that bothers me about it. Can you see what might be bothering me about this strategy?

Well, the problem with it is that it has two breakeven points. It has a lower breakeven point—I'm okay with that. But it has a second breakeven point as well. And if you want to be able to profit from volatility, then this particular risk curve isn't exactly going to be helpful because in order to make a profit from it, our stock must remain within the bounds of those breakeven points. Furthermore, if implied volatility decreases, then those breakeven points will narrow. Conversely, if implied volatility increases, then the gap between the breakevens will widen. We'll see as we go along how volatility is your friend with the calendar spread, but the stock will typically have to remain within a range between two breakeven points.

If you look at the chart again, you'll see we have one breakeven around $135 and another around $171. If AAPL has a surge in price between now and the November expiration of our short call, then even though you essentially got the direction right, you could actually make a loss on the trade.

That would be appalling...to be right with your direction (you're essentially bullish here) and yet lose if the stock rises by too much. If you proceed with the calendar call, you must ensure that the stock is highly unlikely to veer outside the range between the breakevens, yet you'd very much like implied volatility to rise at the same time (with the option premiums).

Let's see what happens with AAPL.

During the time of your trade from September 24 to November 16, AAPL has gone way above the $171 mark, almost certainly putting us in a loss-making position (see Figure 6.10). I say "almost certainly" because if the historical volatility of the stock increases from the 43% that it was around the time you entered the trade, such an increase would have helped your position and pushed out the breakeven above that $171 area. We look into that in more detail shortly.

Figure 6.10   AAPL chart

As it happens, on November 16 the January 2008 150 strike call was worth 25.45 at the bid. The stock closed at $166.39, so the short call would have expired $16.39 ITM. You would therefore be exercised at $150 and lose $16.39 against the $9.50 you took in for it as premium.

So the outcome of that trade, had you stayed in it would be as shown in Table 6.10.

Table 6.10

Long call	Paid 14.40	Now worth 25.45	Profit 11.05
Short call	Sold for 9.50	Exercised at $150	Loss: 6.89
Net Position			**Profit: 4.16**

There's something unusual about this trade. Can you sense that we've been rather fortunate to make a good profit from it?

What's happened is that AAPL's volatility has gone bananas, and this has, fortunately for you, also been reflected in the implied volatility of the options.

Around September 24, AAPL's one-month historical volatility was around 43%. This was reflected precisely in the implied volatilities of the option premiums as you entered the trade. The bought 150 strike January call was priced at 14.40, reflecting an implied volatility of 43.17%, and the sold 150 strike November call was priced at 9.50, reflecting an implied volatility of 43.71%.

Fast forward now to November 16. Our short call has expired ITM, obliging us to sell AAPL at the 150 strike price, creating a loss of 6.89 on that leg of the trade. However, the long January 150 call still has two months left to expiration and is now worth 25.45, which reflects an implied volatility of 58%. Compare that with the stock's increased one-month historical volatility of around 64%.

You can clearly see from the chart that AAPL's volatility has increased dramatically. The historical volatility has increased by over 20% from around 43% to 64%. And the increase in the options' implied volatility has also increased from around 43% that you paid on September 24 to 58% on November 16.

This is great news for you because you're long an AAPL call, which has benefited enormously from this surge in implied volatility. What if the implied volatility of your long call hadn't moved from its original 43%? Well, it's fair value would be around 22.00, not 25.45. In such a scenario, our trade would look like what you see in Table 6.11.

Table 6.11

Long call	Paid 14.40	Now worth 22.00	Profit 7.60
Short call	Sold for 9.50	Exercised at $150	Loss: 6.89
Net Position			**Profit: 0.71**

Compare that with your actual profit of 4.16, which you can now see was to a large degree the result of increasing implied volatility, which offset seven weeks' worth of time decay of our long call.

The difference between these two scenarios is striking. Without the increase in volatility, the trade would barely have worked. This real-life scenario created a yield of 85%, whereas if the implied volatility had remained at 43%, the yield would have been only 14.5%. If the implied volatility had decreased, it's possible that despite the stock price increasing from $148.28 to $166.39, you could actually have made a loss on this trade. A steady rise in AAPL could well have created that scenario. As it happens, the real-life scenario entailed a bumpy ride, increasing both the stock volatility and knocking onto the options' implied volatility, which of course helped enormously.

So now you're definitely paying attention to volatility with regard to this strategy. My issue with the calendar spread is the second (higher) breakeven point. The intention is to create a strategy that mimics a covered call without having to buy the stock itself. The calendar enables you to buy a call option instead of the stock, which radically reduces your entry cost, thereby increasing your yield, but you then have the problem of that second breakeven point.

Remember, the 150 strike call you bought was just OTM (the stock was $148.28) and had only about four months to expiration (from September to January). How could you better replicate the stock? Well, in two ways: First, you could buy a call with longer time to run to expiration. And second, you could buy an ITM call. How deep? Preferably an ITM call with less than 15% of the premium attributed to time value. You'd still sell the short-term OTM call against that long position, and you'd be thereby creating a *diagonal call spread*. And as you see later on, it's imperative that the sold leg of that strategy is OTM.

Before we study the diagonal call, let's go through the various scenarios of the calendar call, just so you know what to do if you ever decide to do such a trade. I emphasize, however, that my preferred strategy is the *diagonal* for reasons that will be revealed later in this chapter.

Calendar Call Scenarios

AAPL is trading at $148.28 on September 24 with historical volatility at around 43%.

● Buy January 2008 150 strike calls at 14.40 (43% implied volatility)
● Sell November 2007 150 strike calls at 9.50 (43% implied volatility)

At November expiration

1. Scenario: stock falls to $130.00
   Implied volatility at 43%

   * The long calls are worth approximately 3.20; loss so far = 11.20
   * The short calls expire worthless; profit 9.50

   No exercise

   Total position = 3.20 - 14.40 + 9.50 = loss of 1.70

   What if implied volatility rises to 55%?

   * The long calls are worth approximately 5.45; loss so far = 8.95
   * The short calls expire worthless; profit 9.50

   No exercise

   Total position = 5.45 - 14.40 + 9.50 = profit of 0.55

   Do you see how a change in implied volatility can make the difference between success and failure? Its significance must be appreciated.

2. Scenario: stock falls to $135.76
   Implied volatility at 43%

   * Long calls worth approximately 4.90; loss so far = 9.50
   * The short calls expire worthless; profit 9.50

   Total position = 4.90 - 14.40 + 9.50 = breakeven
   Now, again, what if implied volatility rises to 55%?

   * The long calls are worth approximately 7.45; loss so far = 6.95
   * The short calls expire worthless; profit 9.50

   No exercise
   Total position = 7.45 - 14.40 + 9.50 = profit of 2.55
   The increase in implied volatility made a huge difference to the trade. Being able to assess the likelihood of volatility swings is a crucial part of being a successful options trader.

3. Scenario: stock stays at $148.28
   Implied volatility at 43%

   * The long calls are worth approximately 10.27; loss so far = 4.13
   * The short 150 strike calls expire worthless; profit 9.50

   No exercise
   Total position = 10.27 - 14.40 + 9.50 = profit of 5.37
   We know that an increase in implied volatility would increase the value of the trade significantly.

4. Scenario: stock rises to $150.00 (i.e. the strike price)
   Implied volatility at 43%

   * The long calls are worth approximately 11.19; loss so far = 3.21

   * The short 150 strike calls expire worthless; profit 9.50

No exercise

Total position = 11.19 - 14.40 + 9.50 = profit of 6.29
Where the stock is at the strike price at the sold call's expiration, you make the greatest profits with this strategy.

5. Scenario: stock rises to $160.00

   * The long calls are worth approximately 17.39;
     profit so far = 2.99

   * The short calls expire $10.00 ITM

Procedure: Sell bought calls; buy stock at current price and sell at strike price.
The short calls are exercised at $150.00.

Buy stock at 160.00

Sell stock at 150.00

Loss = 10.00

Sell long call for a profit = 2.99

Keep short call premium = 9.50

Loss on exercise = 10.00

Total position = 2.49 profit

Notice that although the stock price is higher, the profit is lower than when the stock rose to the strike price. If the stock goes much higher then you could be losing money.

What if you tried to exercise the long call instead of the given procedure?

(In the scenario 5, you sold your long calls, bought the stock at the new market price, and sold the stock at the short call strike price.)

Procedure: Exercise long calls at $150.00; deliver stock at $150.00 for exercised sold call.

Buy call at 14.40

Sell call at 9.50

Net cost = 4.90

Exercise our long call: buy stock at 150.00

Exercised on our sold call: sell stock at 150.00

Net profit = 0.00

Total = -4.90 - $0.00 = loss of 4.90

Lesson: Never exercise a long term option because you'll miss out on time value.

6. Scenario: stock rises to $170.00

- The long calls are worth approximately 24.81; profit so far = 10.41

- The short calls expire $20.00 ITM

Procedure: Sell bought calls; buy stock at current price and sell at strike price.

The short calls are exercised at $150.00.
> Buy stock at 170.00
> Sell stock at 150.00
> Loss = 20.00
> Sell long call for a profit = 10.41
> Keep short call premium = 9.50
> Loss on exercise = 20.00

Total position = 0.09 loss

So even when the stock price has risen substantially, we can face a situation where the calendar call loses money.

If the implied volatility also rose to 55%, the situation would be that the long call would be worth 27.39, meaning an extra profit of 2.58 from the preceding scenario. This would be enough to put the entire position into profit. So instead of it making a loss of 0.09, the position would make a profit of 2.49.

If you tried to exercise your long call, then the position would be in a loss position regardless of the increase in volatility. Remember, by exercising the long call, you forego the time value, and the implied volatility of an option is all bound in with the time value. Let's see what would happen if you exercised the long call in this example where implied volatility rose to 55%.

Procedure: Exercise long calls at $150.00; deliver stock at $150.00 for exercised sold call.
> Buy call at 14.40
> Sell call at 9.50
> Net cost = 4.90
> Exercise our long call: buy stock at 150.00
> Exercise our sold call: sell stock at 150.00
> Net profit = 0.00

Total = -4.90 - $0.00 = loss of 4.90

Do you see how by exercising your long call, you gain no benefit at all from the increase in implied volatility? By exercising the long call, you forego that benefit and any time value in your long call option. Even if the long call is now mostly made up of intrinsic value, the portion of time value (however small in percentage terms) may be enough to make the difference between a profit and a loss.

So this concludes the section on calendar calls. We can see that the strategy delivers better yields than the covered call. But we can also see that the strategy can run into trouble if the stock price rises too far. While an increase in implied volatility helps, we still are left with a second breakeven point as the risk profile descends and as the stock price exceeds the strike price of both call legs.

As suggested earlier, we can eliminate the second breakeven point by buying a deep ITM call option. This will cost more than the ATM or OTM calls we would buy with the calendar calls, and therefore our yield will suffer. However, we will benefit from a much more suitable risk profile to support our outlook of increasing volatility combined with our context of wanting to generate income.

Diagonal Calls

We've finally reached the diagonal call strategy! The context for this strategy is that we're bullish, and increasing volatility might help us as well.

The diagonal call involves buying and selling equal numbers of calls with different strikes and expiration dates. We buy the lower strike longer term expiration date, and we sell the higher strike shorter term expiration date. In buying a deep ITM call instead of the stock we reduce our trade cost, though it's more expensive than the calendar call strategy. However, when we get the diagonal call right, the risk profile will only have one breakeven point, and we won't get punished if the stock price gaps up.

The key to getting this strategy right is to

● Get the buy leg right.

● Get the sell leg right.

As you'll see as we go along, we should buy our first leg deep enough ITM to almost replicate buying the stock even though we'll be paying far less than the stock price. And we must also sell our second leg OTM in order to enable our long call to appreciate in value. In addition, we should aim to buy a lower implied volatility than we sell.

We'll continue using AAPL to illustrate how the strategy works. The stock price is $148.28 on September 24 with historical volatility at around 43%.

● Buy January 2008 110* calls at 42.10

● Sell November 2007 150** calls at 9.50

Let's look at the risk profile in Table 6.12.

Table 6.12   Diagonal call risk profile

Maximum risk	Net debit paid (32.60 here)
Maximum reward	[Long call value at the time of the short call expiration when the stock price is at the short call (higher) strike price - net debit]
Lower breakeven	Depends on the value of the long call at the time of the short call expiration.
Higher breakeven	If there is one, it will depend on the value of the long call at the time of the short call expiration. Ideally we'd like to construct a diagonal call, which doesn't have this second breakeven point.

The success of this trade depends greatly on the value of the long call at the time of the short call's expiration. The maximum reward occurs when the stock price is equal to the short call's strike price at the time of the short call's expiration. Remember that the implied volatility behavior will have a big impact on the result of our trade.

Look at the risk profile in Figure 6.11, and you'll see that it looks more like a covered call than a calendar spread. That's good because we don't have the problem of the second (higher) breakeven point. That in itself is primarily a function of the two strike prices we select for our long and short calls, as we'll see.

---

* The 115 strike is the highest strike where the time value was less than 10% of the option premium. The premium is 42.10. The call is ITM by 38.28 [148.28 - 110 = **38.28**] meaning that time value is 3.82 [42.10 - 38.28 = **3.82**]. The time value percentage of the premium is 9.07% [3.82 / 42.10 = **9.07%**].
** The November 150 calls are only just OTM (by $1.72). This may not be far enough OTM to enable our long calls to grow in value, so we'll compare it with a higher strike or two.

Figure 6.11   AAPL 110-150 November-January diagonal call spread

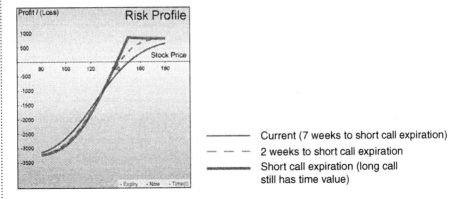

Current (7 weeks to short call expiration)

2 weeks to short call expiration

Short call expiration (long call still has time value)

Table 6.13

Maximum risk	32.60
Maximum reward	8.44
Breakeven	141.14
Initial yield on long call spend	22.57%
Maximum yield on risk	25.89%

The risk on this trade if it went seriously wrong is $32.60, or in real terms with one contract, $3,260. This is significantly more than the risk of the original calendar call we looked at that cost only $4.90 or in real terms, $490. Again, we should acknowledge that it's virtually impossible that AAPL would drop to zero during the time of our investment. A more realistic worst-case bottom is the stock's tangible book value.

With the options' implied volatility remaining around 43%, our breakeven is around $141.14, though we already know that if volatility increases, this breakeven should become "friendlier" or in this case, lower (we'll be verifying this later on). We can also see that our maximum profit occurs at the short call strike price of 150. At this point, with volatility at 43%, our maximum profit is around 8.44, or in real terms, with one contract per leg, $843.88. This produces a maximum yield of 25.89%. Our call is worth only 41.04 (a loss of 1.06), but we lose nothing on the exercise of our short call and keep the 9.50 premium we received for it.

[9.50 - 1.06 = 8.44]
[8.44 / 32.60 = **25.89%** maximum yield on **risk**]

The initial yield on what we paid for the long call is 9.50 / 42.10 = 22.57%, and if we're not exercised, we can always sell another call if the November short call expires worthless.

You may have noticed that there is only a small difference between the initial yield here and the maximum yield. This is because the higher strike price is only just OTM. In order to have a higher maximum yield in relation to the initial yield, our short call must be further OTM. However, by doing so, our initial yield will suffer. The decision all depends on what you think is going to happen with the stock. If you're aggressively bullish, then you'll want a higher strike for the short call, and if you're mildly bullish, you'll keep that strike reasonably close but still OTM. As with the calendar call, it's actually possible for the initial yield to be higher than the maximum yield on the trade. This will happen if the higher (short) strike price is too close to the stock price when the trade is initiated. Therefore the maximum yield is the most important yield to consider with calendars and diagonals.

Before we examine changing the strikes, let's see the results of our trade if implied volatility increases to 55% in Table 6.14.

Table 6.14

	43% IV	55% IV
Maximum risk	32.60	32.60
Maximum reward	8.44	9.21
Breakeven	141.14	139.86
Initial yield on long call spend	22.57%	22.57%
Maximum yield on risk	25.89%	28.26%

Look at the difference in the maximum rewards, breakevens, and maximum yields. An increase in implied volatility makes our breakeven easier to achieve and increases the maximum returns significantly.

Now let's see what happens if we were to raise the short call higher strike price from 150 to 155. We'll base our calculations on our original volatility figure at 43%. We're still buying the 110 strike January 2008 call for 42.10, but we're now selling the 155 strike November 2007 call for 7.30 (see Figure 6.12).

Figure 6.12   AAPL 110-155 November-January diagonal call spread

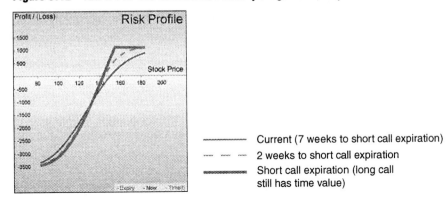

——————— Current (7 weeks to short call expiration)

– – – –   2 weeks to short call expiration

━━━━━   Short call expiration (long call
still has time value)

So by moving the sold call strike out to 155 and keeping everything else the same (see Table 6.15), we see that the trade is quite different, although the basic risk profile shape is the same. Our initial yield and breakevens have suffered, but our maximum returns have gained. It's easy to understand that if we bring in less premium (7.30 as opposed to 9.50), then of course our initial yield will be lower, and our breakeven will be higher (which is to our disadvantage here).

Table 6.15   110-150 versus 110-155 strike diagonal call comparison

	110–150 diagonal	110–155 diagonal
Maximum risk	32.60	**34.80**
Maximum reward	8.44	**11.11**
Breakeven	141.14	**143.48**
Initial yield on long call spend	22.57%	**17.34%**
Maximum yield on risk	25.89%	**31.91%**

Our maximum returns will be much greater though, and this is because we've raised the strike price of our short call. The effect of this is that we'd now be exercised on that short call at a higher price (155 as opposed to 150), which means our long call is able to become more valuable before we have to unravel the entire trade because of the short call being exercised.

The procedure for taking profits if the short call is exercised is almost exactly the same as with the calendar call: Sell bought calls; buy stock at current price and sell at short call strike price.

If the stock rises above 155 at the November expiration, the short call will be exercised, meaning we're obligated to deliver stock at 155 to the call buyer. We'll therefore have to sell our long 110 strike call, buy the stock at the new current market price in order to fulfill our short call obligation, and deliver the stock back at 155. We suffer a loss on the stock transaction but a profit on the long call while also benefiting from the 155 short call premium we sold in the first place.

Let's see how each procedure plays out assuming the stock rises to $160 at the November expiration, which means our short call is exercised in both scenarios. We'll assume that implied volatility is still at 43% for the purpose of valuing the long call.

Table 6.16   110-150 versus 110-155 diagonal call comparison when stock rises to 160 and IV remains at 43%

Stock rises to $160, and we sell the long call. IV remains at 43%.		
	110–150 diagonal call	110–155 diagonal call
Short call exercised at	150	155
Buy stock at market price	160	160
Sell stock at strike price	150	155
Profit / (loss) on exercise	**(10)**	**(5)**
Sell long call for	50.82	50.82
Profit on long call	[50.82 - 42.10] = **8.01**	[50.82 - 42.10] = **8.01**
Keep short call premium	**9.50**	**7.30**
Total profit / (loss)	**7.51**	**10.31**
Initial yield	22.57%	17.34%
Maximum yield *	25.89%	31.91%
Yield with stock at $160	17.84%	24.49%

* The maximum yield occurs when the stock price is at the short call strike price on the short call expiration date.

As we can see in Table 6.16, our long 110 strike call is worth around 50.82 at the time of the November short call expiration when the stock price is $160. In each scenario we sell the long call for the same premium; however, we make more money the higher strike short call because we lose less on fulfilling our exercise on the short side. In the first trade we are obligated to sell the stock at 150, whereas in the second trade we're obligated to sell the stock at 155, thereby gaining an extra $5. The difference in the short call premiums received was only $2.20 [9.50 - 7.30), so our profits differ by $2.80 [5.00 - 2.20].

We can also see that as the stock climbs further without any change in implied volatility, both positions make slightly less profit. However, the 110–155 trade is significantly more profitable than the 110–150 trade as the stock price rises.

What if we decided to exercise our long call instead of selling it? Well, as with the calendar call scenario, we would forego any time value left in the long premium and any increase in implied volatility as well. So let's say the stock has risen to $160 and play out the scenarios again, this time exercising the long call.

Notice how our returns are less when we exercise the long call instead of selling it with time value. We can see that the time value in the long call when the stock has risen to $160 is $0.82. Our original profits were 7.51 and 10.31 for the two trades, and these figures are 0.82 higher than if we exercise our long calls (6.69 and 9.49 in the Table 6.17).

Table 6.17   Exercising the long call side

| | Stock rises to $160, and we sell the long call. IV remains at 43%. | |
	110–150 diagonal call	110–155 diagonal call
Short call exercised at	150	155
Buy stock at market price	160	160
Sell stock at strike price	150	155
Profit / (loss) on exercise	**(10)**	**(5)**
Exercise long call at	110	110
Profit on long call exercise	[160 - 110 - 42.81] = **7.19**	[160 - 110 - 42.81] = **7.19**
Keep short call premium	**9.50**	**7.30**
Total profit / (loss)	**6.69**	**9.49**
Initial yield	22.57%	17.34%
Maximum yield on risk	22.70% *	29.31% **
Yield with stock at $160	15.89%	22.54%

* The maximum yield occurs when the stock price is at the short call strike price on the short call expiration date. If we exercise our long 110 strike call at the strike price of $150, then we gain $40. However, the long call cost us 42.10, so we lose 2.10 by exercising the long call. We make and lose nothing on the exercise of the short call and we keep the 9.50 premium. Our total profit if we exercise the long call would be 7.40, which gives us a maximum yield on risk of 22.70% when we divide 7.40 into 32.60. In the earlier scenario our maximum yield was 25.89% for the 110–150 trade when we sold the long call instead of exercising it.

** If we exercise our long 110 strike call when the stock is at the short strike price of $155, we gain $45 on the exercise. We subtract the 42.10 that we paid for the call, leaving us with 2.90 of net profit. The short call expires ATM, worthless and unexercised, and we keep the entire premium of 7.30. Our maximum profit if we chose to exercise the long call is therefore 10.20, which gives us a maximum yield on risk of 29.31% when we divide 10.20 into 34.80. This compares unfavorably with the scenario where we don't exercise our long call but sell it instead, achieving a yield of 31.91%.

In some cases it's actually possible that by foregoing the time value and exercising the long call side, you can turn a winning trade into a losing trade. So the lesson is, don't exercise early, especially when there's plenty of time left to expiration.

What happens if implied volatility rises to 55% after we enter these trades and we want to see the difference between exercising our long calls and not exercising our long calls? Again, we'll assume the stock is at $160 at the November short call expiration.

Table 6.18   110-150 versus 110-155 diagonal call comparison when stock rises to $160 and IV rises to 55%

	Not exercising our long calls. IV rises to 55%. Stock rises to $160	
	110–150 diagonal call	**110–155 diagonal call**
Short call exercised at	150	155
Buy stock at market price	160	160
Sell stock at strike price	150	155
Profit / (loss) on exercise	**(10)**	**(5)**
Sell long call for	51.29	51.29
Profit on long call	[51.29 - 42.10] = **9.19**	[51.29 - 42.10] = **9.19**
Keep short call premium	**9.50**	**7.30**
Total profit / (loss)	**8.69**	**11.49**
Initial yield	22.57%	17.34%
Maximum yield on risk	28.25% *	33.68% **
Yield with stock at $160	20.64%	27.29%

* The maximum yield occurs when the stock price is at the short call strike price on the short call expiration date. With the table's parameters, the long call would be worth 41.81 if the stock is at $150, representing a loss of 0.29. There would be no loss on exercise of the short call at $150, and we keep the 9.50 premium, so the net profit is 9.50 - 0.29 = 9.21. The maximum yield on risk is therefore 9.21 / 32.60 = 28.25%.

** Similarly, the long call would be worth 46.52 when the stock is at $155. This represents a profit of 4.42. Therefore the maximum profit would be 7.30 + 4.42 = 11.72, and the maximum yield on risk is 11.72 / 34.80 = 33.68%.

With the stock at $160, the long calls are now valued at 51.29 instead of 50.82, meaning an extra 0.47 profit.

Now let's see the results if we exercise our long call instead (Table 6.19).

Table 6.19   Exercising the long call side

	Exercising the long call; IV rises to 55%	
	110–150 diagonal call	110–155 diagonal call
Short call exercised at	150	155
Buy stock at market price	160	160
Sell stock at strike price	150	155
Profit / (loss) on exercise	**(10)**	**(5)**
Exercise long call at	110	110
Profit on long call exercise	[160 - 110 - 42.81] = **7.19**	[160 - 110 - 42.81] = **7.19**
Keep short call premium	**9.50**	**7.30**
Total profit / (loss)	6.69	9.49

We gain nothing by exercising the long call; in fact, we lose. We get neither the time value nor the benefit of increased implied volatility. Compare our profits of 6.69 and 9.49 for the two diagonals where we do exercise our long call, with 8.69 and 11.49 for the exact same trades where we don't exercise the long call and where implied volatility rises to 55% (see Table 6.20).

Table 6.20   Diagonal comparisons

	Exercise long call; IV at 43%		Sell the long call; IV at 55%	
	110–150	110–155	110–150	110–155
Profit / (loss)	6.69	9.49	8.69	11.49
Initial yield	22.57%	17.34%	22.57%	17.34%
Maximum yield *	22.70%	29.31%	**28.25%**	**33.68%**
Yield with stock at $160	15.89%	22.54%	20.64%	27.29%

* The maximum yield occurs when the stock price is at the short call strike price on the short call expiration date.

The reason that our maximum profits occur at the short call strike price is that we get to keep the entire short call premium without being exercised because it expires ATM.

This last table demonstrates that we should never exercise our long calls because we forego (a) time value and (b) any increase in implied volatility.

In reality AAPL was at 166.39 on the November expiration day. Here's how our diagonal call turned out: On September 24 AAPL is trading at $148.28. Historical volatility is around 43%.

● Buy 110 strike January call for 42.10 (implied volatility = 50.73%)

● Sell 155 strike call for 7.30 (implied volatility = 43.07%)

Already we can see something we don't like, and that is that we've paid 50.73% implied volatility and received only 43.07% implied volatility. We've bought a relatively expensive call and sold a relatively cheap call. This explains why our yields are low compared with what we might have expected.

At the November expiration AAPL is at $166.39, and our long January 110 strike call is worth **58.05** at the bid, meaning its implied volatility is **65.28%**. This is a great result and significantly better than our scenarios above where we compared 43% and 55%. Even though we paid 50.73% implied volatility for the long call, we are now benefiting from the significant appreciation of volatility in the stock, which has transferred to the options prices. Interestingly, the 150 and 155 strike calls were only priced at around 57%. This means that the deeper ITM calls were positively skewed in that their implied volatilities were higher than the higher strike calls.

See the difference now on November 16 in Table 6.21.

Table 6.21

Long 110 January strike call	Paid 42.10	Now worth 58.05	Profit 15.95
Short 155 November strike call	Sold for 7.30	Exercised at $155	Loss: 4.09 *
Net Position			**Profit: 11.86**

* [166.39 - 155 + 7.30 = 4.09 loss]

Now, what if we'd exercised the long call instead of selling it with the time value and increase in implied volatility (see Table 6.22)?

Table 6.22

Long 110 January strike call	Paid 42.10	Exercise for profit of 166.39 - 110	Profit 14.29 *
Short 155 November strike call	Sold for 7.30	Exercised at $155	Loss: 4.09
Net Position			**Profit: 10.20**

* [166.39 - 110 - 42.10 = 14.29 profit]

So the difference between the two scenarios is 1.66, which is very significant.

We're now going to compare this with the calendar (see Table 6.23). Remember that AAPL's price was $148.28 on September 24 when the stock initially broke out. By the November expiration it had risen to $166.39.

Table 6.23   150 calendar call compared with 110-150 diagonal call with stock rising to $166.39

Stock rises from $148.28 to $166.39 and we sell the long call. IV as per market.		
	150 strike calendar call	**110–155 diagonal call**
Long call cost	14.40	42.10
Short call premium	9.50	7.30
Risk (net cost of trade)	4.90	34.80
Short call exercised at	150	155
Buy stock at market price	166.39	166.39
Sell stock at strike price	150	155
Profit / (loss) on exercise	**(16.39)**	**(11.39)**
Sell long call for	**25.45** (IV = 58.11%)	**58.05** (IV = 65.28%)
Profit on long call	[25.45 - 14.40] = **11.05**	[58.05 - 42.10] = **15.95**
Keep short call premium	**9.50**	**7.30**
Total profit / (loss)	**4.16**	**6.22**
Initial yield	22.57%	17.34%
Yield on risk with stock at $166.39	84.90%	17.87%
Lower breakeven	126.30	140.91
Higher breakeven	185.99	n/a

In this case, on November 16, it seems clear that the calendar looks superior to the diagonal.

However, let's take a look the AAPL chart again in Figure 6.13, and you'll see that the stock price closed at $191.79 on November 7, just eight traded days before expiration.

Figure 6.13 AAPL chart before and after earnings

TC2000.com. Courtesy of Worden Brothers Inc.

Even more intriguing is that on that day, the historical volatility of the stock was running at around 33.55%.

The 150 strike January call was priced at around 44.85, and the 110 strike January call was priced at 82.80 at the bid. The respective implied volatilities are 46.86% and 58.93%. If the trades were to be closed at this time, the outcome would be slightly different (see Table 6.24).

Table 6.24 150 calendar call compared with 110-150 diagonal call with stock rising to $191.79

Stock rises from $148.28 to $191.79 and we sell the long call. IV as per market.		
	150 strike calendar call	110–155 diagonal call
Long call cost	14.40	42.10
Short call premium	9.50	7.30
Risk (net cost of trade)	4.90	34.80
Buy back short call for	42.25	37.30
Profit / (loss) on short call leg	**(32.75)**	**(30.00)**

Volatile Markets Made Easy

Table 6.24   (continued)

Stock rises from $148.28 to $191.79 and we sell the long call. IV as per market.		
	150 strike calendar call	**110–155 diagonal call**
Sell long call for	**44.85** (IV = 46.86%)	**82.80** (IV = 58.93%)
Profit on long call	[44.85 - 14.40] = **30.45**	[82.80 - 42.10] = **40.70**
Total profit / (loss)	**(2.30)**	**10.70**
Initial yield	22.57%	17.34%
Yield on risk with stock at $191.79	(46.94)%	30.75%
Lower breakeven	c. 126.30	c. 140.91
Higher breakeven	c. 189.49	n/a

Do you see how we are actually making a loss with the calendar call in this situation? Just eight days before the November expiration our calendar call is losing 46.94%. If the stock had continued rising, it's likely that it would have continued to be the case on the November expiration date. A sharp retracement in the stock price combined with an increase in implied volatility brought the calendar call spread back into a profitable position by the expiration date. The diagonal call had no such problems; in fact, its profitability benefited by the greater increase in implied volatility of the long call. Notice how in this table we buy back our short calls for a loss as opposed to being exercised.

Just say we'd reached the November expiration and the stock price was at $191.79. Instead of buying back our short calls for a loss, they would be exercised for a loss. The position would have been roughly as shown in Table 6.25:

Table 6.25   Calendar call versus diagonal call comparison when stock rises from $148.28 to $191.79, having the short calls exercised

Stock rises from $148.28 to $191.79 and we sell the long call. IV as per market.		
	150 strike calendar call	**110–155 diagonal call**
Long call cost	14.40	42.10
Short call premium	9.50	7.30
Risk (net cost of trade)	4.90	34.80
Short call exercised at	150	155
Buy stock at market price	191.79	191.79
Sell stock at strike price	150	155
Profit / (loss) on exercise	**(41.79)**	**(36.79)**

Sell long call for	**44.85** (IV = 46.86%)	**82.80** (IV = 58.93%)
Profit on long call	[44.85 - 14.40] = **30.45**	[82.80 - 42.10] = **40.70**
Keep short call premium	**9.50**	**7.30**
Total profit / (loss)	**(1.84)**	**11.21**
Initial yield	22.57%	17.34%
Yield on risk with stock at $191.79	(37.55)%	32.21%
Lower breakeven	126.30	140.91
Higher breakeven	185.99	n/a

Again, we'd still be taking a loss on the calendar call. So the question is, which strategy is better, the calendar or the diagonal? We know that they are both influenced by the strike prices, the implied volatilities, and the expiration dates used, but it really comes down to personal taste. When you get the calendar spread trade right, it's very rewarding, but there's always the risk of the stock rising too far and the trade making a loss. That doesn't happen with diagonals, provided your long call is deep enough ITM and the short call is enough OTM.

Personally, I prefer diagonals. They're more conservative for sure, but I know I cannot get into much trouble if the stock gaps up in a big way, and that makes me breathe a lot easier.

We've covered a lot of ground with regard to calendar and diagonal call spreads. You should be beginning to feel reasonably comfortable with the concept of them and how we want to replicate the shape of a covered call but significantly improve our yield. We accomplished that most satisfactorily with the diagonal, which achieved an initial yield of 17.24% and maximum yields of over 30% in less than two months, compared with the covered call right at the beginning of the chapter, which achieved corresponding yields of 4.92% and 9.46%.

Before we finish with the diagonal call, I want to go through one more example of the various scenarios that can occur with this strategy. To trade diagonals and calendars well consistently, you really do need to *see* what is going on and how your risk profile changes as the parameters such as implied volatility change. You should also be aware of the Greeks, which I also cover in upcoming sections.

Diagonal Call Scenarios

ACME is trading at $26.00 on March 19, with historical volatility at 40%.

● Buy January 2010 25 calls at 6.60

● Sell April 2008 27.50 calls at 0.55

In this example I've deliberately made it so our bought call is only just ITM with a 25 strike call on a $26.00 stock. You'll see how this will affect the trade as we go through the scenarios.

The risk profile in Figure 6.14 resembles the calendar call doesn't it? The reason for this is that the long call side is not deep enough ITM. As the stock price rises, the long call doesn't immediately go at the speed of 1 delta, but more like 0.5 deltas as the long call is virtually ATM in this example. This means it will be cheaper than a deep ITM call so the initial yields may be higher, but the trade may actually lose money if the stock rises too far. We'll see how the scenarios all play out.

Figure 6.14   ACME 25 - 27.50 April–January diagonal call spread

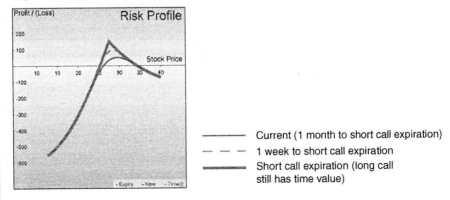

Current (1 month to short call expiration)

1 week to short call expiration

Short call expiration (long call still has time value)

The procedure for the diagonal when we're exercised is as follows:

● Sell bought calls; buy stock at current market price and sell stock at short call strike price.

So for every dollar the stock goes up beyond the short call strike price, our long call only rises at half the rate at first and doesn't catch up speed with the stock until the option is deeper ITM.

At the April expiration

1. Scenario: stock falls to $23.00
   - Long calls worth approximately 4.28; loss so far = 2.32
   - Short calls expire worthless; profit 0.55

No exercise

Total position = -2.32 + 0.55 = loss of 1.77

2. Scenario: stock falls to $25.00
   - Long calls worth approximately 5.46; loss so far = 1.16
   - Short calls expire worthless; profit 0.55

No exercise

Total position = -1.16 + 0.55 = loss of 0.61

3. Scenario: stock stays at $26.00
   - Long calls worth approximately 7.09; loss so far = 0.49
   - Short calls expire worthless; profit 0.55

No exercise

Total position = -0.49 + 0.55 = profit of 0.04

4. Scenario: stock rises to $27.50
   - Long calls worth approximately 7.09; profit so far = 0.49
   - Short calls expire worthless; profit 0.55

No exercise

Total position = 0.49 + 0.55 = profit of 1.04

5. Scenario: stock rises to $30.00
   - Long calls worth approximately 8.82; profit so far = 2.22
   - Short calls expire $2.50 ITM

Procedure: Sell bought calls; buy stock at current price and sell at short call strike price.

Exercised at $27.50

Buy stock at 30.00
Sell stock at 27.50
Loss = 2.50
Sell long call for a profit = 2.22
Keep short call premium = 0.55
Loss on exercise = 2.50
Total position = 0.27 profit

If you tried to exercise the bought call:
Procedure: Exercise bought calls at $25.00; deliver stock at $27.50 for exercised sold call.

> Buy call at 6.60
> Sell call at 0.5
> Net cost = 6.05
> Buy stock at 25.00
> Sell stock at 27.50
> Net profit at 2.50

Total = 2.50 - 6.05 = loss of 3.55

This is a bit more of a stark lesson. But as we know already, never exercise a long-term option because you would miss out on time value and any increases in implied volatility. And make sure you buy reasonably deep ITM calls for the long leg of the diagonal trade. Virtually ATM is not going to be good enough.

Greeks for Diagonal Calls

The AAPL and ACME diagonal call trades are very different, so we'll look at both sets of Greeks so you can appreciate how dynamic they can be.

Starting with AAPL, the trade was initiated on September 24. AAPL was trading at 148.28. We bought the deep ITM 110 strike January 2008 call for 42.10 and sold the 155 strike November call for 7.30 (see Figure 6.15).

Now compare with the ACME diagonal call Greeks (Figure 6.16). The trade was initiated on March 19, 2008. ACME was trading at 26.00. We bought the 25 strike January 2010 call for 6.60 and sell the 27.50 strike November call for 0.55.

Notice the subtle differences between each of the Greeks visuals. The main ones to notice are delta and vega.

For the ACME trade, delta becomes negative as the risk profile starts to lose money. With the AAPL trade delta doesn't quite go into negative territory; it simply goes down to zero as the speed of the position slows down as the stock price rises.

Figure 6.15   AAPL diagonal call risk profile and Greeks

Risk Profile
Maximum profit is achieved when the stock is at the higher strike price at the time of the short call expiration date.

Delta
Delta (speed) is at its fastest around the higher strike price, indicating the increasing speed of the position as it approaches that level.

Gamma
Gamma (acceleration) peaks inversely around the higher strike price, showing where the delta curve is steepest.

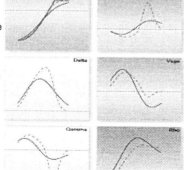

Theta
Theta is positive; illustrating that time decay is most helpful to the position around the higher strike price, where the position is most profitable.

Vega
Increasing volatility is helpful because it will mean the long call's residual value should be higher.

Rho
Higher interest rates become more helpful because we're effectively long calls as the underlying asset price rises.

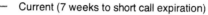

———————   Current (7 weeks to short call expiration)

— — —   1 week to short call expiration

═══════   Short call expiration

Figure 6.16   ACME diagonal call risk profile and Greeks

Risk Profile
Maximum profit is achieved when the stock is at the higher strike price at the time of the short call expiration date.

Delta
Delta (speed) is at its fastest around the higher strike price, indicating the increasing speed of the position as it approaches that level.

Gamma
Gamma (acceleration) peaks inversely around the higher strike price, showing where the delta curve is steepest.

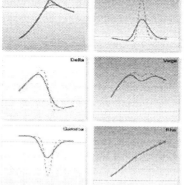

Theta
Theta is positive; illustrating that time decay is most helpful to the position around the higher strike price, where the position is most profitable.

Vega
Increasing volatility is helpful because it will mean the long call's residual value should be higher.

Rho
Higher interest rates become more helpful because we're effectively long calls as the underlying asset price rises.

———————   Current (7 weeks to short call expiration)

— — —   1 week to short call expiration

═══════   Short call expiration

The ACME trade vega remains above the line throughout showing that volatility is helping the trade. This is because the long call has almost two years to expiration and the short call has only one month left. The long call can therefore be helped far more than the short call can be harmed by an increase in volatility. (Remember that increasing volatility helps long options and hurts short options.) Conversely with AAPL, when the stock is around the strike price, the vega lines dip into the negative area, suggesting that increasing volatility may actually harm the trade in that area. This is because the time differential between the long and short calls is only three months, and the long call, being so far deep ITM with a delta of 1, simply cannot be helped by volatility as it will move 1:1 with the stock regardless of increasing volatility. The short call will be harmed by volatility, and this will be most sensitive around its strike price. Therefore with the deep ITM long call not responding much to volatility and the NTM short call being highly responsive to volatility, the net effect is that volatility harms the position.

Theta is mainly positive because the closer we get to the short call expiration date, the nearer we are to keeping the entire short call premium. In this way we see time decay is largely helpful to this strategy.

That concludes the section on diagonal calls. We can see that the strategy delivers better yields than the covered call and a safer return than the calendar call, particularly as the stock price rises.

Let's now take quick look at the exact opposite of a diagonal call.

Diagonal Puts

The opposite of a diagonal call spread is a *diagonal put* spread. We do exactly the same thing but in reverse, and we use puts (see Table 6.26 and Figure 6.17).

Table 6.26   Diagonal put components

	Diagonal calls	Diagonal puts
Options	Calls	Puts
Buy	Lower (ITM) strike Longer time to expiration	Higher (ITM) strike Longer time to expiration
Sell	Higher (OTM) strike Shorter time to expiration	Lower (OTM) strike Shorter time to expiration

Figure 6.17 Diagonal put components

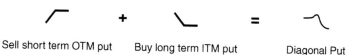

Sell short term OTM put   Buy long term ITM put   Diagonal Put

With both diagonal strategies we buy ITM options and sell OTM options. Remembering the Rule of the Opposites from Chapter 1, "Introduction to Options," we know that for puts, strikes lower than the stock price are OTM, and strikes higher than the stock price are ITM. Conversely for calls, strikes lower than the stock price are ITM, and strikes higher than the stock price are OTM.

1. Buy higher ITM strike puts with longer time to expiration
2. Sell lower OTM strike puts with less time to expiration

Description

The diagonal put spread creates an income strategy from a stock about which we are bearish. As with the diagonal call, if we place the trade correctly, then volatility is more likely to help us with this strategy. That means buying deep ITM puts and selling shorter term OTM puts. We don't want to cut corners and create a trade where we lose money even if we get the direction right. Therefore it's important to not be greedy with the initial yield, so we buy deep ITM options with the diagonal strategy. The best outcome is for the stock to fall gradually and for us to sell the OTM puts month after month.

Let's say we're looking to trade a diagonal put on a $25.00 stock. The six-month 30.00 strike put is say, 7.50, and we sell next month's 22.50 call for $0.75, giving us an initial cash yield of 10%. If the share falls to $20.00, our long put will be worth at least $10.00 (intrinsic value alone), meaning a gain of at least 2.50. Our short put will be worth a minimum of 2.50, meaning a loss of at least 1.75. The net position is still profitable, and if there is an increase in volatility, then our profits are likely to increase as the long put will benefit more than the damage done to the short put. Remember the long option benefits from increasing volatility, and the short option will be hurt by increasing volatility.

Figure 6.18   22.50-30.00 diagonal put risk profile

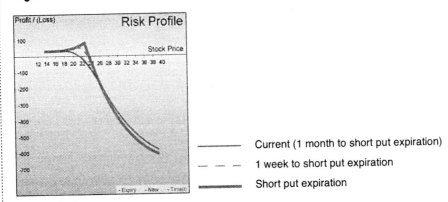

Current (1 month to short put expiration)

1 week to short put expiration

Short put expiration

At the short put expiration, our short put obligation means we'll have to buy the stock for $22.50 if and when exercised. Our long put enables us to exercise our right to sell at $30.00; however, we know that it would be better instead to sell the option if there's plenty of time left.

We go through a real example later, but the main point is this: Because we're buying reasonably deep ITM puts, the long option will have a higher (negative) delta and will move -1:1 against the stock as it falls. Remember that puts have a negative delta, i.e., the put will rise in value as the stock price falls. In buying a reasonably deep ITM put, we will still make money even if the stock price plummets dramatically.

The bought option is longer-term and ITM, and the short option is short-term and OTM. If the stock falls below the lower (short) strike, the short put will be exercised. This means we're obligated to buy the stock at the strike price of 22.50. We'd sell the stock simultaneously at the current market price of $20.00, making a loss on the exercise of $2.50. However, that simply offsets the $2.50 we received for the short put in the first place, and we'll be making money on the long put, which must be worth at least $10 in intrinsic value alone. Remember we paid 7.50 for the long put, which would have included both time value and intrinsic value. Now that the stock price is $20, the put must be worth a minimum of $10, and that's before counting the time value element.

Context

Outlook

With a diagonal put, your outlook is *bearish*.

Rationale

To generate income against your longer-term long put position by selling OTM puts and receiving the premium.

Net Position

This is a **net debit** transaction because your bought puts will be more expensive than your sold puts, which are OTM and have less time value.

Your maximum risk on the trade is limited to the net debit of the bought puts less the sold puts. Your maximum reward occurs when the stock price is at the sold put (lower) strike price at the expiration of the sold put.

Effect of Time Decay

Time decay affects the diagonal put in a mixed fashion. It erodes the value of the long put but helps you with your income strategy by eroding the value faster on the short put.

Appropriate Time Period to Trade

You're safest to choose at least a few months to expiration with the long put and a shorter time (say, one month) for the short put. The aim is to sell an OTM put each month to maximize the income over a period of time.

Selecting the Stock

Choose from stocks with adequate liquidity, preferably over 500,000 Average Daily Volume (ADV), but over 100,000 is sufficient as a minimum.

Seek a downward trend or rangebound stock and identify a clear area of resistance for your stop loss zone. Bear flags are good, particularly when the stock breaks down below support.

Selecting the Option

Choose options with adequate liquidity; open interest should be at least 100, preferably 500.

Table 6.27   Option legs for the diagonal put

Higher strike	Look for either the ATM or ITM (ideally about 10–20% ITM preferred) strike above the current stock price. If you're bearish, choose a higher strike; if neutral choose the ATM strike in anticipation of writing more puts in the future.
Lower strike	Look for OTM by more than one strike to enable the long put to rise in value if you get exercised on the short put.
Expirations	Look at either of the next two expirations for the short option and compare monthly yields. Look for over six months for the long option.

Risk Profile

Table 6.28   Diagonal put risk profile

Maximum risk	Limited to the net debit paid
Maximum reward	[Long put value at the time of the short put expiration when the stock price is at the lower strike price] less [net debit]
Breakeven down	Depends on the value of the long put option at the time of the short put expiration.
Breakeven up	Depends on the value of the long put option at the time of the short put expiration.

Greeks

Figure 6.19 **Diagonal put risk profile and Greeks**

Risk Profile
Maximum profit is achieved when the stock is at the lower strike price at the time of the short put expiration date.

Theta
Theta is positive; illustrating that time decay is most helpful to the position around the lower strike price, where the position is most profitable.

Delta
Delta (speed) is at its fastest either side of the strike price, indicating the increasing speed of the position in one direction and then the other.

Vega
Increasing volatility is mainly helpful because it will mean the long put's residual value should be higher.

Rho
Higher interest rates become more damaging as the underlying asset price fails.

Gamma
Gamma (acceleration) peaks inversely around the lower strike price, showing where the delta line is steepest.

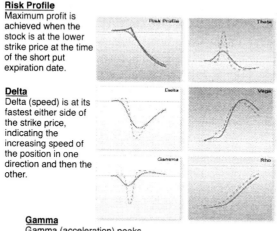

Advantages

You can generate monthly income with a bearish strategy and can profit from rangebound and falling volatile stocks, making a similar yield as with a diagonal call.

Disadvantages

You have a capped upside if the stock falls—ensure you buy a deep ITM put so you don't lose if the stock falls "too much."

High yield does not necessarily mean a profitable or high probability profitable trade, as we saw with the diagonal call.

Example

Typically we like to use this strategy with falling stocks or stocks that are exhibiting a potential to fall in price. So we can use this strategy when we see bear flag patterns that are breaking to the downside.

Staying with AAPL, if you follow the stock to mid-January 2008, AAPL's uptrend grinds to a halt and on January 14, the stock exhibits a very attractive looking bear flag pattern. Notice also in Figure 6.20 how volume tails off as the flag pattern is forming. This shows us that there is little buying appetite at this level, and if the stock falls through support, the sellers are likely to return in force, potentially sending the stock further down with some force.

Figure 6.20   AAPL bear flag chart

TC2000®.com. Courtesy of Worden Brothers Inc.

AAPL is trading at $178.78 on January 14 with historical volatility at 45%.

● Buy July 230 puts at 58.60 (implied volatility = 51%)

● Sell February 170 puts at 8.85 (implied volatility = 62%)

Notice that we're buying lower implied volatility here at 51% compared with the 62% that we're selling. This is exactly what we want—buy low IV and sell high IV.

At the February expiration the stock has fallen to $124.63...this is a massive drop (see Figure 6.21).

Figure 6.21 **AAPL chart at $124.63**

TC2000®.com. Courtesy of Worden Brothers Inc.

With the stock's fall in price, the historical stock volatility has increased to almost 55%, and this will be reflected in the long put premium.

● The long puts are at 105.20 in the market; profit = 46.60 (implied volatility has increased from 51% to **69.29%**; this is fantastic for us and demonstrates how implied volatility can also rise as stock prices fall)

● The short puts expire ITM by $45.37. This means you are obligated to buy AAPL at $170.00, thereby sustaining a loss on the shares of $45.37. The net loss on this leg is $36.52 because you brought in 8.85 of premium when you sold the put at the outset of the trade.

Total position = 46.60 - 36.42 = **10.18** profit

Remember, the maximum profit for the diagonal put occurs when the stock price is at the short put (lower) strike price of 170 at the time of the short put expiration date. Assuming that the implied volatility of the long put had remained at 51%, the maximum profit at the February expiration date would have been around $13.78 if the stock price had been at $170.

Figure 6.22 provides a close up of the risk profile of the 170–230 diagonal put trade on January 14.

Figure 6.22   170-230 diagonal put risk profile

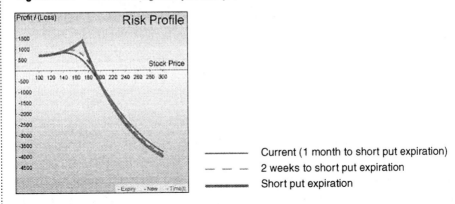

_____ Current (1 month to short put expiration)

_ _ _ _   2 weeks to short put expiration

_____ Short put expiration

Here's how we arrive at that maximum profit figure of 13.78:

● Assume the long put implied volatility remained at 51% for the long put, and the stock is at $170 at the time of the short put's expiration date, 170 being the short put strike price (in reality it shot up because the stock plummeted so far).

● With those parameters the long put value on February 15 would be 63.53, representing a profit of 4.93.

● The short put would have expired ATM and worthless, therefore we'd keep the 8.85 premium with no exercise.

● Therefore our maximum profit would have been 13.78.

When you look at the risk profile, you'll notice that as the stock price falls below the short put strike price, our profits tail off slightly but never enough for us to lose money. This is because we bought a deep ITM put. Had we bought a slightly ITM put, our risk profile would have looked like the calendar spread we looked at earlier.

For example, let's say that instead of having bought the 230 strike July put, we'd bought the 190 strike July put, which was only ITM by $11.22 (remember the stock was $178.78 on January 14). The market price for this long put was 30.55, which coincidentally reflected implied volatility of 51%.

The second leg of the trade still involves selling the 170 strike February put, but look at the different shapes of the two risk profiles in Figure 6.23.

Figure 6.23 170-230 versus 170-190 diagonal put spread

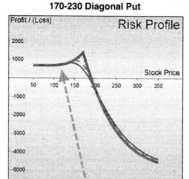

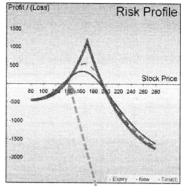

see how the risk profile flattens out even as the stock declines by a large amount ... this is because we have bought a deep ITM put

see how the risk profile turns sharply down and even starts to make a loss as the stock declines sharply ... this is because our long 190 strike put is not deep enough in the money

———————— Current (1 month to short put expiration)

— — — 2 weeks to short put expiration

▬▬▬▬▬ Short put expiration

As we can see, the 170–190 diagonal put has two breakeven points, one at 135.01 and the other at 194.50. In reality we would have made a loss as AAPL was 124.23 on the February expiration date. How galling would that have been...to get the direction right but make a loss because the 190 strike long put wasn't deep enough ITM from the outset.

So, as with the diagonal call earlier, you can now see the wisdom of buying deep ITM options for the long leg of a diagonal spread. The idea is that the long leg of the strategy must be deep enough ITM to have a high delta. Remember, long puts have negative deltas. In this case, the 230 strike put has a much "higher" negative delta (-0.68) than the 190 strike put (-0.47). This means that the 230 strike put will be much more responsive, which is what we want, especially if we're right about the direction of the stock.

Summary

You've seen how to do things the wrong way and then the right way. I've done this to give you some free experience without you having to lose any money. If you've taken these examples to heart and followed each example through, this will stand you in good stead. From here you will gain your own experience in the markets and particularly with my two preferred strategies, the diagonal call and the diagonal put.

These are directional strategies that combine high income returns together while volatility is our friend. The diagonal call is bullish, and the diagonal put is bearish.

You've also discovered which strike prices and expiration dates are preferable, and we've tried other strategies that didn't work so well in terms of safety. The two preferred strategies combine healthy returns with the safety you require to ensure you never get into any trouble that would be unmanageable.

To trade these strategies successfully, it helps to be able to see what's happening with each strategy in terms of their risk profile and the Greeks. You can view the risk profiles in color and see further information about other strategies for free in the Strategy Guides section on www.optioneasy.com (see Figure 6.24).

Figure 6.24   OptionEasy free online options education

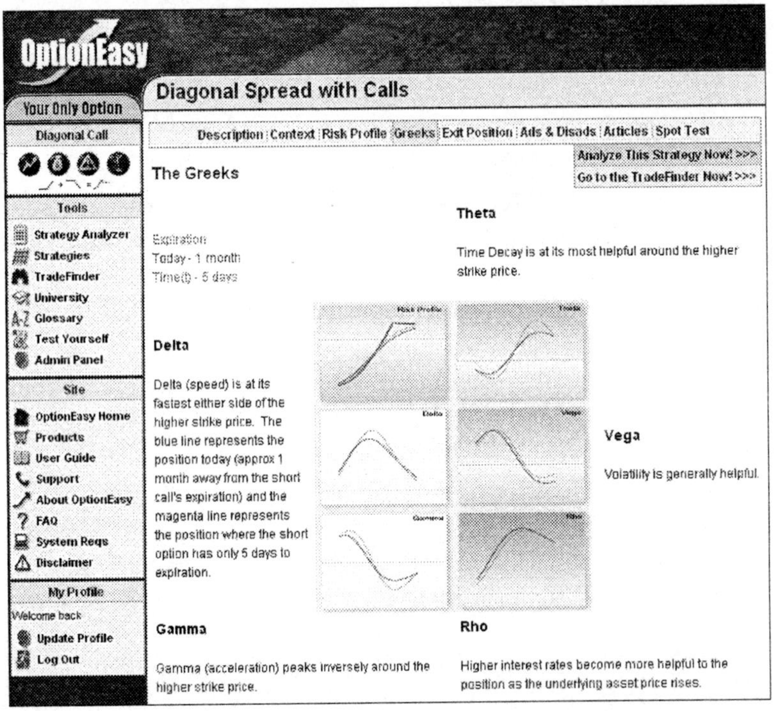

You can also analyze strategies dynamically for a small monthly subscription on www.optioneasy.com (see Figure 6.25).

Figure 6.25   OptionEasy online Strategy Analyzer

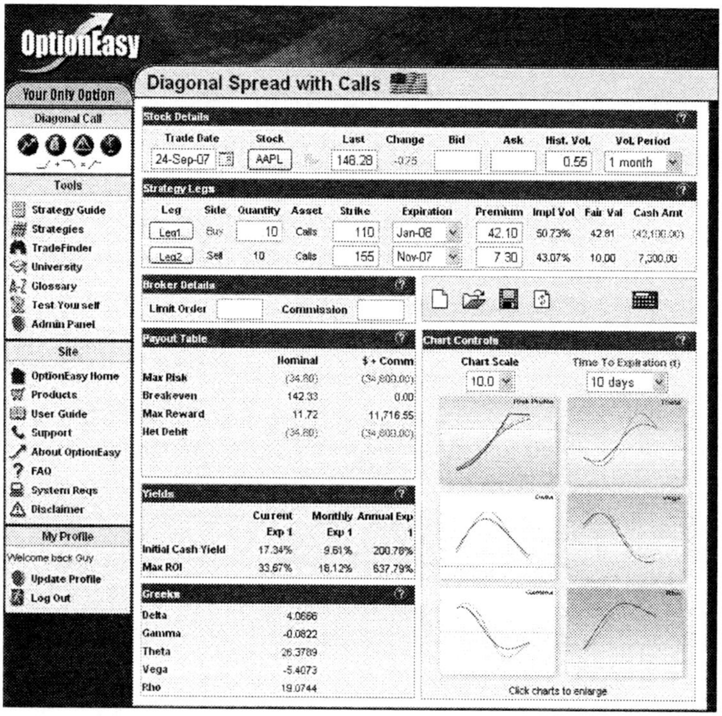

In the coming chapters we get practical with the strategies that we know we can make money from—namely, straddles, strangles, call ratio backspreads, put ratio backspreads, diagonal calls, and diagonal puts.

chapter 7

The Practical Way to Trade Volatility

In the past professionals on Wall Street have had a huge advantage over the private investor/trader, but the gap is closing fast. The combination of broadband and mega-powerful PCs with massive storage and memory capacity means that you can create software that enables you to find suitable candidates to trade consistently and successfully and in real time.

This has become my work focus…to create tools to help me identify great looking trades that fit my criteria and are within my trading comfort zone. My comfort zone involves trading stocks that are trending and forming flag patterns. From there I can easily determine which strategy to employ.

In this chapter we go through the necessary steps to finding a potential trade candidate and then deciding the strategy. In Chapter 9, "Trading Plans and Putting It All Together," we build trading plans for each strategy (straddle, strangle, call ratio backspread, put ratio backspread, diagonal call, and diagonal put).

Steps

1. **Find the tradable chart pattern.**

   Always look for a neat looking pattern. Also be mindful of the general direction of the market. This means you should be looking at the S&P 500 and the Dow Jones Industrial Average. If they're trending up, then focus on uptrending stocks forming bull flags. If they're trending down, focus on downtrending stocks forming bear flags. That's just common sense, but it's a step that many traders simply don't do.

The safest bet is to follow the trend of the overall market and look for stocks that are in sync with that. Trading against the trend is akin to trying to catch a falling knife.

Is it wise to look for bull flags in a downtrending market and vice versa? Well, if you believe that the trend is about to change direction or already has done so, then maybe. But I would suggest that you study and watch the markets for a few months and become accustomed to their undulations first. There are times where you can catch the beginnings of a trend and ride it up to the moon, but you just have to follow the rules about entry, stop positioning, targets, and trade management of the pattern you're trading. Remember, even a simple trendline can be enough to keep you on the straight and narrow.

Figure 7.1 Finding flag candidates using www.flag-trader.com

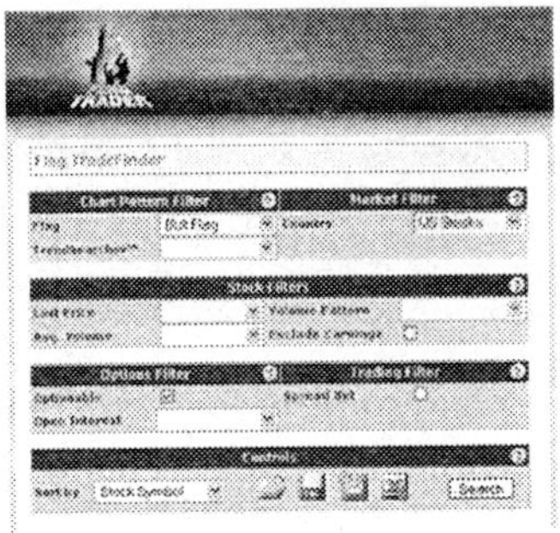

This application makes it easy to quickly identify flag patterns occurring in the markets. Of course, the number of good looking flag patterns will vary according to market conditions, but every one of them has at least satisfied a complex mathematical algorithm. From here you now need to use discretion and decide what constitutes a neat looking flag pattern and what doesn't.

Figure 7.2 is an example of a bull flag in a bearish market. The stock is HSII, the date is February 19, and earnings are announced on February 26.

Figure 7.2 Bull flag in bearish market

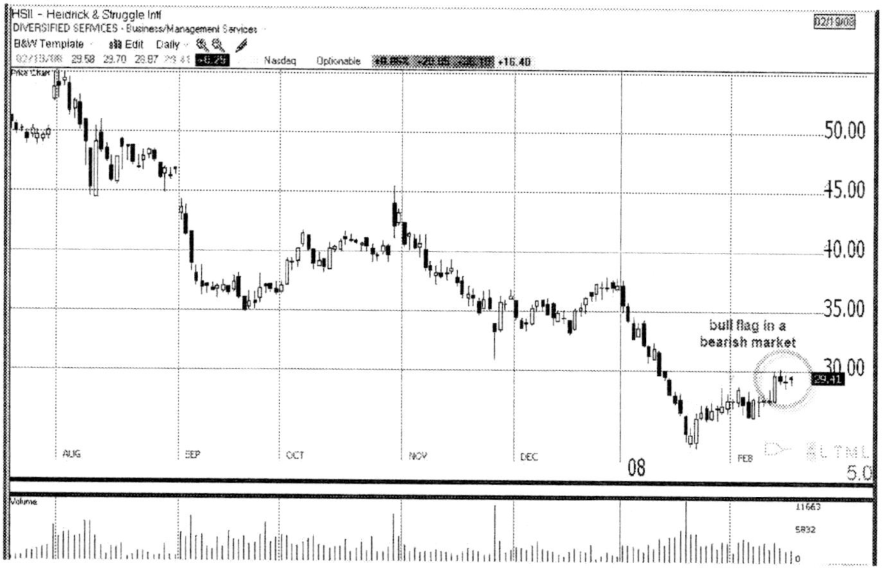

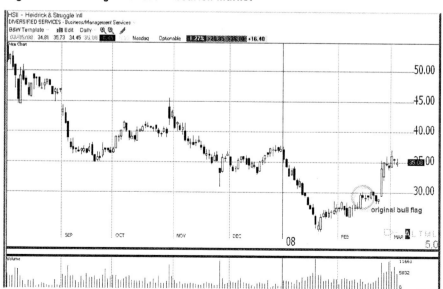

TC2000®.com. Courtesy of Worden Brothers Inc.

Sure enough, the earnings are a nice surprise to the market, and the stock rises over 20% to over $37, as shown in Figure 7.3.

Figure 7.3 Bull flag breakout in bearish market

TC2000®.com. Courtesy of Worden Brothers Inc.

But as can often happen with counter trend moves, the rise is short-lived, at least in the short term as support needs to be tested.

With this stock the diagonal trendline intersects with the horizontal line, marking the low of $33.84, which occurred on February 29 (see Figure 7.4). This would be the natural exit point if you hadn't already exited with a profit.

Figure 7.4 **Taking profits from bull flag breakout in bearish market**

TC2000®.com. Courtesy of Worden Brothers Inc.

Let's now look at an example of a bear flag in a bearish market in Figure 7.5. The stock is IRIS, viewed on February 13, with earnings on February 26. The pattern doesn't get a lot better than this.

Figure 7.5 Bear flag in bearish market

TC2000.com®. Courtesy of Worden Brothers Inc.

Now take a look at Figure 7.6 to see what happened next.

Figure 7.6 IRIS bear flag breakout

TC2000®.com. Courtesy of Worden Brothers Inc.

Down it went. You can use the trendline to determine your exit point with profits. Even several days later this trendline hasn't been hit, meaning that the profit is at least $4 (from around the $15 short entry point to around $11 where the trendline would force a buy-to-cover order if the stock consolidates further or rises from that level).

The next example is of a bull flag in a bull market on April 30. The stock is FWLT. This has been looking positive since the bull flag just a few days earlier on April 9 (see Figure 7.7). There is no imminent earnings announcement on this stock.

Figure 7.7 Bull flag in bullish market

TC2000®.com. Courtesy of Worden Brothers Inc.

The chart in Figure 7.8 shows that we have a bull flag forming a double top around $35.00 before retesting the highs and then zooming upward.

Notice how the stock price flies once it breaks the previous highs of just a few days ago. Again we can manage our trade by way of a diagonal trendline.

Before we move onto the next section, let's just acquaint ourselves with an "ugly" chart, seen in Figure 7.9. There is no discernable pattern in this next chart. The bars are long and have big tails, and it's simply a mess!

Figure 7.8 FWLT bull flag breakout

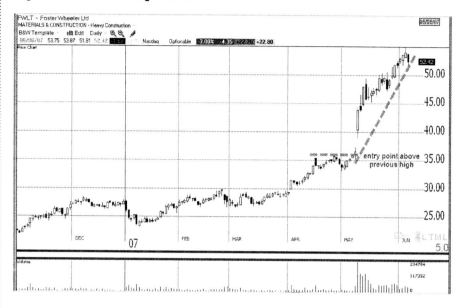

TC2000®.com. Courtesy of Worden Brothers Inc.

Figure 7.9 Ugly chart

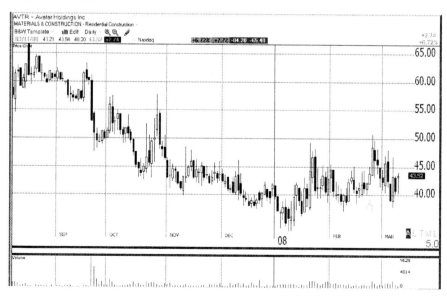

TC2000®.com. Courtesy of Worden Brothers Inc.

It's crucial that you can recognize the difference between a tradable pattern and one that's a mess. This will save you so much time and money in the short, medium, and long term. When you're going through the application and finding flags, the ugly charts should take you no more than a couple of seconds to reject.

2. **Research the news.**

The next step is to see if there's any news out for the stock that you're interested in trading.

Direction neutral trading (straddles and strangles)
When you're trading straddles, you don't want the news to have occurred yet, but you do want a news event (such as an earnings announcement) to be scheduled to occur in the following 1 to 2 weeks. You don't want to know what the news will entail and want it to be a surprise. In this way one of your option legs will rise sharply up, hopefully by more than the other leg moves down.

Directional trading
If you're trading flag patterns, long or short, you want the news to be in the past, and you don't want any news event ahead that may harm your directional trade.

Where to look
The easiest places to look are Yahoo Finance (http://finance.yahoo.com) and SmartMoney (www.smartmoney.com).

When you get to Yahoo Finance, shown in Figure 7.10, simply enter the stock ticker you're looking at and search under Headlines and Company Events. The Illuminati Trader and Flag-Trader software enables you to do this directly with one click of a button.

The same goes for SmartMoney. Enter the ticker symbol and then choose from the various tabs such as News.

With the stocks used as examples so far in this chapter, I discovered that HSII and IRIS both had earnings announcements, but FWLT did not. This will have a bearing on what strategies to trade in each case. The stocks with pending earnings announcements will be suitable for straddles, strangles, and the ratio backspreads. The stocks without pending earnings announcements will be suitable for all the favored strategies including the diagonal, long, and short directional positions.

Figure 7.10 Yahoo! Finance

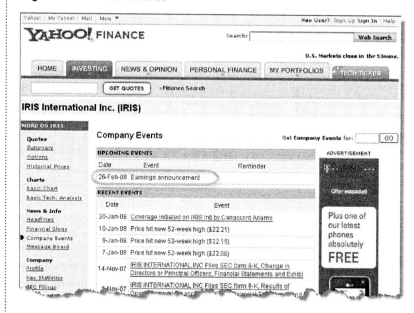

3. **Analyze options prices (if applicable).**

   If you're going to use options for your trade, particularly if you're contemplating a straddle or strangle, you must look at the options prices. An over-expensive straddle is not worth doing, and you should obey the parameters in Chapter 4, "Straddles and Strangles." If you want to trade pure volatility (as opposed to income) and the straddle looks too expensive, you should consider one of the two ratio backspreads.

   You can see how easy it is to view the options series and calculate the cost of your trades from Figure 7.11. Your broker will have a similar display to this.

   To verify that you're not overpaying for your options, you can use the implied volatility filters on www.illuminati-trader.com.

   We're restricted to black and white in these pages, but on the Illuminati-Trader site, the lines are in different colors. The idea is that you can easily distinguish the implied volatility for the front month options and the 2–4 month options that we typically look at for long straddles and strangles (see Figure 7.13).

Figure 7.11 Yahoo! option chain example

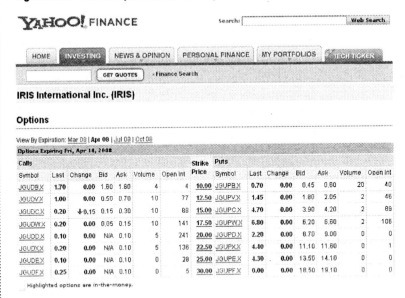

IRIS International Inc. (IRIS)

Options

View By Expiration: Mar 08 | Apr 08 | Jul 08 | Oct 08

Options Expiring Fri, Apr 18, 2008

Calls							Strike	Puts						
Symbol	Last	Change	Bid	Ask	Volume	Open Int	Price	Symbol	Last	Change	Bid	Ask	Volume	Open Int
JGUDB.X	1.70	0.00	1.60	1.60	4	4	10.00	JGUPB.X	0.70	0.00	0.45	0.60	20	40
JGUDV.X	1.00	0.00	0.50	0.70	10	77	12.50	JGUPV.X	1.45	0.00	1.80	2.05	2	46
JGUDC.X	0.20	↓0.15	0.15	0.30	10	88	15.00	JGUPC.X	4.70	0.00	3.90	4.20	2	89
JGUDW.X	0.20	0.00	0.05	0.15	10	141	17.50	JGUPW.X	6.80	0.00	6.20	6.60	2	106
JGUDD.X	0.10	0.00	N/A	0.10	5	241	20.00	JGUPD.X	2.20	0.00	8.70	9.00	0	0
JGUDX.X	0.20	0.00	N/A	0.10	5	136	22.50	JGUPX.X	4.40	0.00	11.10	11.60	0	1
JGUDE.X	0.10	0.00	N/A	0.10	0	28	25.00	JGUPE.X	4.30	0.00	13.50	14.10	0	0
JGUDF.X	0.25	0.00	N/A	0.10	0	5	30.00	JGUPF.X	0.00	0.00	18.50	19.10	0	0

Highlighted options are in-the-money.

Figure 7.12 Implied volatility graph

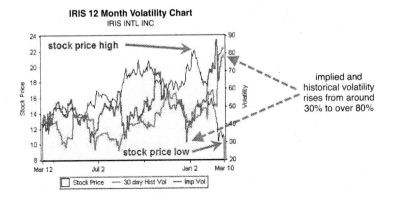

Many traders wrongly measure implied volatility against historical volatility as the Holy Grail. Supposedly if implied is less than historical, the options are a bargain and vice versa. This is not necessarily so. Far more important is what implied volatility is doing against itself. So if implied volatility is low compared with its own average for the last few months, and there's a flag pattern and an earnings report coming, then you might be very interested. If we had the same circumstances but implied volatility was high in comparison with itself, then you'd be more cautious. As you can see in the volatility chart in Figure 7.12, implied volatility is rising from March 11. However, at the end of December implied volatility was relatively low (and the corresponding stock price was at a high).

What a great trade buying long-term puts would have been at the time. Not only would they have risen as the stock halved from around $23, but the options implied volatility rises from around 30% to over 80%, so you would have benefited from that positive double whammy. It's often the case that as stocks rise, volatilities fall and vice versa. So when you buy puts on a high priced stock that's about to fall, you can often make a mint because the put intrinsic value will rise as the stock falls, and the implied volatility of the put will rise, driving up the time value portion of the put premium.

Where the options premiums are high (because of high implied volatilities), it's more likely that straddles and strangles will be prohibitively expensive. The ratio backspreads will therefore be a good alternative because with the backspreads you're buying *and* selling option premiums, which offset each other. The sold-legs effectively hedge your exposure to the high implied volatility of the bought legs.

Figure 7.13   Implied Volatility for Near-the-Money Options with 2-4 months left to expiration

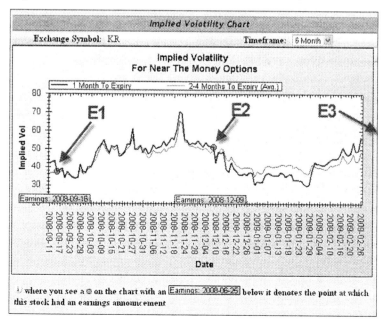

In Figure 7.13, see how Implied Volatility is rising as the stock now approaches a new earnings report (E3). Compared with the previous two earnings reports shown (E1 and E2), this may mean the options become prohibitively expensive for the purposes of trading a straddle or strangle.

We're now in a position to decide on our strategy.

4. Decide strategy.

Our choice of strategy depends on a number of factors:

- The chart pattern of the stock and the overall direction of the market (step 1).
- Whether news is in the past or future and the overall state of the market (step 2).
- The options prices where applicable* (step 3).

For example if you have a bull flag, news has been quiet but earnings will be coming in two weeks' time, and implied volatility is low compared with that of the prior three months, then you're likely to be interested in trading a straddle or strangle.

If you have a bear flag, earnings were reported a month ago, there's no news in the foreseeable future, and implied volatility is high, then you may be interested in trading a put ratio backspread once the support of the bear flag has broken down.

Table 7.1 is not meant to be definitive per se, but it gives you a feel for the factors you need to consider in order to arrive at your preferred volatility strategy.

Table 7.1 Strategies and associated chart patterns

Chart pattern	News	Volatility	→	Strategy
Bull flag	Earnings in two weeks' time, no news in the last month	Implied volatility low compared with last three months	→	Straddle or strangle if options prices permit according to rules in Chapter 4
Bear flag	Earnings four weeks ago, no news anticipated	Implied volatility low compared with last three months	→	Long put or put diagonal, contingent on break of bear flag support

* You can always choose to trade the stock long or short.

Double bottom	Earnings in two weeks time, no news in last month	Implied volatility high compared with last three months	➡	Consider put ratio backspread if stock breaks support
Cup and handle	Earnings three weeks ago, no news anticipated	Low implied volatility compared with last two months	➡	Call ratio backspread, diagonal call contingent on stock price breaking up through the flag resistance

5. **Place the trade.**

So here's where you put your analysis to the test. You may have noticed my mentioning placing trades contingent upon support or resistance being broken. You can place trades online in advance and "contingent" upon an event taking place. This makes trading flags so much easier where you only want to enter the trade upon support or resistance being broken to your specific price requirements. Several years ago, you'd have to have been stuck to the screens to have been able to place the trade on the break.

In the case of spread trades (that is, trades involving more than one leg), you can also specify a limit price at which to place the trade. For example, let's say you have a bull flag where the top of the flag is at $50.24. If you want to trade a diagonal call that is priced at $12.75 net debit (using the ask price for the buy leg and the bid price for the sell leg), you can specify through your online platform to execute the trade only at a limit price of $12.50 net debit for the diagonal call spread, contingent on the stock price breaking higher than say $50.35 (where the stock price has broken up through the top of the flag).

Most brokers offer virtual trading systems, so you can learn how to use their platforms before you start risking real money. I'd urge you to spend several hours getting used to the broker trading platform because it's all too easy to press the wrong button in the heat of trading with real money.

6. **Manage the trade.**

Once you're in the trade, you need to manage it.

With straddles, strangles, and the ratio backspreads, you have a time stop as opposed to a traditional price stop loss. If the stock hasn't moved shortly after the news event, you should exit the trade with a small loss. If the trade becomes profitable, you need to manage that profit by taking partial profits at logical targets. For straddles, strangles, and the ratio backspreads, these targets can be set by the trendline being breached. So in the case of a bull flag/straddle combination, if the stock breaks out after an earnings report, you should be able to draw an upward trendline (see Chapter 2, "Trends and Flags"). Make sure it's not too steep because you don't want to get stopped out too soon in case there's more of a move to follow. You want to give the stock every chance to keep going up, making your calls more valuable.

In terms of managing your money, go to www.manageyourtrade.com where you can use a free calculator to ensure you're managing your trade properly in terms of both risk and profits, according to the parameters in this book.

Learning Points

In this chapter you've seen how to arrive at the point where you select your strategy. The main criteria are

● The chart pattern of the stock and the overall direction of the market.

● Whether news is in the past or future and the overall state of the market.

● The options prices. The options price analysis includes analysis of the implied volatility of the option series you're looking to trade.

Once you've identified your chosen strategy, then it's time to trade and see if you can get a fill at the price you want. Sometimes you will, and sometimes you won't—that's just part of trading.

In the next chapter I get a bit more technical. It's not rocket science but is a little more mathematical in terms of understanding the formulas behind what we're doing. If you're math-phobic, just give it a glance over. If you're a math fiend, then take a look at the other references I provide so you can conduct deeper studies.

chapter 8

The Science of Volatility

I always try to keep things simple and explain things with pictures where possible. The aim of this chapter is to explain more about the mechanisms behind option pricing and how they might affect you as a trader. Frankly it would take an entire book to explain all the different methodologies, which are evolving all the time, but we certainly cover the essentials here.

The overall goal is to improve your trading performance, not make you a math egghead.

Options play a significant role in the financial markets, particularly during times of instability and increased market volatility. This is because they can be used by investors to hedge their positions in a highly leveraged fashion. Hedging risk is another way of saying reducing or mitigating risk. Admittedly some institutions are more responsible than others when it comes to hedging their risk exposures, but provided there is enough liquidity, there's always a way to limit risk.

For example, consider buying 100 shares of Bear Stearns (BSC) at $62.97 on March 11, 2008. Now, despite what CNBC was saying, if you're in the middle of a credit crunch, buying shares in banking stocks shouldn't seem like a good idea. But some people did just that. When you buy shares, theoretically speaking, your risk is what you pay for them, as the stock price could potentially fall to zero—although it's unlikely. The maximum risk on 100 shares at $62.97 is $6,297.

Options give you the ability to hedge such a position. You could hedge those long shares by buying a put, thereby creating what's known as a "synthetic call" or "married put" strategy. Let's say you only needed a couple of weeks of protection against a news report of some kind that you were feeling uneasy about. You could buy 1 contract of 60 strike April puts at 5.40, giving you "insurance" at that strike price level. The total paid for the insurance premium is $540 (5.40 x 100 x 1). The put option on that day was trading at an implied volatility of 86%, whereas its average for the past year was around 50% and had been as low as that in February. To give you an idea of the impact on the premium, if the implied volatility for the 60 strike April put was at 50%, the put premium would be 2.60. That's less than half of the 5.40 you'd have to have paid on March 11. You can be sure that someone somewhere was in the know about something, though it's also fair to say that the stock had already been falling precipitously in the weeks prior.

The risk profile of this trade looks like a long call (see Figure 8.1), but the leverage is completely different. You're long the stock and long puts, so your base cost is high. What you have, though, is protection against a catastrophic event where your risk is capped as the stock price hits the 60 strike price.

Figure 8.1 Synthetic long call risk profile

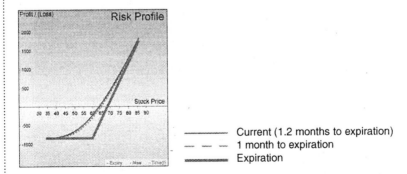

- Your risk on such a trade would be the premium paid and the difference between the stock price and the strike price:
  5.40 + 2.97 = 8.37

  This equates to $837 of risk on a total investment of $6,837. Remember the shares cost $6,297, and the put premium cost $540.

- Your maximum reward for the trade is unlimited because if the stock rises, your profits are not capped.

  Your breakeven point at expiration is the stock price plus the put premium:
  62.97 + 5.40 = 68.37
  In other words, the stock would have to rise by the amount you've insured it for.

So as you can see, a small investment of $540 can hedge a much larger one of $6,297, and remember, you can select different expiration dates that will correspond to the likely time length of your exposure. Also remember that you'd typically not hold the long put until expiration, so you'd get something back for that if you closed the entire position with time to spare. The point is that with a highly speculative play like BSC was at the time, it's crazy not to use options to hedge your position and reduce your overall risk.

Historical and Implied Volatility

At this point it would be a good idea to reacquaint yourself with the section on vega from Chapter 3, "Options and the Greeks," where volatility was discussed in some depth.

Remember there are two categories of volatility, historical and implied, as described in Table 8.1.

Table 8.1 Historical versus implied volatility

Historical volatility	Derived from the standard deviation of the stock price movement over a known period of time.
Implied volatility	Derived from the market price of the option itself.

Historical Volatility

Remember, historical volatility is an indication of how a security's price is moving and is recognized as a measure of risk. Higher volatility translates to greater uncertainty and greater risk.

Historical volatility is calculated by measuring the standard deviation of closing prices expressed as an annualized percentage figure. Volatility is not directional. If a stock is priced at $50 and has volatility of 20%, then we expect the stock to trade in the range of $40–$60 for the next year.

Standard deviation measures the changes in the past price of a security. The higher the standard deviation, the more volatile the security.

For example, say we have two stocks:

● Stock 1 typically gives returns of 10% with a standard deviation of 10%.
● Stock 2 typically gives returns of 15% with a standard deviation of 20%.

Our assessment of the two investments is based on risk and return. Stock 2 has much higher risk and only a modestly greater return. On the basis of the balance of risk and return, you may decide that Stock 1 is the better choice because Stock 2's additional 5% of return comes at the price of an extra 10% of risk (expressed by the standard deviation).

Calculating Historical Volatility in Excel

You can calculate the historical volatility of a stock on www.optioneasy.com or www.illuminati-trader.com. If, however, you want to evaluate the historical volatility of a stock and you can't find it anywhere, here's what you can do:

1. Get the data. Go to http://finance.yahoo.com, input the ticker of the stock, click the "historical prices" link on the left, and select the relevant dates (see Figure 8.2).

Figure 8.2 Yahoo! Price data

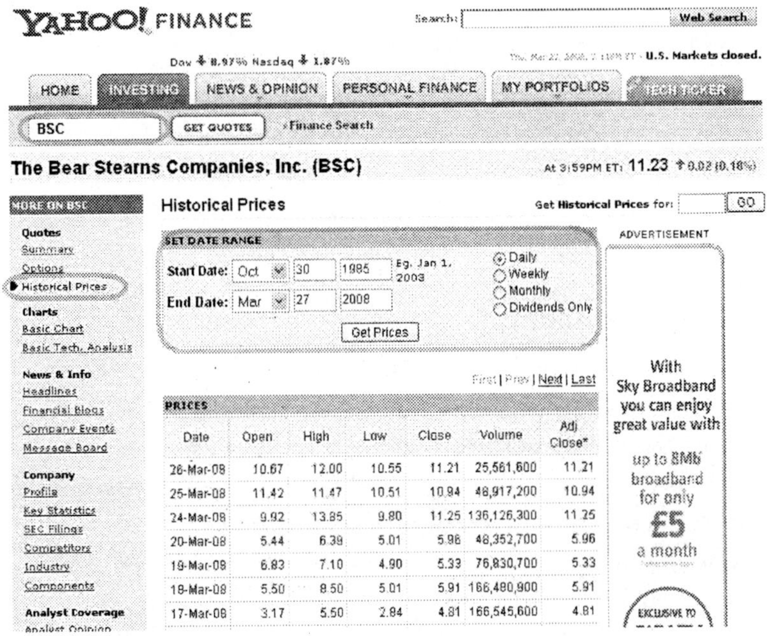

2. Choose the "download to spreadsheet" option at the bottom of the data series.

3. Now you have a spreadsheet that looks like the one in Figure 8.3:

Figure 8.3 Yahoo! data on spreadsheet

	A	B	C	D	E	F	G
1	Date	Open	High	Low	Close	Volume	Adj Close
2	26/03/2008	10.67	12	10.55	11.21	25561600	11.21
3	25/03/2008	11.42	11.47	10.51	10.94	48917200	10.94
4	24/03/2008	9.92	13.85	9.8	11.25	136126300	11.25
5	20/03/2008	5.44	6.39	5.01	5.96	46352700	5.96
6	19/03/2008	6.83	7.1	4.9	5.33	76830700	5.33
7	18/03/2008	5.5	8.5	5.01	5.91	166480900	5.91
8	17/03/2008	3.17	5.5	2.84	4.81	166545600	4.81
9	14/03/2008	54.24	54.79	26.85	30	186985600	30
10	13/03/2008	57.64	59.6	50.48	57	70720800	57
11	12/03/2008	65.5	67.82	61.35	61.58	26803300	61.58
12	11/03/2008	66.02	68.24	55.42	62.97	54966600	62.97
13	10/03/2008	70.28	70.59	60.26	62.3	32465300	62.3
14	07/03/2008	68.71	73	68.3	70.08	8034400	70.08
15	06/03/2008	75.21	76.59	69.86	69.9	9757600	69.9
16	05/03/2008	77.75	79.31	75.03	75.78	6809100	75.78
17	04/03/2008	76.76	78.03	74.69	77.17	5282100	77.17
18	03/03/2008	79.62	79.89	76.62	77.32	5408800	77.32
19	29/02/2008	68.7	73.55	8	8	5644300	6

4. Using the "Adj Close" as your closing price, enter four new columns of calculated data with the following headings (leave column H blank), as shown in Table 8.2.

Table 8.2

H	I	J	K	L
	Log Change	Mean	Deviation from mean	Deviation squared

5. In the first "log change" cell, input the following formula, referencing the first "Adj Close" cell:

=LN(G2/G3)

Copy the formula down to row 22 so that you've calculated 21 days worth of log changes.

6. In the first "mean" cell, input the following formula, which is going to calculate the average for 21 days of the log change.

=AVERAGE($I$2:$I$22)

Copy the formula down as far as you did before. The values should all be the same because of the "$" within the formula.

7. In the first "dev from mean" cell, input the following formula, which calculates the deviation from the mean of the log change for 21 days.

=I2-J2

Copy the formula down as far as you did before.

8. In the first "dev sq'd" cell, input the following formula, which calculates the deviation squared.

=K2 ^ 2

Copy the formula down as far as you did before.

9. In cell L24, under the "dev sq'd" column, input the following formula, which calculates the sum of 21 days of deviations squared:

    =SUM(L2:L22)

10. In cell L25, input the following formula, which calculates the standard deviation of the average day's change:

    =SQRT(L24/20)

11. In cell L26, input the following formula, which calculates the annualized volatility using 252 traded days:

    =L25*SQRT(252)

    Now, that's the long way to do it. Let's now do it the short way, and we should end up with the same number!

12. In cell L28, input the following formula, which calculates the annualized volatility in just one formula.

    =STDEV($I2:$I22)*SQRT(252)

Figure 8.4 Excel spreadsheet volatility calculation

	A	B	C	D	E	F	G	H	I	J	K	L	M
1	Date	Open	High	Low	Close	Volume	Adj Close		log change	mean	dev from mean	dev sq'd	
2	26-Mar-08	10.67	12	10.55	11.21	25561600	11.21		0.02438044	-0.09742	0.121803216	0.01483602	
3	25-Mar-08	11.42	11.47	10.51	10.94	48917300	10.94		-0.02794233	-0.09742	0.069480445	0.00482753	
4	24-Mar-08	9.92	13.85	9.8	11.25	136126300	11.25		0.635297648	-0.09742	0.732720424	0.53667922	
5	20-Mar-08	5.44	6.39	5.01	5.96	48352700	5.96		0.111719243	-0.09742	0.209142019	0.04374038	
6	19-Mar-08	6.83	7.1	4.9	5.33	76930200	5.33		-0.10329459	-0.09742	-0.005871817	3.4478E-05	
7	18-Mar-08	5.5	8.5	5.01	5.91	166480900	5.91		0.205948747	-0.09742	0.303371524	0.09203428	
8	17-Mar-08	3.17	5.5	2.84	4.81	166545600	4.81		-1.8305003	-0.09742	-1.733077521	3.00355769	
9	14-Mar-08	54.24	54.79	26.85	30	186886800	30		-0.64185389	-0.09742	-0.54443111	0.29640523	
10	13-Mar-08	57.64	58.6	50.48	57	70720800	57		-0.07728587	-0.09742	0.020135902	0.000040549	
11	12-Mar-08	65.5	67.62	61.35	61.58	26803300	61.58		-0.02332128	-0.09742	0.075101496	0.00564023	
12	11-Mar-08	60.02	60.24	55.42	62.97	54366600	62.97		0.010696997	-0.09742	0.108119773	0.01168908	
13	10-Mar-08	70.28	70.59	60.26	62.3	32466300	62.3		-0.11767602	-0.09742	-0.020253245	0.00041019	
14	07-Mar-08	68.71	73	68.3	70.08	8034400	70.08		0.002571797	-0.09742	0.099994574	0.00999091	
15	06-Mar-08	75.21	76.59	69.88	69.9	9757600	69.9		-0.08076876	-0.09742	0.01665402	0.00027736	
16	05-Mar-08	77.75	79.31	75.03	75.78	6809100	75.78		-0.01817637	-0.09742	0.079246401	0.00627999	
17	04-Mar-08	76.76	78.03	74.69	77.17	5292100	77.17		-0.00194187	-0.09742	0.095480902	0.0091166	
18	03-Mar-08	79.62	79.99	76.82	77.32	5408600	77.32		-0.03232245	-0.09742	0.065100329	0.00423805	
19	29-Feb-08	82.7	83.56	78.6	79.86	5544300	79.86		-0.05315732	-0.09742	0.044265455	0.00195943	
20	28-Feb-08	86.8	86.6	83.85	84.22	4186900	84.22		-0.03631304	-0.09742	0.061504736	0.00378283	
21	27-Feb-08	85.88	89.62	84.8	87.3	5245700	87.3		0.00943729	-0.09742	0.106860066	0.01141907	
22	26-Feb-08	85.93	87.62	85.37	86.48	4789500	86.48		-0.00277136	-0.09742	0.094651412	0.00895889	
23	25-Feb-08	84.11	87.44	82.94	86.72	6845700	86.72						
24	22-Feb-08	82.41	85.27	80.21	85.16	7266400	85.16					4.0664918	sum of deviations squared
25	21-Feb-08	83	85.29	82.02	82.23	5892300	82.23					0.45091528	standard deviation
26	20-Feb-08	78.9	83.39	78.06	93.05	7336500	83.05					7.15805817	annualized volatility
27	19-Feb-08	82.91	83.6	78.9	80.02	7214800	80.02						
28	15-Feb-08	79.36	84.03	77.57	82.79	20030500	82.79					7.15805817	annualized volatility check
29	14-Feb-08	80.15	80.15	77.53	78.47	5542400	78.47						

In this example using BSC, you can see how high the historical volatility was, largely because of the drop from $61.58 to $4.81 in just three days. Such a collapse is going to create a huge figure for volatility. Here, the 21-day figure for February 26 to March 26 is 715.81%—enormous by any standard.

Just so you can compare, the 21-day historical volatility of BSC from February 6 to March 6 is 47.64% where the price range of the stock moved from $69.90 to $87.30, still a healthy range in turbulent times.

Now let's look at the volatility view in Figure 8.5, and we can see graphically what's happened both to the historical and implied volatilities.

Figure 8.5 BSC implied versus historical volatility

You can see on the chart how historical volatility has gone over 600%. One of the conundrums we have in attempting to calculate the theoretical fair value for the option is what timeframe to use for historical volatility. In other words, what is the correct period of time to use for historical volatility when you're trying to calculate fair value?

Also notice that implied volatility reached a peak of over 250%. At www.illuminati-trader.com we're careful to select the strikes and expirations that are relevant to the straddles that we might want to trade. We also should assess volatility from earnings season to earnings season to see if we can spot a relative bargain in terms of implied volatility prior to an earnings announcement. This makes our research highly targeted to our specific strategy.

Normal Distribution and Random Walk

We already know that historical volatility is calculated by measuring the standard deviation of closing prices expressed as an annualized percentage figure. We can therefore define historical volatility as a one standard deviation of price change at the end of one year, expressed as a percentage.

Although this is not absolutely critical to your trading success by any means, if you want to understand the mechanics behind options pricing, you'd need to understand mathematical concepts such as the normal distribution function.[1]

---

[1] For a more detailed yet concise and relevant explanation, refer to *The Volatility Edge in Options Trading* by Jeff Augen (FT Press).

Before I explain the normal distribution, let's put it in the context of the stock market.

In the book *A Random Walk Down Wall Street*, Burton Malkiel asserted that market prices cannot be predicted. Since its publication in 1973, there have been countless books and software products published that claim the complete opposite of this. I like to remember Warren Buffett's quote: "Forecasting says much about the forecaster but nothing about the future." I'm a real student of the markets, and for my money both Gann and Elliott Theory, two methods that aspire to predict, are a complete waste of time, so potentially there's something to this random walk theory! That said, I've found certain patterns to work consistently in certain conditions (flag patterns for example), but a pattern on its own won't work. You need the pattern in the context of trend and a properly formulated trading plan that includes money management.

Another theory, the efficient market hypothesis (EMH) claims that all known information about a company is factored into the current stock price. However

● A market inefficiency occurs when the share price does not reflect all the available information at any given moment in time.

● "Strong form" efficiency asserts that share prices reflect all information at any given moment in time, and so all the information must be priced into the market. This can lead to some interesting discussions regarding insider trading, given that strong form efficiency asserts that all information, including information not known to the general public, is priced into the markets.

The random walk model states that stock price returns are similar to coin tosses and that future returns fit the standard normal distribution.

The *normal distribution*, also called the Gaussian distribution, is a probability distribution function that is applicable in many fields. The normal distribution is the most widely used family of distributions in statistics, and many statistical tests are based on the assumption of normality. The basic idea is as follows:

● 68.27% of all returns fall within 1 standard deviation of the mean

● 95.45% of all returns fall within 2 standard deviations of the mean

● 99.73% of all returns fall within 3 standard deviations of the mean

● 99.99% of all returns fall within 4 standard deviations of the mean

If you have a continuous random variable such as a stock price, this random variable can take on an infinite number of values, with the characteristic that there are no gaps between the values (in theory). Other examples of a continuous random variable are the speed of a car or the time of the day. It can be argued that stock prices are noncontinuous because gaps can and do happen between the close and the open of the markets. However, the counter to that argument is that gaps can be seen as "illusions" and that in reality the stock price really did move continuously at the time when the market was closed. As such, intraday gaps are relatively infrequent compared with overnight gaps. However, gaps may occur intraday when important economic news is released during trading hours.

A random variable is said to have a normal distribution if it has a probability distribution that is symmetric and bell-shaped, as in Figure 8.6.

Figure 8.6 Normal distribution curve

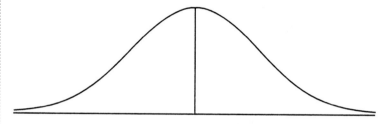

There are two critical factors about this diagram.

1. The total area under the curve represents one, or 100%. In other words, all possibilities reside under the curve.

2. The area is what will be used to measure probabilities of a random variable's likelihood of occurring. This will correlate directly with its distance from the mean, which is located at the center of the diagram where the bell curve peaks.

In practice, the big assumption is that the data is from an approximately normally distributed population. This is frequently justified by the classical central limit theorem, which says that sums of many independent, identically distributed random variables tend toward the normal distribution as a limit. If that assumption is justified, then about 68% of the values are within one standard deviation of the mean, about 95% of the values are within two standard deviations, and about 99.7% lie within three standard deviations. This is known as the *empirical rule*.

With σ standing for standard deviation, the confidence intervals for the normal distribution are as shown in Table 8.3.

Table 8.3 Normal distribution confidence intervals

SD	Probability	Interpretation
1σ	68.27%	68.27% of the values will be within 1 standard deviation of the mean
2σ	95.45%	95.45% of the values will be within 2 standard deviations of the mean
3σ	99.73%	99.73% of the values will be within 3 standard deviations of the mean
4σ	99.99%	99.99% of the values will be within 4 standard deviations of the mean

The mean and the standard deviation of a series of data are usually reported together. Obviously, for a data point right at the mean, the standard deviation from the mean is smaller than from any other point in the series if the center of the data is measured around the mean value (see Figure 8.7).

Figure 8.7 Normal distribution curve with probabilities

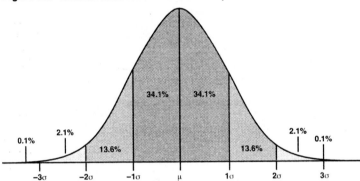

Example

If a stock trades at $100 with a volatility of 40%, then a one standard deviation change during a one-year time period will see the stock price rise to $140 or fall to $60. The normal distribution assumes there is a 68.2% chance that the final price will fall within this range, although strictly speaking, an adjustment for interest rates is also required. If base rates are 4%, a one standard deviation price change at year end will be $104 x 40% = $41.60. So there would be a 68.2% chance that the stock would trade between $62.40 and $145.60. This is a highly simplistic example. A more accurate definition for volatility is the annualized standard deviation of the return using *continuous compounding*.

When I say that returns are normally distributed, I'm saying that they conform to a symmetrical bell-shaped curve. So for every possible upward price movement, there must be the possibility of an equal downward price movement. This clearly cannot be the case for future prices given that a $15 stock can rise by $20 to $35 but cannot fall by $20 to -$5. This is where continuous compounding comes into play.

If a $50 stock were to rise five times by moves of 10% each, the stock would rise to $80.53, a total increase of 61.05%. For each time the stock increases by 10%, the base figure has risen by more than the one before, the formula for the final figure being $50 \times (1.10^{\wedge}5) = 80.53$.

Table 8.4

	$50	55	60.50	66.55	73.05	80.53
% increase ➜		+10%	+10%	+10%	+10%	+10%
$ increase ➜		+5	+5.50	+6.05	+6.50	+7.48

If the same stock were to fall five times by moves of 10% each, the stock would fall to $29.52, representing a fall of 40.95%. For each time the stock decreases by 10%, the base figure has fallen by less than the one before, the formula here for the final figure being $50 \times (0.90^{\wedge}5) = 29.52$.

Table 8.5

	$50	45	40.50	36.45	32.81	29.52
% decrease ➜		-10%	-10%	-10%	-10%	-10%
$ decrease ➜		-5	-4.50	-4.05	-3.64	-3.29

In this way, the distribution of final prices is skewed so that no price can ever fall below zero. Therefore the continuous compounding of normally distributed price changes will cause prices at maturity to be lognormally distributed. The lognormal hypothesis is the key to options pricing theory and looks more like what you see in Figure 8.8.

Figure 8.8 Skewed normal distribution curve

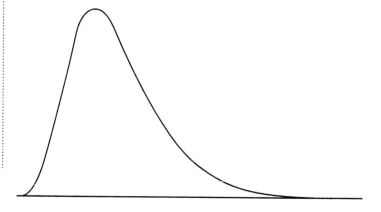

The big debate is whether it's sound to assume that stock prices are distributed normally. There's an argument to suggest that in a practical sense they are because the normal distribution function seems to work much of the time. However, this argument is technically incorrect because large movements in prices (surges and crashes) are more frequent than would be predicted in a normal distribution. Such observations have encouraged modified theories such as Lévy Flight, a random walk that is occasionally disrupted by large movements. In 1995, Rosario Mantegna and Gene Stanley analyzed one million records of the S&P 500 market index, calculating the returns over a five year period. Their conclusion was that stock market returns are more volatile than a Gaussian distribution but less volatile than a Lévy Flight.

Implied Volatility

Remember how I mentioned that the option pricing models use historical volatility to estimate the theoretical value of an option? We do this by inputting the historical volatility figure into the options pricing model as shown in Figure 8.9.

Figure 8.9 Calculating the theoretical value of an option

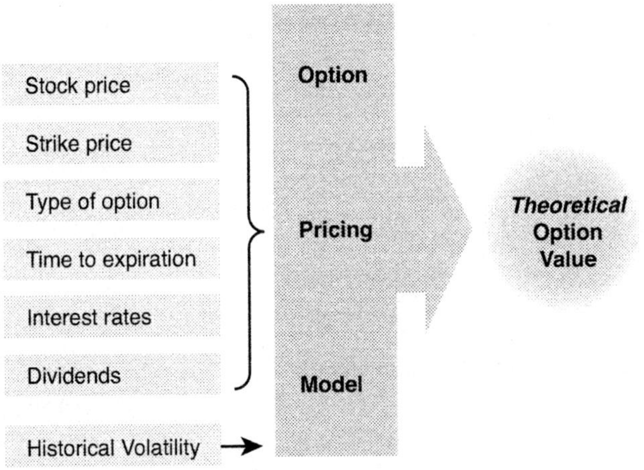

We get onto specific option pricing models later, but for now we know that the theoretical option value isn't necessarily the option value that is quoted on the exchanges. Real-life option prices are determined by forces such as demand and supply for a particular strike and expiration at a particular time.

From a simplistic viewpoint, implied volatility gives the price of an option, whereas historical volatility gives an indication of its actual value. For instance, if you're anticipating greater historical volatility than the current implied volatility, then you might consider current options premiums to be under-valued, particularly if you think that implied volatility will mimic the action of historical volatility. This may lead you toward the strategies we've studied so far such as straddles, ratio backspreads, or diagonals, all of which benefit from increasing volatility once you're in the trade. However, it's worth noting again that a better technique is to compare implied volatility against itself for the relevant strikes and expirations to see if you're getting good value from the options you're trading.

Figure 8.10 Calculating the implied volatility of an option

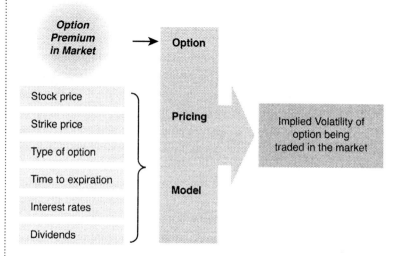

In the meantime, it's quite feasible that tell-tale price action in the options market may precede events in the stock market. In fact this was one of the main observations of the October 1987 crash where the derivatives markets were ahead of the game and in some quarters were blamed for the crash itself. The tell-tale signs are

● Large movements in implied volatility, especially for the near month options

● Large increase in option volumes

● Large changes in open interest

● Unusual imbalance changes between calls and puts.

Is it possible that stocks could be influenced in advanced by derivatives traders? Or do option traders predict the movements about to occur in stock pricing? The phenomenon of strike price pinning, where the stock latches onto a strike price, is evidence that the presence of options could have a significant impact upon the stock price itself.

Option Pricing Models

Up until equity options were launched on the Chicago Board Options Exchange (CBOE) in 1973, options had traded in small numbers on an over the counter (OTC) basis. At the time there was also no generally accepted pricing methodology for these instruments.

Since that time various option pricing models have come into existence. In chronological order, in 1973 Fischer Black and Myron Scholes published a new model for pricing options that has become the cornerstone for how most markets would price options on equities, indices, and futures for years to come. The model has been extended and tweaked to include iterations for dividends and other factors. The key to the model was that the interaction of time and uncertainty could be quantified so that derivative values could be easily calculated with reasonable precision. The Black-Scholes options pricing model is the best known and the most widely used but by no means the only model out there, nor necessarily the most accurate.

In 1979 John Cox, Stephen Ross, and Mark Rubenstein constructed a binomial tree approach representing the different possible paths that a stock price may follow during an option's lifetime until expiration. Subsequent extensions and refinements of binomial trees have overcome some of the limitations that restricted this model and that continue to hamper Black-Scholes.

Let's look briefly at both the Black-Scholes model and the Cox Ross Rubenstein model and examine their relative merits.

Black-Scholes

The Black-Scholes model is used to calculate a theoretical option price (ignoring dividends paid during the life of the option) using the five key determinants of an option's value: stock price, strike price, volatility, time to expiration, and the risk-free interest rate (central bank base rates).

The formula for calculating the theoretical call price is as follows:

$$C = S_0 e^{-qt} N(d_1) - Xe^{-rt} N(d_2)$$

Where:

$$d_1 = \frac{\ln (S_0 / X) + (r - q + \sigma^2 / 2)\, t}{\sigma\sqrt{t}}$$

And:

$$d_2 = d_1 - \sigma\sqrt{t}$$

For puts the equation is:

$$P = Xe^{-rt} N(-d_2) - S_0 e^{-qt} N(d_1)$$

Table 8.6 displays the variables in these equations.

Table 8.6 Black-Scholes formulae components

C	Call price
P	Put price
S_0	Stock price at time = 0
X	Strike price
t	Time until expiration expressed as a percentage of a year
r	Risk-free interest rate
σ	Historical volatility of the stock
ln	Natural logarithm
N(x)	Standard normal cumulative distribution function
e	The exponential function

The d_1 and d_2 relationship exists because:

$$\ln (S_0 e^{-qt} / X) = \ln (S_0 / X) - qt$$

Puts and calls are related by way of "put-call parity." Where this is violated there may be arbitrage (risk-free profit taking) opportunities, which typically vanish rapidly.

$$C + Xe^{-rt} = P + S_0$$

The Black-Scholes model is based on a normal distribution of underlying asset returns, which is the same thing as saying that the underlying asset prices themselves are log normally distributed. As we know from before, the lognormal distribution has a longer right tail compared with a normal, or bell-shaped, distribution because stock prices can only go down as far as zero. The lognormal distribution allows for a stock price distribution between zero and infinity and has an upward bias, representing the reality that a stock price can fall by a maximum of 100% but can rise by an infinite amount.

Of course there are equations for all the Greeks as well, as shown in Table 8.7.

Table 8.7 Black-Scholes Greeks formulae components

Greek	Formula
Delta $\triangle$ c	$= N(d_1)$
Delta $\triangle$ p	$= N(d_1) - 1$
Gamma Γ c	$= N_1(d_1) / S\sigma \sqrt{t}$
Gamma Γ p	$= N_1(d_1) / S\sigma \sqrt{t}$
Theta Θ c	$= [S\sigma / 2\sqrt{t}] N_1(d_1) + Xe - (rt) r N(d_2)$
Theta Θ p	$= [S\sigma / 2\sqrt{t}] N_1(d_1) - Xe - (rt) r N(-d_2)$
Vega c	$= S[\sqrt{t}] N_1(d_1)$
Vega p	$= S[\sqrt{t}] N_1(d_1)$
Rho c	$= t Xe - (rt) N(d_2)$
Rho p	$= -t Xe - (rt) N(-d_2)$

For more details on the Greeks refer back to Chapter 3.

As mentioned earlier, stock price distributions often do not follow the lognormal distribution. Lévy addressed this phenomenon with his model. Historical distributions of underlying asset returns often have fatter left and right tails than a normal distribution, indicating that dramatic market moves (both up and down) occur with greater frequency than would be predicted by a normal distribution of returns.

As a direct result of this, ATM options may sometimes experience lower implied volatility than deep OTM or deep ITM options. This is as a result of increased demand or floor traders pricing up the far away strike options to compensate themselves for the extra potential risk they perceive of a wild price swing in the stock. That extra risk arises because wild stock price swings could cause the local floor trader to make a significant loss or be exercised when selling those options.

This phenomenon is known as the *volatility smile*, as depicted in Figure 8.11.

Figure 8.11 Volatility smile

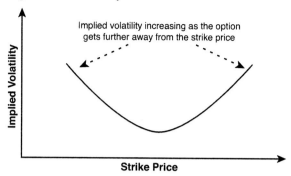

In practice, the volatility smile is asymmetrical for equity and index options and symmetrical for commodity options only.

Where you find a volatility smile, you may become interested in strategies like diagonal spreads and ratio backspreads, where you buy the NTM options and sell the further away strike options. If you can do this and combine the right chart pattern and news event (or non-event) to the equation, you're really marrying practice and theory in a powerful way.

To assess whether a trade is good value, experienced options traders will compare implied volatility against both the historical volatility of the stock and the historical implied volatility of comparable strikes and expiration periods.

We already know that options prices are highly sensitive to changes in volatility, and we've identified that for the purposes of options pricing models, volatility cannot be directly observed and must therefore be estimated.

The chief criticism of Black-Scholes is that a fixed figure for volatility must be priced into an options contract. Remember from Chapter 1, "Introduction to Options," the seven factors that affect an option's premium:

1. The type of option (call or put)

2. The stock price

3. The strike price

4. The expiration date

5. Volatility—implied and historical

6. Risk-free interest rate

7. Dividends

Volatility will vary from day to day, so a fixed figure for volatility is unrealistic. The Black-Scholes model was designed around options that can only be exercised at expiration (European-style). U.S. equity options allow the option buyer to exercise before expiration (American-style), which in theory adds extra value to the option. However, early exercise of an ITM option means that time value is thrown away, so it rarely happens and in my opinion carries little practical value other than when a big dividend is payable on the stock.

An American-style call on a non-dividend paying asset is worth the same as its European-style equivalent as there is rarely any advantage in exercising early. In theory the stock price will drop by the amount of the dividend as soon as the stock goes ex-dividend. This means that calls will drop in value and puts will gain in value.

Example

- Stock = $60
- You own a deep ITM 50 strike call expiring in ten days. The option is trading at $11.00, and we'll assume its delta is 1.00.
- Tomorrow the stock will open ex-dividend with a $0.50 dividend payable.

Your three choices are as follows:

1. Hold the option
2. Exercise the option early
3. Sell the option.

- The stock price will fall by $0.50 when the stock goes ex-dividend, and because the call has a 100% delta, in theory it would fall by at least $0.50 in value, say 5%. However, if this happened in reality, option traders would jump on the opportunity to sell naked calls and realize a riskless 5% profit at the market open the very next morning. Arbitrage traders would simply sell naked calls prior to every ex-dividend date for every dividend paying stock.

The reality is that certain market mechanisms make this impossible. Options prices anticipate every announced event including dividend payments. Reductions in implied volatility are the prevailing mechanism for offsetting impending dividend payments. Deep ITM options with little excess time premium left on the ex-dividend date will exhibit large bid-ask spreads that make it impossible for a call holder to avoid the price decrease. In these circumstances it's not uncommon for a $10 ITM option to have a bid price lower than $10, thereby rendering it impossible for the naked call seller to take advantage of the ex-dividend price decrease.

In our example the option has $1.00 of excess time premium. This price necessarily reflects a combination of reduced implied volatility and an abnormally wide gap between the bid and ask. The adjustment will be reversed and the price restored the moment the dividend is paid. The same applies to any distortions with the bid-ask spread.

In reality, no investor would purchase call options that are guaranteed to immediately lose 5% of their value.

- If you exercise early, you buy the stock at $50 when it's worth $60, meaning a $10 benefit. The stock would fall by $0.50 in value, but that would be negated as you'd receive the $0.50 dividend. Your sale value here is effectively $10.

- If you sell the option, you benefit from both time and intrinsic value. In theory you sell the option for $11, which is a better result than exercising it and receiving only $10. However, you have to factor in the likely bid-ask distortion, which at worst would mean selling below $10 depending on the level of distortion.

A dividend arbitrage typically involves buying both stock and ITM puts, typically where the remaining time premium of the puts is smaller than the impending dividend payment. This can occur when the market anticipates that the stock will fall less than the dividend amount.

Another weakness of Black-Scholes is that it doesn't cater well for lumpy, irregular dividend payments. The formula can be adjusted for a continuous dividend payment, but dividends are typically never paid out in this way.

The main advantage of the Black-Scholes model is its efficiency. It allows you to calculate a very large number of option prices in a very short time. When you consider how many optionable U.S. stocks there are (around 2,000) and how many strikes and expirations they all have, you're talking millions of rows of data over an assessable period of time, requiring a lot of processing power.

Various adjustments are sometimes made to the Black-Scholes price to enable it to approximate American option prices (e.g., the Fischer Black Pseudo-American method), however these only work well within certain parameters and don't work so well for puts.

Cox Ross Rubinstein (the Binomial Model)

The binomial options pricing model is highly versatile and simple. It involves creating a *binomial tree* diagram that represents the different paths that an outcome (option price) may follow during a certain time period (the time to expiration).

Because each step is documented and passed through in order to reach the end valuation, the binomial method is able to handle a variety of conditions that other models cannot cope with. This is mainly because the binomial model is able to adjust itself along with the underlying instrument over the discreet period of time, whereas other models are limited by a snapshot approach. In practical terms this means that volatility can be adjusted as we move through the binomial lattice tree.

As the name suggests, the binomial model involves a series of binary outcomes. Over a period of time the option price is faced with junctures (nodes) at which it can either move up or down by a given amount. Each node represents a possible price of the stock at a particular point in time. This price evolution forms the basis for the option valuation. The end result is a binomial tree with many possible price outcomes. The span of the tree (the number of possible outcomes) relates directly to the number of discrete timeframes chosen. This process is iterative in nature, starting at each final node and working backwards through the tree to the first node (the valuation date) where the calculated result will be the option value.

The probability of an up mode is denoted as "p." Therefore the probability of a down move must be "1 – p." Let's value an option using the binomial method:

- Stock = $70

- Over the next discreet time period the stock will either move up by $3 (u = 3) or down by $3 (d = 3).

- There is a 50/50 chance of both u and d occurring.

- Time is the only one (node) left before expiration, and we'll ignore interest rates and dividends for this example.

  - 70 strike call = 0.50 x (73 – 70) + 0* = $1.50

  - 65 strike call = 0.50 x (73 – 65) + 0.50 x (67 – 65) = 4 + 1 = $5.00

Both strikes here are ITM, so we'd expect positive values.

---

* The zero here is achieved by the equation: 0.50 x (67 - 70), where 67 - 70 will equal zero as we cannot have a negative intrinsic value.

In constructing the binomial tree, if the probability of an up or down move remains equal at each node, we can calculate the probability of each outcome at expiration. The expected return for any particular ITM option will be equal to

(stock price – strike price) x probability of that outcome

Let's create our own tree now.

Figure 8.12 demonstrates a four-time-step binomial tree with nodal probabilities of p and 1 - p. At each node the value can rise or fall by 5%. The value of each node is equal to the up or down ratio multiplied by the previous node's value. The up ratio is 1.05, and the down ratio is 0.95.

Figure 8.12 Binomial tree

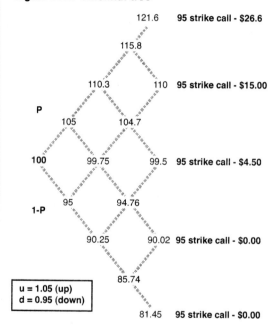

This example is very simplified. In practice, the lifespan of an option contract will usually be divided into 30 or more steps with each node containing a binomial stock price fork.

Because of its step-by-step approach, the binomial model can used to value American style options, which can be exercised at any point.

Although slower than the Black-Scholes model, this is considered more accurate, particularly for longer-dated options and options on securities with dividend payments. Also you can make adjustments for volatility as you move along the tree, making the model far more responsive and reflective of real market conditions than Black-Scholes.

For options with several sources of uncertainty or for exotic options with complicated features, this lattice style approach is not practical. Instead Monte Carlo option models are more suitable. However, Monte Carlo simulation is time-consuming in terms of computation and is not used when the binomial or Black-Scholes methods will suffice.

So let's recap: The binomial model breaks down the time to expiration into a number of time intervals or steps. A tree of stock prices is initially produced working forward from the present to expiration. At each step it is assumed that the stock price will move up or down by an amount calculated using volatility and time to expiration. This produces a binomial distribution of underlying stock prices. The tree represents all the possible paths that the stock price could take during the life of the option.

At the end of the tree (at expiration), all the nodal option prices for each of the final possible stock prices are known as they equal their intrinsic values.

Next the option prices at each step of the tree are calculated working back from expiration to the present. In the preceding example only the five option prices at the end of the fourth node are filled, as these are the (intrinsic) values at expiration. The option prices at each step are used to calculate the option prices at the next step of the tree using a risk neutral valuation based on

● The probabilities of the stock prices moving up or down

● The risk-free interest rate

● The time interval of each step

Any adjustments to stock prices (e.g., dividends) or option prices (e.g., early exercise in the case of American style options) are incorporated into the calculations at the required point in time. At the top of the tree you are left with one option price.

A binomial tree that approximates the lognormal distribution is built on probabilities and up/down ratios defined as follows:

$$u = e^{\sigma\sqrt{\Delta t}}$$
$$d = 1/u$$
$$p = \frac{e^{r\Delta t} - d}{u - d}$$

Table 8.8 provides the meaning of the variables.

Table 8.8 Binomial tree formulae components

u	Up ratio
d	Down ratio
p	Inter-nodal probability
Δt	Length of time in years (time in years/number of time steps)
σ	Annualized volatility
r	Expected return of the stock (% per annum)

The classic binomial model is based on fixed volatility (like Black-Scholes), however it is possible to extend the binomial model so that volatility can vary with time and the underlying stock price at each node. Sophisticated traders refer to a "volatility surface" that has a three-dimensional shape that maps time, price, and volatility. Quantitative analysts are able to create customized volatility maps for individual stock behavior for specific events such as earnings, FOMC meetings, and the various economic reports.

The big advantage the binomial model has over the Black-Scholes model is that it can be used to accurately price American-style options. This is because the binomial model enables us to check every step in an option's lifespan for the possibility of early exercise. Early exercise may occur because of a dividend or in a situation where a deep ITM option is priced in the market at less than its intrinsic value. In such a case of mispricing, early exercise is the only way of extracting the full intrinsic value from the position.

The main limitation of the binomial model is its relatively slow speed compared with Black-Scholes. It's great for a few calculations at a time, but even with today's most powerful PCs, the binomial model is not a practical solution for the calculation of tens of thousands of prices in a few seconds.

Other models have been developed specifically to deal with American-style option pricing in an efficient manner. If you want to investigate further, three of the better models are described in Table 8.9.

Table 8.9   Other options pricing models

Roll, Geske, and Whaley	This is an analytic solution that can be used for pricing an American-style call on a stock paying discreet dividends.
Black's model for American-style calls	An iterative analytic solution that makes adjustments to the stock price and expiration date in order to account for early exercise. This model uses Black-Scholes and adds a few bells and whistles.

Table 8.9 continued

Barone-Adesi and Whaley	This is another analytic solution for American-style options but assumes a continuous dividend is paid (which isn't realistic but is the best an analytic solution can probably achieve when it comes to lumpy dividend payments). As with the RGW formula, it involves solving equations iteratively, so it is much slower than Black-Scholes but much faster than the binomial model.

Learning Points

We've only scratched the surface in this chapter, but you now have an idea of the complexity that can be involved in valuing option prices.

The binomial and Black-Scholes models converge as they both assume that stock prices follow a lognormal distribution. As a result of this, for European-style options the binomial model must cope with a greater number of iterations (as there is no early exercise) and therefore converges toward Black-Scholes. For European-style options Black-Scholes can be seen as a binomial model with an infinite number of steps. Put another way, the binomial model provides discrete approximations to the continuous process underpinning the Black-Scholes (analytic) model.

If you're analyzing vast amounts of data comprising several stocks, then analytic models like Black-Scholes are the practical solution for pricing options. Mathematically speaking these analytical models are perfectly adequate for European-style options but are more limited when it comes to the pricing of American-style options other than calls on non-dividend paying assets. For American-style options the binomial approach is technically the most sound.

The modeling of prices and the formula base involved is interesting for all option traders. But in practice if you can find an appropriate stock (say, a trending stock that is forming a flag pattern) and you can pick up the options trade at a real bargain, then you have a phenomenal chance of making great profits.

While theory is useful as a foundation to your knowledge, it isn't going to make you a great trader. Practical implementation of a workable trading plan is going to make you a great trader. So that's what we're going to focus on in the final chapter, which will help you put everything together in a practical framework.

chapter 9

Trading Plans and Putting It All Together

You're now armed with two stock strategies and six major options strategies to take advantage of volatile markets.

Stock strategies:

- Bull flags (long stock)
- Bear flags (short stock)

Options strategies:

- Straddles
- Strangles
- Call ratio backspreads
- Put ratio backspreads
- Diagonal calls
- Diagonal puts

You could add to this list the long call and long put provided you trade them deep ITM and contingent on a breakout of the stock price. You'd trade the long call contingent on the bull flag breakout and the long put contingent on the bear flag breakout.

Ideally you want to enter your trades while volatility is low and exit after a surge of volatile action in the markets.

In Chapter 8, "The Science of Volatility," we went through the practical steps of how to find suitable candidate stocks and then trade as follows:

1. Find the tradable chart pattern.

2. Research the news.

3. Analyze the option prices (if applicable).

4. Decide strategy.

5. Place the trade.

6. Manage the trade.

Now let's go through each strategy in turn and work through a sample trading plan for each.

Flag Trades

We'll create separate trading plans for bull and bear flags.

Bull Flag

● **Find the tradeable chart pattern.**
EOG is an oil stock that is demonstrating very bullish signals during a very bearish market. This counter trending stock is one of the few bull flags around during February 2008. We wouldn't typically buck the trend of the market by trading a bull flag in a bear market (or vice versa), but this is clearly a stock that has been getting stronger (see Figure 9.1).

Figure 9.1 EOG bull flag

TC2000®.com. Courtesy of Worden Brothers Inc.

- **Research the news (on Yahoo Finance or Smartmoney.com).**
  Earnings were released on February 7 and were very positive with a 51%
  increase in profits. No further announcements are pending as we view this
  chart.

- **Analyze the option prices (if applicable).**
  With this stock, if we were going to trade options, we would buy calls or
  look at a diagonal call as this is looking bullish. For illustration purposes,
  we should simply buy the stock here.

- **Decide strategy.**
  As of February 21 the earnings announcement is now two weeks in the
  past, so we should be satisfied that there are no surprises on the way. This
  means we would lean toward a directional strategy, such as buying stock or
  deep ITM calls.

- **Place the trade.**
  The bull flag chart pattern is strong here, so we're interested. It needs to
  clear past $101 for any trade to be entered. We enter a buy stop limit to
  open at $101.25 together with an attached (or if done) stop loss order at
  $93.60, which is below the low of $93.80. This is an area of controversy.
  The low bar in this flag pattern occurred on February 15 and is a bit out of

whack with the rest of the pattern. As such we could actually ignore it, particularly as it's a "rogue" bar that probably took out a lot of stop orders before the price ran back upward. Interestingly, February 15 was a Friday, and volume was down that day. We have two other choices. Either ignore that bar completely and enter the stop below the low of February 19 as the low of the flag or enter the stop loss just below the close of the February 15 bar. Whichever one we use will impact the number of shares we can buy. Refer to www.manageyourtrade.com for the free online trade management calculator.

If we have $50,000 of trading capital available, then we may choose to risk only 3% on this trade, or $1,500. Our risk is the difference between our entry ($101.25) and our stop ($93.60), which would be $7.65 per share (1,500/7.65 = 196 shares) and will cost $19,853 plus commissions. That's almost 40% of our trading capital spent on just one trade. Therefore we may also decide that we will not spend more than 20% of our trading capital on any one position (20% x 50,000 = $10,000). This means we can buy 98 shares (10,000/101.25), call it a round 100 shares we can buy here. Our maximum risk barring a completely unexpected calamity is 100 x 7.65 = $765, which is 7.55% of what we spent on the trade ($10,125) and only 1.53% of our $50,000 trading capital. That's pretty safe.

When it comes to placing orders, different brokers have different terminology, so you need to ensure you're completely familiar with your broker's trading platform. You only want to buy the stock as it trades up past $101.25 and your limit order is $101.25. You also have your stop loss in place the instant you're in the position, so you're covered unless it gaps against you. This is unlikely with news already in the past and with a strong uptrend in place together with the strong bullish pattern. If this stock were to gap down, it's unlikely that you'd be affected as it would have to break out upward first to trigger your buy order.

Here's how the stock price broke out to the upside (see Figure 9.2).

Figure 9.2 EOG flag breakout and stop loss positioning

TC2000®.com. Courtesy of Worden Brothers Inc.

If we place the order on February 21, we may have to re-enter the trade on subsequent days if the stock remains in the consolidation pattern. On February 25 the stock clears $101.25, and our order is executed. Our stop order also goes live into the market but is not executed unless the stock price falls to $93.60. This is highly unlikely given the surge upward in the stock price.

● **Manage the trade.**

As the stock rises we can do three things:

- Partially exit the trade as it reaches a predefined target.
- Raise your initial stop loss to near our trade entry point.
- Put in a trendline to stop ourselves out with profits.

If we look at the pattern again, we can see that the stock moves sharply from $90 to just over $100. Using the 1:1 rule, the stock could feasibly reach $110. However, we're conservative, so we'll target the halfway point at $105. This is reached on February 26, only two days after your trade is executed (see Figure 9.3).

Figure 9.3 EOG bull flag initial profit target

TC2000®.com. Courtesy of Worden Brothers Inc.

So we've exited half our position, selling 50 shares for $5,250, the profit being a mere $187.50, but don't knock it. We want to get used to taking profits. If we don't the market will swipe them back! At this point we'll also raise the stop to just below the top of the flag. Again, barring a complete catastrophe, we now cannot suffer a loss on this trade. If the stock comes back to the flag, then we'll lose marginally on the 50 shares we have left in the trade. With our stop raised to $100.75, we would stand to lose only $25 on those 50 shares outstanding, and we'd still make an overall profit of $162.50 on the trade in only a couple of days. Ok, it's not millions at this stage, but this is an illustration. Percentage-wise we're doing well with a minimum return of around 1.6% in just a couple of days. If you keep doing that, you'd be one of the greatest traders who ever lived.

So now we ride the remaining 50 shares until our trendline stops us out. At this point we can put in a trendline. This isn't an exact science, but the general rule is (with an uptrend) to draw the line along the lows of the bars (see Figure 9.4).

We can use some discretion here by adjusting the angle of the trendline, but we should have it in place and enter our sell stop on the 50 remaining shares accordingly. The stop placement will be roughly where the trendline dissects the next trading day (see Figure 9.5). We'll therefore have to adjust it every day—we can do this at the close and outside market hours.

Figure 9.4 EOG trade management with trendline

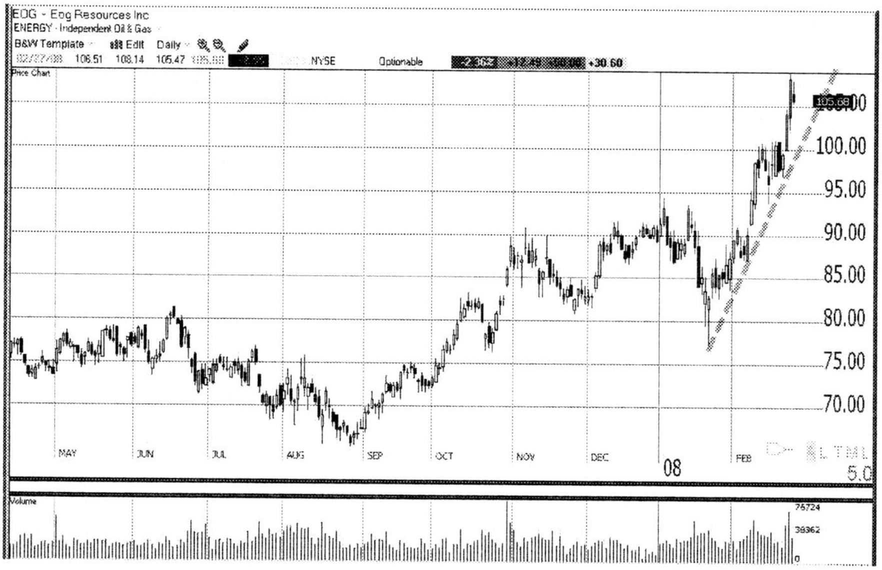

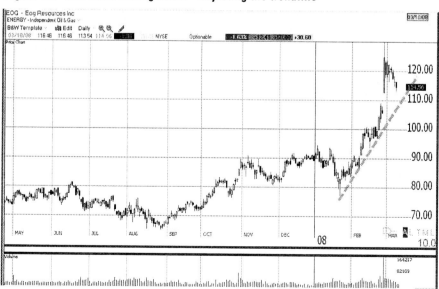

TC2000®.com. Courtesy of Worden Brothers Inc.

Figure 9.5 EOG trade management—adjusting the trendline

TC2000®.com. Courtesy of Worden Brothers Inc.

Moving forward a few days, the stock jumps up and then consolidates again sharply. After the jump we could have stopped ourselves out and taken profits at $118, even though the trendline hadn't been violated. Or we could have stopped ourselves out if the big bar of February 28 retraced by more than 50% of the bar. That would have us stopped out at around $120. As the stock has gone "parabolic," the other alternative is to steepen the trendline (see Figure 9.6).

Figure 9.6 EOG trade management— making the trendline steeper

TC2000®.com. Courtesy of Worden Brothers Inc.

Finally we're stopped out for a big profit at around $118, though the stock has been as high as $128.15 since we steepened our trendline. The profit on the remaining 50 shares is at least $16.75 per share or $837.50 in addition to the profit on the first 50 shares of $187.50 (see Figure 9.7).

Figure 9.7 EOG trade closed with profit

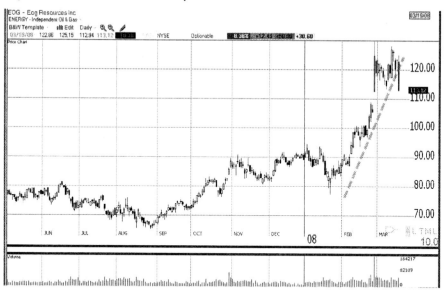

TC2000®.com. Courtesy of Worden Brothers Inc.

That brings our total profit on the trade to $1,025 or just over 10% on our initial outlay. Because of the way in which we managed the trade, we had very little risk on it from the very start, and as the position cleared the first target, we then had virtually no risk at all on the trade, barring a complete Armageddon scenario for oil stocks, which was highly unlikely to happen.

So that's a pretty detailed example of how to execute a trading plan. The remaining examples outline the steps with slightly less detail.

Bear Flag

● **Find the chart pattern.**
IRIS is identified by Flag-Trader on February 1 and is an absolute gem. Unknown to us, the stock is going to provide two opportunities in quick succession to get into a trade.

Figure 9.8 IRIS bear flag

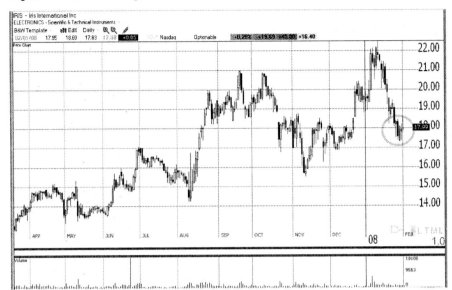

TC2000®.com. Courtesy of Worden Brothers Inc.

● **Research the news.**
Earnings is to be released on February 26.

● **Analyze the option prices (if applicable).**
With this stock, if we were going to trade options, we would buy deep ITM puts or look at a diagonal put as the stock looks bearish. For illustration purposes we're simply going to short the stock here.

● **Decide strategy.**
The earnings announcement is almost four weeks away. There is the chance of a surprise and the stock gapping upward; however, the markets are bearish at this time, and if the stock breaks below the low of the flag around $17.25, then we wouldn't expect it to bounce back any time soon.

● **Place the trade.**
The bear flag chart pattern is strong here, so we're interested. It needs to fall past $17.25 for a short trade to be entered. We enter a sell stop limit to open at $17.15 together with an attached (or if done) buy stop loss order to close at $18.75, which is above the bear flag high of $18.60.

We now calculate how many shares we can short according to our risk management plan by using the free tool at www.manageyourtrade.com.

● **Manage the trade.**

The trade is executed on February 6 as the stock breaks below the bear flag into new lows. The following day the stock makes a huge drop, and our initial profit target around $15.50 is hit. Now we must draw a downward trendline to manage our profits for the other half of the trade (see Figure 9.9).

Figure 9.9 IRIS trade management with downward trendline

TC2000®.com. Courtesy of Worden Brothers Inc.

We're finally stopped out of the remaining short position on March 14 at around $12 as the stock price retraced upward. We made around $1.65 per share with half of our shorted shares and $5.15 with the second half, another very impressive result and achieved with minimum fuss. Of course not all trades go like this, but by taking profits early, we remove stress from our trading even if it means we don't make the maximum amount from each and every successful trade. This trade management method is invaluable when the stock breaks out, triggering our order to be executed, then continues to the first target where we exit half of the trade, and then the stock bounces back to our adjusted stop. In these cases we don't end up suffering a loss, and depending on where we adjust our stop to, we may even make a profit. Without such a trade management strategy, we would end up taking losses on trades that could have been profitable.

Figure 9.10 IRIS trade closed with profit

TC2000®.com. Courtesy of Worden Brothers Inc.

Straddles and Strangles

Let's start with a straddle first.

Straddle

● **Find the chart pattern.**
BWLD is forming a nice bull flag/rounded top on October 10. The stock price is around $41, right in the sweet zone for straddles (see Figure 9.11).

Figure 9.11 BWLD bull flag

TC2000®.com. Courtesy of Worden Brothers Inc.

● **Research the news.**
Earnings is on October 30, and there's no other major news out right now.

● **Analyze the option prices.**
The 40 strike December straddle is priced at 7.60, and the 42.50 strike December straddle is priced at 7.70. These prices are definitely at the upper end of the preferred scale, but this stock has proved to be a big mover around earnings announcements.

The pattern is a bull flag but is showing signs of becoming a rounded top. This may affect which strike price we would go for. If we think the stock is going down, then we'll want to select the 42.50 strike straddle as the calls are cheaper with this strike price, and if they lose value if the stock falls, they'll lose less than the puts would if the stock rises. On the other hand, if we think the stock is more likely to rise, then we'll pick the 40.00 strike as the puts are cheaper and will lose less value than the calls.

● **Decide strategy.**
We'll decide on a straddle and strangle for this one as the stock price is right between the 40 and 42.50 strikes. The 40 strike straddle is the one we're going for.

● **Place the trade.**
  We place the December 40 strike straddle at 7.60 per contract. And we'll be out of the trade within two weeks after the earnings report.

● **Manage the trade.**
  With straddles there's not much to do until the earnings report comes, unless you get a big move beforehand or if you start gamma trading (see Chapter 4, "Straddles and Strangles").

  Earnings are announced on October 30, and the stock gaps down to around $30.00.

Figure 9.12 BWLD earnings breakout

TC2000®.com. Courtesy of Worden Brothers Inc.

Because of the gap down, it's very difficult to draw the downward trendline because it's so steep, but the 40 strike straddle is now worth 11.20 at the bid, so we're sitting on profits of 47% on the original trade, which cost 7.60.

If we'd traded the 42.50 strike, our straddle would be worth 13.70, and our profit would be 78%. No matter—we're grateful for a successful trade that we implemented properly.

Strangle

- **Find the chart pattern.**
  Using the same stock, BWLD is forming a nice bull flag/rounded top on October 10. The stock price is around $41, right in our sweet zone for straddles and strangles.

- **Research the news.**
  Earnings is on October 30, and there's no other major news out right now.

- **Analyze the option prices.**
  The stock is around $41.00. The nearest adjacent strikes are 40.00 and 42.50. The straddles for these strikes were priced at 7.60 and 7.70, respectively. We'd expect the 35–45 strangle to be around half of that level to consider a strangle. Sure enough, the 35–45 strike strangle is priced at 3.70, which is respectable in comparison with the straddle, though we've already conceded that the straddle was on the pricey side to start with.

- **Decide strategy.**
  Let's decide on a straddle and a strangle for this one as the stock price is right between the 40 and 42.50 strikes. In this case we'll go for the 40.00–42.50 strangle.

- **Place the trade.**
  We place the December 40.00–42.50 strangle at 6.50 per contract. We'll be out of the trade within two weeks after the earnings report.

- **Manage the trade.**
  With strangles there's not much to do until the earnings report comes, unless you get a big move beforehand or if you start gamma trading (see Chapter 4).

  Earnings are announced on October 30, and the stock gaps down to around $30.00.

Figure 9.13 BWLD rounded top

TC2000®.com. Courtesy of Worden Brothers Inc.

The strangle is now worth 11.20 at the bid (curiously, the same as the 40 strike straddle), so we're sitting on profits of 72% on our original trade, which cost 6.50. That compares favorably with the 40 strike straddle where our profit was 47%.

Ratio Backspreads

Let's start with the call ratio backspread.

Call Ratio Backspread

● **Find the chart pattern.**
We've already seen one example involving EOG, but there's another one that precedes the one we already looked at. Just a few days before, on February 6, the stock was forming a rather untidy bull flag, but bull flag nevertheless (see Figure 9.14). Being an oil stock with oil prices rising and the rest of the market falling, I'm minded that this looks like it could fly.

Figure 9.14 EOG bull flag

TC2000®.com. Courtesy of Worden Brothers Inc.

- **Research the news.**
  Earnings is tomorrow, on February 7. A positive announcement could rocket this stock up from here.

- **Analyze the option prices.**
  Looking at the options prices, we can sell 20 July expiration 90 strike calls at 7.50 (each) and buy 30 July expiration 95 strike calls at 5.80 (each). This would be a 3:2 call ratio backspread. The implied volatilities for both legs are around 34% with no bias either way.

- **Decide strategy.**
  The call ratio backspread looks interesting. If nothing happens we'll get out of the trade for a very small loss, but if the stock gaps up, we'll be into big profits.

  If we enter a 3:2 call ratio backspread with 20 and 30 contracts, the trade will cost $2,400, and the maximum risk at expiration for this trade is $12,400. If the stock doesn't fall too much, it's highly unlikely we could lose much more than $1,000 on this trade, and for the first three months of the trade it's unlikely that we'd lose more than the $2,400 cost. Our breakeven from the outset is around $88, though this will rise over time. Any increase in implied volatility is going to help enormously, and this is distinctly possible.

Figure 9.14a EOG 3:2, 90-95 call ratio backspread

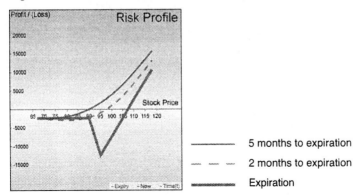

_____   5 months to expiration

_ _ _ _ _   2 months to expiration

_____   Expiration

● **Place the trade.**

This trade has to be placed right away before the earnings report is announced the following day.

● **Manage the trade.**

The stock rises almost uninterrupted until mid-March, where we are stopped out as our trendline is broken at around $113 even though the stock has been as high as 125 on the day that we're stopped (see Figure 9.15).

Figure 9.15 EOG trendline trailing stop broken

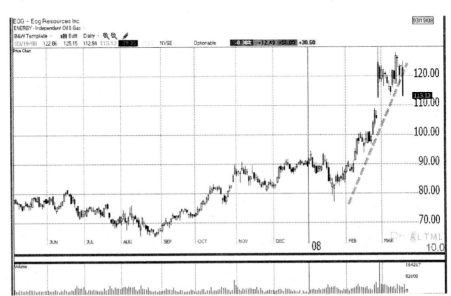

TC2000®.com. Courtesy of Worden Brothers Inc.

To close the trade, we buy back the 90 strike calls for 27.20 each, and we sell the 95 strike calls for 23.10 at a ratio of 2:3 respectively. This means we collect a net credit of 14,900 for closing the position that cost us $2,400 to open. That's a profit of $12,500 or over 600%! Incidentally the implied volatilities have jumped up to between 46% and 48%. That plus the big rise in the stock price has contributed to our windfall profit.

Put Ratio Backspread

● **Find the chart pattern.**
On December 21 MGM is forming a perfect bear flag pattern around $84 (see Figure 9.16).

Figure 9.16 MGM bear flag

TC2000®.com. Courtesy of Worden Brothers Inc.

● **Research the news.**
The last earnings announcement was at the end of October, so we're about a month away from the next earnings announcement.

● **Analyze the option prices**
The June expirations are available. We'll look to sell the 80 strike puts and buy the 75 strike puts at a ratio of three bought and two sold. Our

breakeven is around $75, however that's with no change in volatility, and also our risk is tiny provided we exit the trade within about two months. An increase in the options' implied volatility is going to result in profits even if the stock price doesn't move.

Figure 9.17 shows what the put ratio backspread looks like:

Figure 9.17 MGM 75-80 put ratio backspread

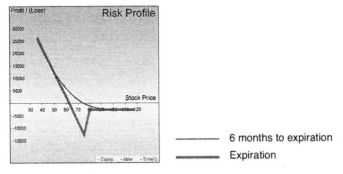

─────────── 6 months to expiration
━━━━━━━━━━━ Expiration

- **Decide strategy.**
  We're happy with an OTM put ratio backspread here and expect a rise in volatility, and in using the 3:2 ratio, we shouldn't be able to lose too much even if nothing happens. The only thing that can really hurt us is if there's a big drop in implied volatility.

- **Place the trade.**
  The trade is placed immediately. We sell 20 x June 80 strike puts and buy 30 x June 75 strike puts for a small net debit of $2,600.

- **Manage the trade.**

  MGM started to plummet on January 2 and only paused in the middle of January (see Figure 9.18).

  If we liquidate the trade on January 22, we buy back the 20 x 80 strike puts and sell the 30 x 75 strike puts for a credit of $4,100, meaning a profit of $1,500. Now that doesn't sound like much, but our "realistic" risk on this trade was never more than $2,600 (the net debit) because we would have been out of the this trade well before time decay would start to kick in. If we were foolish enough to stay in the trade until expiration, then our maximum risk would be $12,600, but that would never have been the case here (though a broker would still require you to have the full amount of margin in your account). As it is, the profit on our "realistic risk" figure is 57%.

Figure 9.18 MGM bear flag—managing profits with a trendline

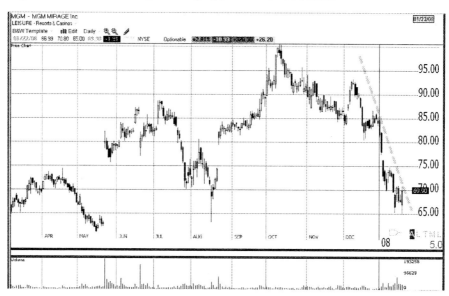

TC2000®.com. Courtesy of Worden Brothers Inc.

Diagonals

Diagonal Call

● **Find the chart pattern.**
We'll use EOG again as we did for our bull flag example earlier. The stock is forming a bull flag around $100–$101 (see Figure 9.19).

● **Research the news.**
As we know from before, earnings was announced on February 7 and was very positive with a 51% increase in profits. There are no announcements pending that we know about.

● **Analyze the option prices.**
We'll combine this with the next task, which is to decide upon our strategy.

Figure 9.19 EOG bull flag

TC2000®.com. Courtesy of Worden Brothers Inc.

- **Decide strategy.**

  As of February 21, the earnings announcement is now two weeks in the past, so I'm satisfied there are no surprises on the way. This means we'll lean toward a directional strategy, like a diagonal call.

  We're going to look to buy the 90 strike July calls and sell the April 110 calls.

- **Place the trade.**

  As the stock price breaks up through $101.25, we're going to buy the 90 strike July calls for 15.60 and sell the April 110 calls for 1.95, giving a net debit of 13.65 and an initial yield of 12.5%. (The equivalent covered call would have given a yield of only 1.93%.)

  The trade is safe in terms of its risk profile, and our breakeven is around $100.93 if volatility remains at around 30%. This means if we're triggered into the trade, the stock would have to reverse straight back in order for us to suffer a loss. My expectation is that if this stock rises through the resistance of $101.25, it won't look back for long, if at all.

  Figure 9.20 shows what the diagonal call for EOG looks like:

Figure 9.20 EOG diagonal call risk profile

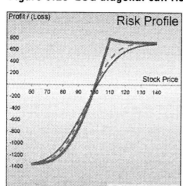

——————— Current (2 months to short call expiration)

—— —— —— 1 month to short call expiration

━━━━━━ Short call expiration (long call still has time value)

● **Manage the trade.**

As the stock rises we can use the rising trendline to keep in the trade until it is violated on March 19 at around $113, even though the stock has been as high as $125 on this day itself (see Figure 9.21). We could wait until the April expiration, but the stock is well past our short call strike of 110, so we might as well take our profits now and move on. We sell the July 90s for 26.80, and we buy back the April 110s for 8.40, giving a net credit of 18.40, which is a profit of 4.65 or 35%.

Figure 9.21 EOG bull flag—managing profits with a trendline

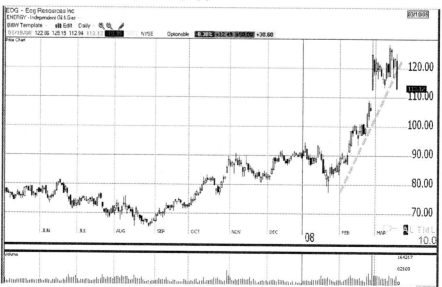

TC2000®.com. Courtesy of Worden Brothers Inc.

Diagonal Put

● **Find the chart pattern.**
As before, on December 21, MGM is forming a perfect bear flag pattern around $84 (see Figure 9.22).

Figure 9.22 MGM bear flag

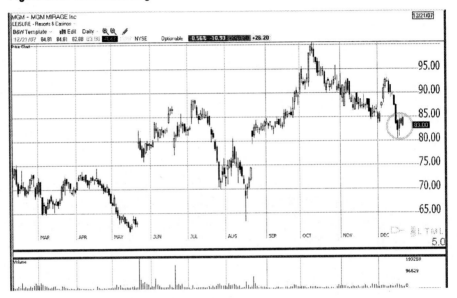

TC2000®.com. Courtesy of Worden Brothers Inc.

● **Research the news.**
The latest earnings announcement was at the end of October, so we're about a month away from the next earnings announcement.

● **Analyze the option prices.**
Assuming the stock breaks down past $80.00, we like the look of buying the June 95 strike puts (deep ITM) and selling the March 75 strike puts for a diagonal put spread.

- **Decide strategy.**
  This is a candidate for four of our favorite strategies, the straddle, strangle, put ratio backspread, and diagonal put. The stock is forming a bear flag within an upside-down cup and handle, and we're only going to place the trade if the stock breaks the low of $80.50. On balance we should be happy with a diagonal put spread here.

- **Place the trade.**
  On January 2, as the stock falls past $80.50, we buy the 95 strike June put for 16.70 and sell the 75 strike March put for 3.40. This is a net debit of 13.30, an initial yield of over 25%, and our breakeven will be around $84.00, meaning that if the stock does nothing, we'll make a profit on the trade at the time of the March expiration. This is a good-looking trade (see Figure 9.23).

Figure 9.23 MGM diagonal put risk profile

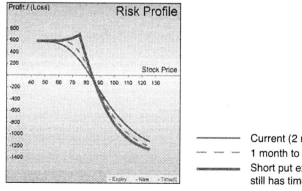

Current (2 months to short put expiration)
1 month to short put expiration
Short put expiration (long put still has time value)

- **Manage the trade.**

  With the trade triggered on January 2, MGM continues falling, and very soon the stock is below our lower strike price (see Figure 9.24).

Figure 9.24 MGM diagonal put—managing profits with a trendline

TC2000®.com. Courtesy of Worden Brothers Inc.

It looks highly improbable that $75 is going to be breached to the upside, so it's best to keep our trade on for a while in order to allow time decay to diminish the short put. This is because our maximum profit occurs at expiration, and so we might as well let time do its work—unless it looks like the stock might come back above $75.00. With the exception of the open on February 4, the stock never even touched $75.00, so we simply keep the trade on to allow time decay to reduce our short put.

The short put expires on the Thursday before Easter, so we'll need to liquidate the day before on March 19. We buy back our short puts at 17.00 and sell our long puts for 36.30. This is a credit of $17.30 which gives us a profit of $4.00 (30%) on our original trade, which cost $13.30.

So that concludes our trading plans. Let's look at a summary of our six preferred strategies in Table 9.1.

Table 9.1 Strategy Matrix

Strategy	Outlook	Rationale	Stock price	Chart pattern	News & fundamentals	Timing	Volatility
Straddle	Direction neutral	Capital gain	$15–$50 is the sweet spot though other prices work fine	Consolidation patterns—flags, pennants, triangles	None in the recent past; an announcement anticipated in the next two weeks or so	Around two weeks before the anticipated announcement or closer provided the implied volatilities haven't been rising too much	Implied volatility to be low compared with its own readings over the past two to three months
Strangle	Direction neutral	Capital gain	$15–$50 is the sweet spot though other prices work fine	Consolidation patterns—flags, pennants, triangles	None in the recent past; an announcement anticipated in the next two weeks or so	Around two weeks before the anticipated announcement or closer provided the implied volatilities haven't been rising too much	Implied volatility to be low compared with its own readings over the past two to three months; cost of strangle needs to be around 50% of the cost of the straddle
Call ratio backspread	Bullish	Capital gain	Anything above $15	Uptrending and consolidation patterns—flags, pennants, triangles	If the trade has been executed at zero cost, then no recent news is preferable, with news anticipated in the next two weeks or so	Within two weeks before the anticipated announcement or closer provided the implied volatilities haven't been rising too much	Preferably low implied volatility for the NTM calls that you're buying and high for the OTM calls you're selling; a net credit or zero cost trade preferable

Table 9.1 Strategy Matrix (continued)

Strategy	Outlook	Rationale	Stock price	Chart pattern	News & fundamentals	Timing	Volatility
Put ratio backspread	Bearish	Capital gain	Anything above $15	Downtrending and consolidation patterns—flags, pennants, triangles	If the trade has been executed at zero cost, then no recent news is preferable, with news anticipated in the next two weeks or so	Within two weeks before the anticipated announcement or closer provided the implied volatilities haven't been rising too much	Preferably low implied volatility for the NTM puts that you're buying and high for the OTM puts you're selling; a net credit or zero cost trade preferable
Diagonal call	Bullish	Income and capital gain	Anything over $5	Uptrending and consolidation patterns—flags, pennants, triangles	Good fundamentals; don't want surprises here	A couple of weeks after an earnings announcement and where no news is anticipated any time soon	Preferably low implied volatility for the deep ITM call that you're buying and high for the OTM call you're selling; volatility to subsequently rise for the deep ITM call

Strategy	Outlook	Rationale	Stock price	Chart pattern	News & fundamentals	Timing	Volatility
Diagonal put	Bearish	Income and capital gain	Anything over $10	Downtrending and patterns—flags, pennants, triangles	Bad fundamentals; don't want surprises here	A couple of weeks after an earnings announcement and where no news is anticipated any time soon	Preferably low implied volatility for the deep ITM put that you're buying and high for the OTM put you're selling; volatility to subsequently rise for the deep ITM put

Learning Points

In this chapter we've seen how to put together a trading plan for each of our favored strategies from start to finish.

Trading is not a game. If you're doing it properly, it's a business. I've given you templates here, but you'll probably want to add your own personal touch to them. Discretionary trading plans are very personal, and each trader's will be different. The most important rule is to keep it simple. Confusion will result in bad performance, whereas clarity will lead to consistent profits.

Too many traders spend all their time experimenting with various kinds of analytical tools, never quite finding the Holy Grail and never actually trading. The truth is that there is no Holy Grail, so you're better off with a straightforward approach that you can adjust as you feel necessary from time to time. Simple patterns with simple trading plans lead to more enjoyment and consistent profits.

Use the sample trading plans here, add whatever you want to them, but keep things simple. Always know your entry points, stop loss areas (where applicable), and how you'll manage your profits. If you do this you'll avoid the most common trading pitfalls.

Now your task is to implement these trading methods for yourself. You achieve this by adhering to a proper trading plan. If you're going to do this, do it properly. Real enjoyment and excitement will follow, but as with many things in life, it takes discipline. Discipline ultimately will give you freedom.

Trading can be fun—but only when you're winning! Lots of incremental wins translate to a healthy looking trading account. If you apply the principles in this book, you'll develop a winning habit, unencumbered by confusion and complexity. This simple approach has arisen out of many years of research, development, self-examination, and studious observation. I discovered that some of the complicated and time-consuming methods I was using with great success years ago actually boiled down to flag patterns but in a different guise. With no compromise on performance, I've been able to simplify my life to such a degree that I enjoy trading now more than ever, and that's a great feeling.

Now it's your turn!

Strategy Table

Strategy	Execution	Benefits	Disadvantages	Component Parts	Risk Profile
Long Call	Buy a call.	Capped risk; uncapped reward; better leverage than stock purchase.	Can lose entire stake if the call expires OTM (out of the money).	╲	╲
Long Put	Buy a put.	Capped risk; uncapped reward; better leverage than straight stock shorting.	Can lose entire stake if the put expires OTM (out of the money).	╲	╲
Short Call (naked)	Sell a call.	Short-term income strategy.	Uncapped risk and capped reward.	╱	╱
Short Put (naked)	Sell a put.	Short-term income strategy.	Uncapped risk and capped reward.	╲	╲
Covered Call	Buy stock and sell call.	Protected income strategy. Profit assured if stock remains static or rises. Calls can be sold on a monthly basis to generate income.	Uncapped risk and capped reward.	╱ + ╲	╲
Collar	Buy stock, buy ATM put, and sell OTM call.	Can be a riskless strategy if executed correctly with the right stock.	Net debit out of your account. Works best for long-term trades where you leave it alone.	╱ + ╲ + ╱	╲

appendix I continued

Strategy	Execution	Benefits	Disadvantages	Component Parts	Risk Profile
Covered Put	Sell stock (short) and sell put.	Net credit into your account.	Uncapped risk and capped reward.		
Synthetic Call	Buy stock and buy put.	Capped risk and uncapped reward. Good insurance tactic.	Expensive strategy.		
Synthetic Put	Short stock and buy call.	Capped risk and uncapped reward.	More complex than simply buying puts.		
Covered Short Straddle	Buy stock and sell put and call with same strike and expiration date.	Enhanced income (compared with Covered Call).	Very high risk and capped reward. Not recommended.		
Covered Short Strangle	Buy stock and sell lower strike put and higher strike call with same expiration date.	Enhanced income (compared with Covered Call).	Very high risk and capped reward. Not recommended.		
Bull Call Spread	Buy lower strike calls and sell higher strike calls (same expiration).	Capped risk; lower breakeven point than simply buying a call.	Capped reward.		
Bull Put Spread	Buy lower strike puts and sell higher strike puts (same expiration).	Capped risk; lower breakeven point than simply buying a put; net credit into your account.	Capped reward.		

Strategy	Execution	Benefits	Disadvantages	Component Parts	Risk Profile
Bear Call Spread	Sell lower strike calls and buy higher strike calls (same expiration).	Capped risk; bearish income strategy.	Capped reward.		
Bear Put Spread	Sell lower strike puts and buy higher strike puts (same expiration).	Capped risk.	Capped reward.		
Bull Call Ladder	Buy lower strike calls, sell higher strike calls, and sell even higher strike calls (all same expiration).	Cheap strategy.	Uncapped risk if stock rises sharply; confusing as to whether this is a bullish or bearish strategy.		
Bull Put Ladder	Buy lower strike puts, buy higher strike puts, and sell even higher strike puts (all same expiration).	Uncapped reward as the stock falls.	Expensive; confusing as to whether this is a bullish or bearish strategy.		
Bear Call Ladder	Sell lower strike calls, buy higher strike calls, and buy even higher strike calls (all same expiration).	Uncapped reward as the stock rises.	Expensive; confusing as to whether this is a bullish or bearish strategy.		

appendix I continued

Strategy	Execution	Benefits	Disadvantages	Component Parts	Risk Profile
Bear Put Ladder	Sell lower strike puts, sell higher strike puts, and buy even higher strike puts (all same expiration).	Cheap strategy.	Uncapped risk as the stock falls; confusing as to whether this is a bullish or bearish strategy.		
Straddle	Buy puts and calls with same strike price and expiration.	Capped risk; profitable if stocks rises or falls significantly; uncapped reward.	Expensive; low volatility required for entry whereas high volatility required once you are in.		
Short Straddle	Sell puts and calls with same strike and expiration.	Net credit into your account; profitable if stock shows low volatility and does not move.	Uncapped risk on either side.		
Strangle	Buy lower strike puts and buy higher strike calls (same expiration).	Capped risk; profitable if stocks rises or falls significantly; uncapped reward.	Low volatility required for entry whereas high volatility required once you are in.		
Short Strangle	Sell lower strike puts and sell higher strike calls (same expiration).	Net credit into your account; profitable if stock shows low volatility and does not move.	Uncapped risk on either side.		

Strategy	Execution	Benefits	Disadvantages	Component Parts	Risk Profile
Strip	Buy 2 puts and 1 call with same strike and expiration.	Capped risk; profitable if stocks rises or falls significantly; uncapped reward.	Expensive; low volatility required for entry whereas high volatility required once you are in.	*(diagram)*	*(diagram)*
Strap	Buy 1 put and 2 calls with same strike and expiration.	Capped risk; profitable if stocks rises or falls significantly; uncapped reward.	Expensive; low volatility required for entry whereas high volatility required once you are in.	*(diagram)*	*(diagram)*
Long Call Butterfly	Buy 1 lower strike call, sell 2 middle strike calls, and buy 1 higher strike call. All strikes evenly apart.	Capped risk and a cheap strategy to enter; can be very profitable if stock shows low volatility after you are in.	Capped reward; awkward to adjust.	*(diagram)*	*(diagram)*
Long Put Butterfly	Buy 1 lower strike put, sell 2 middle strike puts, and buy 1 higher strike put. All strikes evenly apart.	Capped risk and a cheap strategy to enter; can be very profitable if stock shows low volatility after you are in.	Capped reward; . awkward to adjust	*(diagram)*	*(diagram)*
Short Call Butterfly	Sell 1 lower strike call, buy 2 middle strike calls, and sell 1 higher strike call. All strikes evenly apart.	Capped risk; profitable if stock shows high volatility after you are in.	Capped reward; awkward to adjust.	*(diagram)*	*(diagram)*

appendix I continued

Strategy	Execution	Benefits	Disadvantages	Component Parts	Risk Profile
Short Put Butterfly	Sell 1 lower strike put, buy 2 middle strike puts, and sell 1 higher strike put. All strikes evenly apart.	Capped risk; profitable if stock shows high volatility after you are in.	Capped reward; awkward to adjust.		
Modified Call Butterfly	Buy 1 lower strike call, sell 2 middle strike calls, and buy 1 higher strike call. Middle strike closer to higher strike than to lower strike.	Capped risk and a cheap strategy to enter; can be very profitable if stock shows low volatility or rises modestly after you are in.	Capped reward; awkward to adjust.		
Modified Put Butterfly	Buy 1 lower strike put, sell 2 middle strike puts, and buy 1 higher strike put. Middle strike closer to higher strike than to lower strike.	Capped risk and a cheap strategy to enter; can be very profitable if stock shows low volatility or rises modestly after you are in.	Capped reward; awkward to adjust.		
Call Ratio Backspread	Sell 1 or 2 lower strike calls and buy 2 or 3 higher strike calls. Buy greater number of higher strike calls in ratio of 0.67 or less.	Capped risk; uncapped and highly geared reward if stock rises significantly.	Lots of volatility required after entry and in the right direction (upward) for your trade to be profitable.		

Strategy	Execution	Benefits	Disadvantages	Component Parts	Risk Profile
Put Ratio Backspread	Buy 2 or 3 lower strike puts and sell 1 or 2 higher strike puts. Buy greater number of lower strike puts in ratio of 0.67 or less.	Capped risk; uncapped and highly geared reward if stock falls significantly.	Lots of volatility required after entry and in the right direction (downward) for your trade to be profitable.		
Ratio Call Spread	Buy lower strike call and sell greater number of higher strike calls (ratio of 0.67 or less).		Uncapped risk; capped reward.		
Ratio Put Spread	Buy higher strike put and sell greater number of lower strike puts (ratio of 0.67 or less).		Uncapped risk; capped reward.		
Long Call Condor	Buy lower strike call, sell middle strike call, sell next middle strike call, and buy higher strike call. All strikes evenly apart.	Capped risk and a cheap strategy to enter; can be very profitable if stock remains rangebound after you are in.	Capped reward; awkward to adjust.		

appendix I continued

Strategy	Execution	Benefits	Disadvantages	Component Parts	Risk Profile
Long Put Condor	Buy lower strike put, sell middle strike put, sell next middle strike put, and buy higher strike put. All strikes evenly apart.	Capped risk and a cheap strategy to enter; can be very profitable if stock remains rangebound after you are in.	Capped reward; awkward to adjust.		
Short Call Condor	Sell lower strike call, buy middle strike call, buy next middle strike call, and sell higher strike call. All strikes evenly apart.	Capped risk; profitable if stock shows high volatility after you are in.	Capped reward; awkward to adjust.		
Short Put Condor	Sell lower strike put, buy middle strike put, buy next middle strike put, and sell higher strike put. All strikes evenly apart.	Capped risk; profitable if stock shows high volatility after you are in.	Capped reward; awkward to adjust.		
Long Call Synthetic Straddle	Sell 1 stock and buy 2 ATM calls.	Capped risk; profitable if stock rises or falls significantly; uncapped reward; cheaper than doing a normal Straddle.	Low volatility required for entry whereas high volatility required once you are in.		

Strategy	Execution	Benefits	Disadvantages	Component Parts	Risk Profile
Long Put Synthetic Straddle	Buy 1 stock and 2 ATM puts.	Capped risk; profitable if stocks rises or falls significantly; uncapped reward.	Even more expensive than normal Straddle; low volatility required for entry, whereas high volatility required once you are in.	/ + ⌣ + ⌣	⌣
Short Call Synthetic Straddle	Buy 1 stock and sell 2 ATM calls.	Profitable if stock shows low volatility and does not move.	Uncapped risk on either side; expensive because you are buying the stock.	/ + ⌢ + ⌢	⌢
Short Put Synthetic Straddle	Sell 1 stock and 2 ATM puts.	Cheap strategy that brings in a net credit to your account; profitable if stock shows low volatility and does not move.	Uncapped risk on either side; large margin required.	\ + / + /	⌢
Long Iron Butterfly	Buy lower strike put, sell mid strike put, sell next mid strike call, and buy higher strike call. (Middle strikes can be the same.)	Cheap strategy that brings in a net credit to your account; capped risk; profitable if stock doesn't move much; capped risk.	Capped reward; margin required.	⌐ + ⌢ + ⌢ + ⌣	⌐⌣

appendix I continued

Strategy	Execution	Benefits	Disadvantages	Component Parts	Risk Profile
Short Iron Butterfly	Sell lower strike put, buy mid strike put, buy next mid strike call, and sell higher strike call. (Middle strikes can be the same.)	Capped risk.	Expensive strategy.		
Calendar Call	Buy long-term call and sell shorter-term call (same strikes).	Capped risk; can sell the shorter-term calls on a monthly basis in order to generate income.	Capped reward; can become loss-making if the underlying asset rises too much.		
Calendar Put	Buy long-term put and sell shorter-term put (same strikes).	Capped risk; can sell the shorter-term calls on a monthly basis in order to generate income.	Capped reward; can become loss-making if the underlying asset rises too much.		
Diagonal Call	Buy long-term lower strike call and sell shorter-term higher strike call.	Capped risk; can sell the shorter-term calls on a monthly basis in order to generate income.	Capped reward.		
Diagonal Put	Sell shorter-term lower strike put and buy longer-term higher strike put.	Capped risk; can sell the shorter-term calls on a monthly basis in order to generate income.	Capped reward.		

Strategy	Execution	Benefits	Disadvantages	Component Parts	Risk Profile
Guts	Buy lower strike calls and higher strike puts.	Capped risk; profitable if stocks rises or falls significantly; uncapped reward.	Expensive because you're buying ITM options.		
Short Guts	Sell lower strike calls and higher strike puts.	Net credit into your account; profitable if stock shows low volatility and does not move.	Uncapped risk on either side.		
Long Synthetic Future	Buy ATM call and sell ATM put.	Simulates going long on a stock with no or very little net debit or credit.	Same leverage as the underlying.		
Short Synthetic Future	Sell ATM call and buy ATM put.	Simulates going short on a stock with no or very little net debit or credit.	Same leverage as the underlying.		
Long Combo	Sell OTM (lower) put and buy OTM (higher) call.	Almost simulates going long on a stock with no or very little net debit or credit.	Same leverage as the underlying.		
Short Combo	Buy OTM (lower) put and sell OTM (higher) call.	Almost simulates going short on a stock with no or very little net debit or credit.	Same leverage as the underlying.		

308

appendix I continued

Strategy	Execution	Benefits	Disadvantages	Component Parts	Risk Profile
Long Box	Buy one low strike call, sell one same strike put; sell one higher strike call, and buy one same higher strike put; all same expiration dates.	Create a completely hedged position where the ultimate profit is known with certainty ahead of time.	Complicated, requires many contracts to be effective. Bid/Ask spread makes it difficult to guarantee a profitable position.		

Glossary

American Stock Exchange (AMEX)	Securities exchange that handles approximately 20% of all securities trades within the USA.
American-style option	An option contract that can be exercised at any time before the Expiration Date. Stock options are American-style.
Arbitrage	Where the simultaneous purchase and disposal of a combination of financial instruments is such that a guaranteed profit is made automatically.
Ask	The price that you buy at and the price that market makers and floor brokers are willing to sell at. The Ask stands for what the market makers and floor traders ask you to pay for the stock (or options or other instrument).
ATM (at the money)	Where the option Exercise price is the same as the asset price.
At the Opening order	An order that specifies execution at the market opening or else it is cancelled.
Automatic Exercise	The automatic exercise of an In the Money (ITM) option by the clearing firm at Expiration.
Backspread	A spread where more options (calls or puts) are bought than sold (the opposite of a Ratio Spread).
Bear Call spread	A net credit spread only using calls where the trader buys a higher Strike call and sells a lower Strike call. The higher Strike call is cheaper, hence the net credit. Bear Call spreads have limited risk and reward and are more profitable as the underlying asset price falls to the lower Strike price.

Bear Put spread	A net debit spread only using puts where the trader buys a higher Strike put and sells a lower Strike put. The higher Strike put will be more expensive, hence the net debit. Bear Put spreads have limited risk and reward and are more profitable as the underlying asset falls to the lower Strike Price.
Bid	The price the trader sells at and the price that market makers and floor traders are willing to buy at. The Bid stands for the price at which the market maker will bid for your stock (options, or other instrument).
Bid–Ask Spread	The difference between the Bid and Ask prices. Generally you will buy at the Ask, and sell at the Bid. The Ask is always higher than the Bid.
Blow off Top	A large rise in price followed by a quick drop. Often accompanied with high volume. Usually a technical indicator for the end of a bullish trend.
Bond	A debt financial instrument used by governments and corporate entities in order to raise capital. The bond obliges the organization to pay its holders a fixed rate of return (coupon) and repay the principal of the debt at maturity. These bonds are traded (the CBOT is one of the major bond exchanges) and their values are directly correlated with interest rates and interest-rate speculation by the markets. The lower interest rates are projected to be, the more valuable the bond will be.
Breakeven	The point(s) at which a risk profile of a trade equals zero.
Breakout	Where a price chart emerges upward beyond previous price resistance.
Broker	A person who charges commission for executing a transaction (buy or sell) order.
Bull	Someone who expects the market to rise.
Bull Call spread	A net debit spread only using calls where the trader buys a lower Strike call and sells a higher Strike call. The lower Strike call is more expensive, hence the net debit. Bull Call spreads have limited risk and reward and are more profitable as the underlying asset rises to the higher Strike price (see Chapter 7).
Bull market	A rising market over a period of time (usually a few years).
Bull Put spread	A net credit spread only using puts where the trader buys a lower Strike put and sells a higher Strike put. The lower Strike put is less valuable, hence the net credit. Bull Put

	spreads have limited risk and reward and are more profitable as the underlying asset rises to the higher strike price (see Chapter 7).
Butterfly spread	A 3-leg option strategy using all calls or all puts (see Chapter 9).
Buy on Close	An order stipulating to buy the security at the close of the trading session.
Buy on Open	An order stipulating to buy the security at the opening of the trading session.
Buy Stop	A buy order where the price stipulated is higher than the current price. The rationale here is when the buyer believes that if the security breaks a certain resistance, the security will continue to rise.
CAC 40 Index	The Paris Bourse index based on 40 stocks.
Calendar spread	A 2-leg option strategy where the trader buys longer-term options and sells shorter-term options. Use all calls or all puts.
Call option	The right, not the obligation, to buy an underlying security at a fixed price before a predetermined date.
Call premium	The price of a call option.
Capital gain	The profit realized from buying and selling an asset.
Capital loss	The loss taken from buying and selling an asset unprofitably.
Chicago Board Options Exchange (CBOE)	The largest options exchange in the world.
Chicago Board of Trade (CBOT)	The oldest commodity exchange in the USA. Known for listings in T-bonds, notes and a variety of commodities.
Chicago Mercantile Exchange (CME)	An exchange in which many types of futures contracts are traded in an open outcry system.
Class of options	Options of the same type, style and underlying security.
Clearing House	A separate institution that establishes timely payment and delivery of securities.
Close	The last price quoted for the day.
Closing purchase	A transaction which closes an open short position.
Closing sale	A transaction which closes an open long position.
Commission	A charge made by the broker for arranging the transaction.

Commodity	A tangible good that is traded on an exchange, for example, oil, grains, and metals.
Commodity Futures Trading Commission (CFTC)	An institution charged with ensuring the efficient operation of the futures markets.
Condor	A 4-leg option strategy using all calls or all puts (see Chapter 9).
Consumer Price Index (CPI)	An index measuring the change in consumer prices. An important inflation indicator.
Contract	A unit of trading for an option or future.
Correction	A post-rise decline in a stock price or market.
Covered Call	An income strategy involving the simultaneous purchase of the underlying asset and sale of call options (see Chapter 5).
Covered Put	A high-risk strategy involving the simultaneous shorting of the underlying asset and put options.
Credit spread	Where the simultaneous buying and selling of options creates a net credit into your account (that is, you receive more for the ones you sell than those you buy).
Day order	An order good for the day only.
Day trade	The acquisition and disposal of an asset in the same day.
Day trading	A trading style where positions are closed by the end of every day.
Debit spread	Where the simultaneous buying and selling of options creates a net debit from your account (that is, you pay more for the ones you buy than those you sell).
Deep In the Money (DITM)	*Calls:* where the price of the underlying security is far greater than the call Strike price.
	Puts: where the price of the underlying security is far less than the put Strike price.
Delayed time quotes	Quotes which are delayed from real time.
Delta	The amount by which an option premium moves divided by the dollar for dollar movement in the underlying asset.
Delta Hedge	A strategy designed to protect the investor against directional price changes in the underlying asset by engineering the overall position delta to zero.
Delta Neutral	Where a spread position is engineered so that the overall position delta is zero.
Derivative	A financial instrument whose value is 'derived' in some way from the value of an underlying asset.

Discount brokers	Low commission brokers who simply place orders, and do not provide advisory services.
Divergence	Where two or more indicators move in different directions indicating different outcomes.
Dividend	A payment made by an organization to its owners (shareholders), hopefully from profits.
Dow Jones Industrial Average (DJIA)	An index of 30 blue chip stocks traded on the New York Stock Exchange (NYSE). This index is often considered a bellwether of overall market sentiment.
Downside risk	The potential risk of a trade if prices decline.
End of day	The close of the trading day when prices settle.
EPS	Earnings per Share. The amount of profits of an organization divided by the number of outstanding shares.
Equity options	The same as stock options.
European-style option	An option which cannot be exercised before the Expiration date.
Exchange	Where an asset or derivative is traded.
Exchange rate	The price at which one currency can be converted into another currency.
Execution	The process of completing an order to trade a security.
Exercise	The activation of the right to buy or sell the underlying security.
Exercise (Strike) price	The price at which the underlying asset can be bought or sold by the buyer of a call or put option.
Expiration	The date at which the option's ability to be exercised ceases.
Expiration Date	The last day on which an option can be exercised.
Extrinsic Value (Time Value)	The price of an option less its Intrinsic Value. Out of the Money (OTM) options are made up entirely of Extrinsic (or Time) Value.
Fair market value	An asset's value under normal circumstances.
Fair value	The theoretical value calculation of an option using a pricing formula such as the Black-Scholes Options Pricing Model.
Fibonacci Retracement	Where prices on a chart move off their latest tops or bottoms in swings of 38.2%, 50%, or 61.8% from their previous bottoms or tops before resuming their original trend direction. The most common and easiest to spot is 50%.

Fill	An order that has been executed.
Fill order	An order that must be filled immediately or cancelled.
Fill or Kill	An order where a precise number of contracts must be filled or the order is cancelled.
Floor broker	A member of an exchange who is paid to execute orders.
Floor trader	An exchange member who trades on the floor of the exchange for their own account.
Fundamental Analysis	Analysis of a stock security based on the ability of the organization to generate profits for its shareholders. Such analysis embraces earnings, PE ratios, EPS, net assets, liabilities, customers, etc.
Futures contracts	Agreement to buy or sell an underlying security at a predetermined date at an agreed price. The difference between futures and options is that with options the buyer has the right, not the obligation. With futures, both parties are obliged to fulfill their part of the bargain.
Gamma	The speed by which delta changes compared with the speed by which the underlying asset is moving.
Gap	Where the opening bar of a price chart opens and stays beyond (lower or higher) that of the spread of the previous bar. Gaps can be lower or higher.
Good Till Cancelled order (GTC)	An order that remains active until either it is filled or cancelled specifically by the trader.
Guts spread	An expensive strategy where the trader buys OTM calls and puts to replicate the risk profile of a Strangle. Far cheaper to trade the Strangle.
Hedge	A term for reducing the risk of one position by taking other positions with options, futures or other derivatives.
Historic (Statistical) Volatility	A measure of the price fluctuation of an asset averaged out over a period of time. A typical and popular period would be 21–23 trading days.
Index	A group of assets (often in a similar class of sector or market capitalization) which can be traded as a single security.
Index options	Options on the indexes of stocks or other securities.
Interest rates	The rate at which borrowed money is charged by the lender, usually annualized into a percentage figure.
In the Money (ITM)	Where you can exercise an option for a profit.
	ITM *calls* are where the current stock price is greater than the call Strike price.

	ITM *puts* are where the current stock price is less than the put Strike price.
Intrinsic Value	The amount by which an option is In the Money.
Iron Butterfly	A 4-leg option strategy using calls and puts together.
Japanese Candlesticks	A popular method of visually depicting price bars where the open, high, low, close are shown explicitly.
	Upward moving price bars are hollow.
	Downward moving price bars are filled.
	Different looking bars and different clusters of price bars can lead to different interpretations of future price movements.
LEAPs	Long-term Equity AnticiPation Securities.
	These are long-term stock options with expirations up to three years in the future. LEAPs are available in calls and puts and are American-style traded options.
Leg	One side or component of a spread.
Leg in/Leg out	*Legging into a spread* entails the completion of just one component part of a spread with the intention of completing the other component parts at more favorable prices later on.
	Legging out of a spread entails the opposite whereby you exit your spread one component part at a time with the intention of completing the other component parts at more favorable prices as the underlying security moves in the anticipated direction.
LIFFE	London International Financial Futures and Options Exchange.
Limit Order	An *order to buy* at a set price which is at or below the current price of the security.
	An *order to sell* at a set price which is at or above the current price of the security.
Liquidity	The speed and ease with which an asset can be traded. Cash has the most liquidity of all assets, whereas property (real estate) is one of the most illiquid assets.
Long	Being long means that you are a buyer of a security.
MACD (Moving Average Convergence Divergence)	Measures the difference between two moving averages and is a measure of momentum. As the moving averages drift apart then momentum is increasing and vice versa.

Margin	An amount paid by the account holder (either in cash or "marginable securities"), which is held by the brokerage against noncash or high risk investments, or where the brokerage has lent the account holder the means to undertake a particular trade.
Margin account	An account where the brokerage lends the customer part of the net debit required to make a trade.
Margin Call	Where the brokerage calls the account holder in order for them to pay more funds into their account to maintain the trade.
	Note that strategies that involve some form of unlimited risk often require a level of margin to be determined by the brokerage.
Margin requirements	The amount of cash or marginable securities (for example, blue chip stocks) that an account holder must have in his account to write uncovered (or naked) options.
Mark to Market	The daily adjustment of margin accounts to reflect profits and losses in such a way that losses are not allowed to accumulate.
Market Capitalization	The number of outstanding shares multiplied by the value per share.
Market if Touched (MIT) order	An order that becomes a market order if the price specified is reached.
Market Maker	A trader or trading firm that buys and sells securities in a market in order to facilitate trading. Market makers make a two sided (bid and ask) market.
Market on Close order	An order that requires the broker to achieve the best price at the close or in the last five minutes of trading.
Market on Open order	An order that must be executed at the opening of trading.
Market order	Trading securities immediately at the best market prices to guarantee execution.
Market price	The most recent transaction price.
Momentum	Where a market direction (up or down) is established.
Momentum indicators	Technical Analysis indicators using price movement and volume to determine market direction.
Momentum traders	Traders who use momentum as their primary criteria to invest.
Moving Average	The average of a security's latest prices for a specific period of time (for example, 50 days). Another Technical Analysis tool.

Mutual Fund	An open-ended investment fund that pools investors' contributions to invest in securities such as stocks and bonds.
Naked	Selling naked options refers to a sold options contract with no hedge position in place. Such a position leaves the option seller (writer) exposed to unlimited risk.
Nasdaq	National Association of Securities Dealers Automated Quotations system.
	This is a computerized system providing brokers and dealers with securities price quotes.
Near the Money (NTM)	Where the underlying asset price is close to the strike price of an option.
New York Stock Exchange (NYSE)	The largest stock exchange in the USA.
Note	A short-term debt instrument. They normally mature in or less than five years.
OEX	Standard & Poor's 100 Stock Index.
Offer	The lowest price at which the market-maker is willing to sell.
	Also can refer to the "Ask" of a "bid–ask" spread. See Ask.
On the Money (At the Money)	See ATM (At the Money).
Open Outcry	Verbal system of floor trading still used at many exchanges (for example, the CME and CBOT).
Opening	The beginning of the trading session at an exchange.
Opportunity Cost	The risk of an investment expressed as a comparison with another competing investment.
Option	A financial instrument which gives the buyer the right, not the obligation to buy (call) or sell (put) an underlying asset at a fixed price before a predetermined date.
Option Premium	The price of an option.
Option Writer	The seller of an option (naked).
Out of the Money (OTM)	Where the option has no Intrinsic Value and where you cannot exercise an option for a profit.
	OTM *calls* are where the current stock price is less than the call Strike price.
	OTM *puts* are where the current stock price is greater than the put Strike price.

Par	The nominal value of a bond that is paid back to the bondholder at maturity.
Position Delta	The sum of all positive and negative deltas within a hedged trade position.
Premium	The price of an option.
Price bar	The visual representation of a securities price fluctuations for a set period of time. Price bars can be for as little as one minute (or less) and as much as one year (or more).
Price Earnings Ratio	The price of a stock divided by the Earnings per Share for that stock.
	The same figure can be calculated by dividing the market capitalization of a stock by the earnings of that company.
Principal	The purchase price of a bond
Put option	The right, not the obligation, to sell an underlying security at a fixed price before a predetermined date.
Quote	The price being bid or offered by a market maker for a security.
Ratio Backspread	A strategy using all puts or all calls whereby the trader buys OTM options in a ratio of 3:2 or 2:1 to the ITM options he sells. In this way the trader is always long in more options than those he is short in.
Ratio Call spread	A bearish strategy that involves the trader being short in more, higher Strike calls than those lower Strike calls he is long in, at a ratio of 3:2 or 2:1. In this way the trader will have an unlimited risk profile with only limited profit potential.
Ratio Put spread	A bullish strategy that involves the trader being short in more, lower Strike puts than those higher Strike puts he is long in, at a ratio of 3:2 or 2:1. In this way the trader will have an unlimited risk profile with only limited profit potential.
Real Time	Data which is updated and received tick by tick.
Relative Strength	A technical indicator comparing a security's price action as compared to that of an index or another stock.
Relative Strength Index (RSI)	A technical indicator which is an oscillator that combines price action with volume. Best to use with trending stocks and can be used to indicate potential tops and bottoms.
Resistance	A ceiling on a price chart which is thought to be difficult for the price to burst up through because of past price movements.

Return	The income profit on an investment, often expressed as a percentage.
Reversal Stop (or Stop and Reverse) order	A stop order which, when activated, reverses the current position from long to short (or vice versa).
Risk	The potential loss of a trade.
Risk Free Rate	The interest chargeable on Treasury Bills (T-Bills) is generally known as the Risk Free Rate, and it is this rate that is used as a component part of the theoretical options valuation model.
Risk Profile	The graphic depiction of a trade, showing the potential Risk, Reward, and Breakeven Points as the underlying security price deviates within a range of prices.
Seat	Membership in a stock or futures exchange.
Securities and Exchange Commission (SEC)	Organization which regulates the US securities markets to protect investors.
Security	An instrument which can be traded (for example, stocks, bonds, and so on).
Series (options)	Option contracts of the same class (underlying asset), same strike price and same Expiration Date.
Shares	Units of ownership in a company or organization.
Short	Selling a security which you don't actually own.
Short selling	Selling a security which you don't actually own beforehand. You will eventually have to buy it back, hopefully at a reduced price, thus making profit.
Small-Cap stocks	Smaller (and sometimes newer) companies associated with high risk and high potential rewards. Can be illiquid to trade with large bid–ask spreads.
Speculator	A trader who aims to make profit by correctly assessing the direction of price movement of the security. Generally distinguished from investors in that speculators are associated with short-term directional trading.
Spread	The difference between the Bid and Ask of a traded security.
	or: A trading strategy which involves more than one leg to create a (hedged) position.
	or: A price spread is the difference between the high and the low of a price bar.
Standard & Poor's (S&P)	A company that rates stocks and bonds and produces and tracks the S&P indices.

Stochastic	A technical indicator, which is an oscillator based on the relationship of the open, high, low, close of price bars.
Stock	A share of a company's stock is a unit of ownership in that company.
Stock Exchange or Stock Market	An organized market where buyers and sellers are brought together to trade stocks.
Stock Split	Where a company increases the amount of outstanding stock, thus increasing the number of shares, reducing the value per share. Generally a sign that the stock has been rising and management's way of assisting the liquidity in the stock.
Stop orders	*Buy stops:* where the order price is specified above the current value of the security.
	Sell stops: where the order price is specified below the current value of the security.
Straddle	A neutral trade that involves simultaneously buying a call and put at the same strike price and with the same Expiration Date. Requires the underlying asset to move in an explosive nature (in either direction) in order to make the trade profitable.
Strangle	A neutral trade that involves simultaneously buying a call and put at different strike prices (the put Strike being lower than the call Strike, that is, both OTM) and with the same Expiration Date. Requires the underlying asset to move in an explosive nature (in either direction) to make the trade profitable.
Strike price (Exercise price)	The price at which an asset can be bought or sold by the buyer of a call or put option.
Support	A floor on a price chart thought to be difficult for the price to fall down through because of past price movements.
Synthetic Long Call	Buying a share and a put, or going long a future and a put.
Synthetic Long Put	Buying a call and shorting a stock or future.
Synthetic Long Stock	Buying a call and shorting a put with the same strike price and Expiration Date.
Synthetic Short Call	Shorting a put and shorting a stock or future.
Synthetic Short Put	Shorting a call and buying a stock or future.
Synthetic Short Stock	Shorting a call and buying a put with the same strike price and Expiration Date.

Synthetic Straddle	Combining stocks (or futures) with options to create a delta neutral trade.
Technical Analysis	Using charts and charting techniques and indicators (such as prices, volume, moving averages, stochastics, etc.) to evaluate future likely price movement.
Theoretical Value (options)	The Fair Value calculation of an option using a pricing formula such as the Black-Scholes Options Pricing Model.
Theta (decay)	The sensitivity of an option price to the variable of time to Expiration. Remember that options only have a finite life (until Expiration), therefore theta is an extremely important sensitivity to consider.
Tick	The least amount of price movement recorded in a security. Was 1/32 until decimalization eliminated the fractions structure.
Time premium	The non-Intrinsic component of the price of an option.
Time Value (Extrinsic Value)	The price of an option less its Intrinsic Value. Out of the Money options are entire made up of Extrinsic (or Time) Value.
Treasury Bill (T-Bill)	A short-term government debt security with a maturity of no more than one year. The interest charged on these instruments is known as the Risk Free Rate.
Treasury Bond (T-Bond)	A fixed interest US government debt security with ten years or more to maturity.
Treasury Note (T-Note)	A fixed interest US government debt security with between one to 10 years to maturity.
Triple Witching Day	The third Friday in March, June, September, and December when US stock options, index options, and futures contracts all expire at the same time. The effect of this is often increased volume and volatility as traders look to close short and long positions.
Type	The classification of an option, either a call or a put.
Uncovered Option	A short position where the writer does not have the underlying security (or call option) to hedge the unlimited risk position of his naked position.
Underlying asset/ instrument/security	An asset (such as a share) that is subject to purchase or disposal upon exercise.
Upside	The potential for a price to increase.
Vega	The sensitivity of an option price to volatility. Typically, options increase in value during periods of high volatility.

Volatility	The measure of the fluctuation in the price movement in a security over a period of time. Volatility is one of the most important components in the theoretical valuation of an option price.
	Historical Volatility: the standard deviation of the underlying security (closing) price movement over a period of time (typically 21 to 23 days).
	Implied Volatility: the calculated component derived from the option price when using the Black-Scholes Option Pricing Model. Traders can take advantage when there is a significant discrepancy between Implied and Historical Volatility.
Volatility Skew	Whereby deep OTM options tend to have higher Implied Volatilities than ATM options. This type of discrepancy again gives the trader the opportunity to make trades whose profits are determined by volatility action as opposed to directional price action.
Volume	The number of underlying securities traded on their particular part of the exchange.
	Where price direction and volume bars are aligned in the same direction, this is a bullish sign (it means that prices are rising with increased volume or that prices are falling with decreased volume).
	Where price direction diverges from volume bars, this is a bearish sign (that is, prices rising with falling volume or prices falling with rising volume).
Whipsaw	A short, sharp price swing that ensures a losing scenario for both sides of a position.
Witching Day	When two or more classes of options and futures contracts expire.
Writer	Someone who sells an option.
Yield	The rate of return of an investment, expressed as a percentage.
Zeta	An option price's sensitivity to Implied Volatility.

Index

trends, 30
    cup and handle pattern,
      51-54
    downtrends, 30
    flags, 38-41
    reverse cup and handle
      pattern, 54-55
    uptrends, 30

U

uptrending stock, 30
uptrends, 30

V

valuation of options, 4
vega, 60, 82-83, 89-90
    call ratio backspread, 152
    implied volatility, 83
    put ratio backspreads, 167
    theoretical option pricing,
      84-89
    volatility, 88
volatility
    historical versus implied, 245
    historical volatility, 245-246
      calculating in Excel,
        246-249

    normal distribution,
      249-254
    vega, 83
    implied volatility, 254-255
    vega, 83
    straddles, 98-100
    strangles, 98-100
    vega, 88
volatility smile, 258-259

W-X-Y-Z

week only, 25
whipsaws, 26
Yahoo Finance, 237
Zeta, 60